STAR WARS®

❖ L E G A C Y ❖

❧ L E G A C Y ❧

(Forty years after the Battle of Yavin and beyond)

As this era began, Luke Skywalker had unified the Jedi Order into a cohesive group of powerful Jedi Knights. It was a time of relative peace, yet darkness approached on the horizon. Now, Skywalker's descendants face new and resurgent threats to the galaxy, and to the balance of the Force.

The events in this story begin approximately 137 years after the Battle of Yavin.

STAR WARS® LEGACY

VOLUME EIGHT
TATOOINE

STORY
John Ostrander and Jan Duursema

SCRIPT
John Ostrander

PENCILS
Jan Duursema and Kajo Baldisimo

INKS
Dan Parsons

COLORS
Brad Anderson and Jesus Aburto

LETTERS
Michael Heisler

COVER ART
Chris Warner and Brad Anderson

BACK COVER ART
Jan Duursema and Brad Anderson

DARK HORSE BOOKS®

PUBLISHER
Mike Richardson

EDITOR
Randy Stradley

COLLECTION DESIGNER
Scott Cook

ASSISTANT EDITOR
Freddye Lins

Special thanks to Jann Moorhead, David Anderman, Troy Alders,
Leland Chee, Sue Rostoni, and Carol Roeder at Lucas Licensing.

STAR WARS: LEGACY VOLUME EIGHT—TATOOINE

Star Wars © 2010 Lucasfilm Ltd. & ™. All rights reserved. Used under authorization. Text and illustrations for Star
Wars are © 2010 Lucasfilm Ltd. Dark Horse Books® and the Dark Horse logo are registered trademarks of Dark
Horse Comics, Inc. All rights reserved. No portion of this publication may be reproduced or transmitted, in any form
or by any means, without the express written permission of Dark Horse Comics, Inc. Names, characters, places, and
incidents featured in this publication either are the product of the author's imagination or are used fictitiously. Any
resemblance to actual persons (living or dead), events, institutions, or locales, without satiric intent, is coincidental.

This volume collects issues #37–#41 of the
Dark Horse comic-book series *Star Wars: Legacy*.

Published by
Dark Horse Books
A division of Dark Horse Comics, Inc.
10956 SE Main Street
Milwaukie, OR 97222

darkhorse.com
starwars.com

To find a comics shop in your area, call the Comic Shop Locator Service toll-free at 1-888-266-4226

Library of Congress Cataloging-in-Publication Data

Ostrander, John.
Star wars, legacy. volume eight : Tatooine / story, John Ostrander and Jan Duursema ; script John Ostrander ; pencils
Jan Duursema, Kajo Baldisimo ; inks Dan Parsons ; colors Brad Anderson,
Jesus Aburto ; letters Michael Heisler ; front cover art Chris Warner and Brad Anderson ; back cover art Jan
Duursema and Brad Anderson. -- 1st ed.
p. cm.
"This volume collects issues #37-#41 of the Dark Horse comic-book series Star Wars: Legacy."
Summary: "Legacy (Forty years after the Battle of Yavin and beyond) - As this era began, Luke Skywalker had unified
the Jedi order into a cohesive group of powerful Jedi Knights. It was a time a relative peace, yet darkness approached
on the horizon. Now, Skywalker's descendants face new and resurgent threats to the galaxy, and to the balance of the
Force. The events in this story begin approximately 137 years after the Battle of Yavin."
ISBN 978-1-59582-414-1
1. Comic books, strips, etc. I. Duursema, Jan. II. Title. III. Title: Tatooine.
PN6728.S73O885 2010
741.5'973--dc22
2009036455

First edition: March 2010
ISBN 978-1-59582-414-1

1 3 5 7 9 10 8 6 4 2
Printed in China

MIKE RICHARDSON president and publisher NEIL HANKERSON executive vice president TOM WEDDLE
chief financial officer RANDY STRADLEY vice president of publishing MICHAEL MARTENS vice president of
business development ANITA NELSON vice president of marketing, sales, and licensing DAVID SCROGGY vice
president of product development DALE LAFOUNTAIN vice president of information technology DARLENE VOGEL
director of purchasing KEN LIZZI general counsel DAVEY ESTRADA editorial director SCOTT ALLIE senior
managing editor CHRIS WARNER senior books editor DIANA SCHUTZ executive editor CARY GRAZZINI
director of design and production LIA RIBACCHI art director CARA NIECE director of scheduling

Rumors of the death—or possible survival—of Sith Emperor Darth Krayt ripple throughout the galaxy. The Sith's enemies, notably the remnants of the Galactic Alliance and emperor-in-exile Roan Fel's loyalist followers, see this moment as the opportunity they've been waiting for.

Within the Sith Empire itself, various factions are preparing for a power struggle. Control of the galaxy is at a tipping point.

But the man who brought the galaxy to this point has turned his back on it. Cade Skywalker, fleeing the consequences of his own selfish desires, has returned to his old piratical ways. Along with the crew of the *Mynock*, he seeks plunder in the Outer Rim—but with a twist . . .

STAR WARS

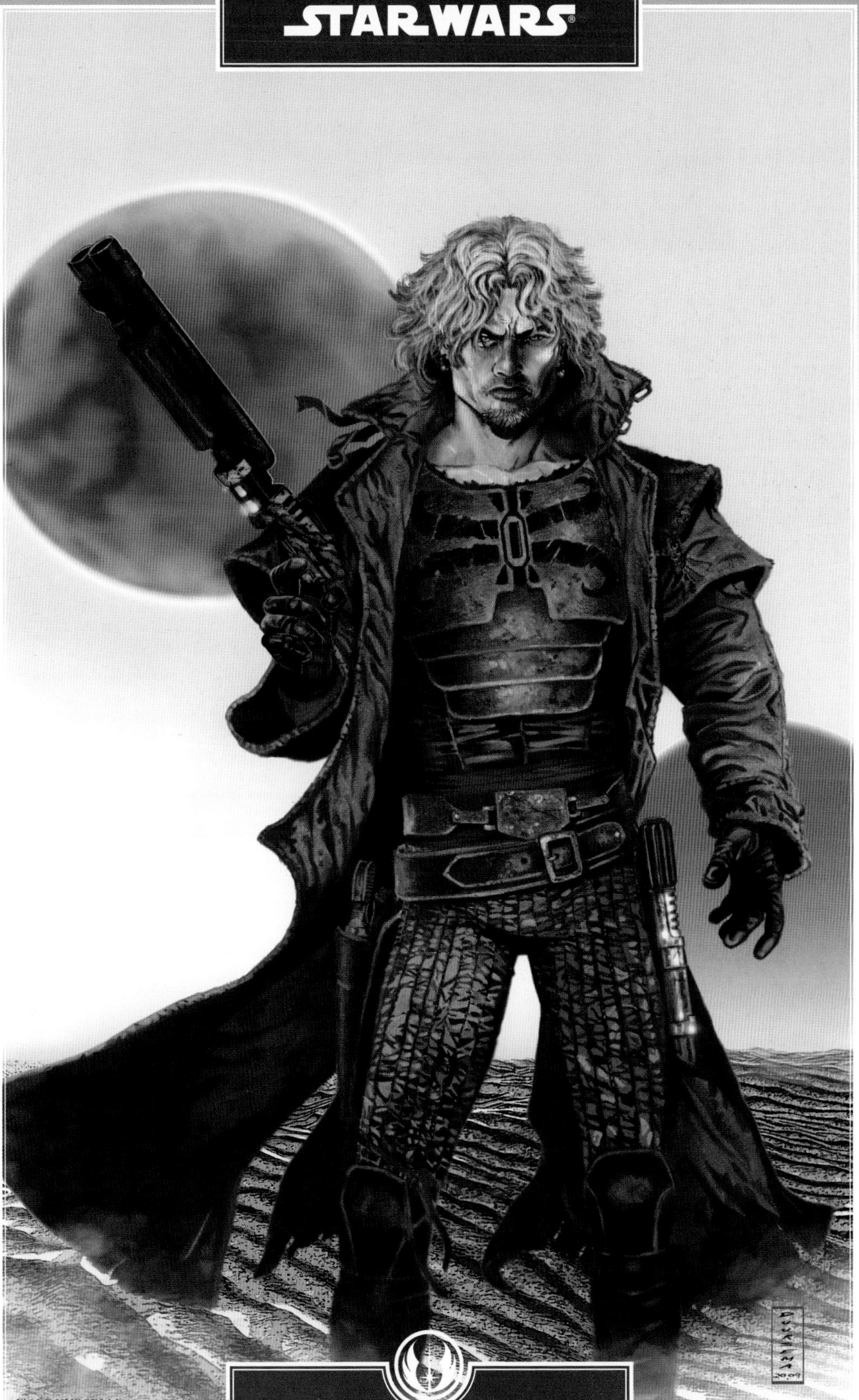
JAN DUURSEMA

TATOOINE

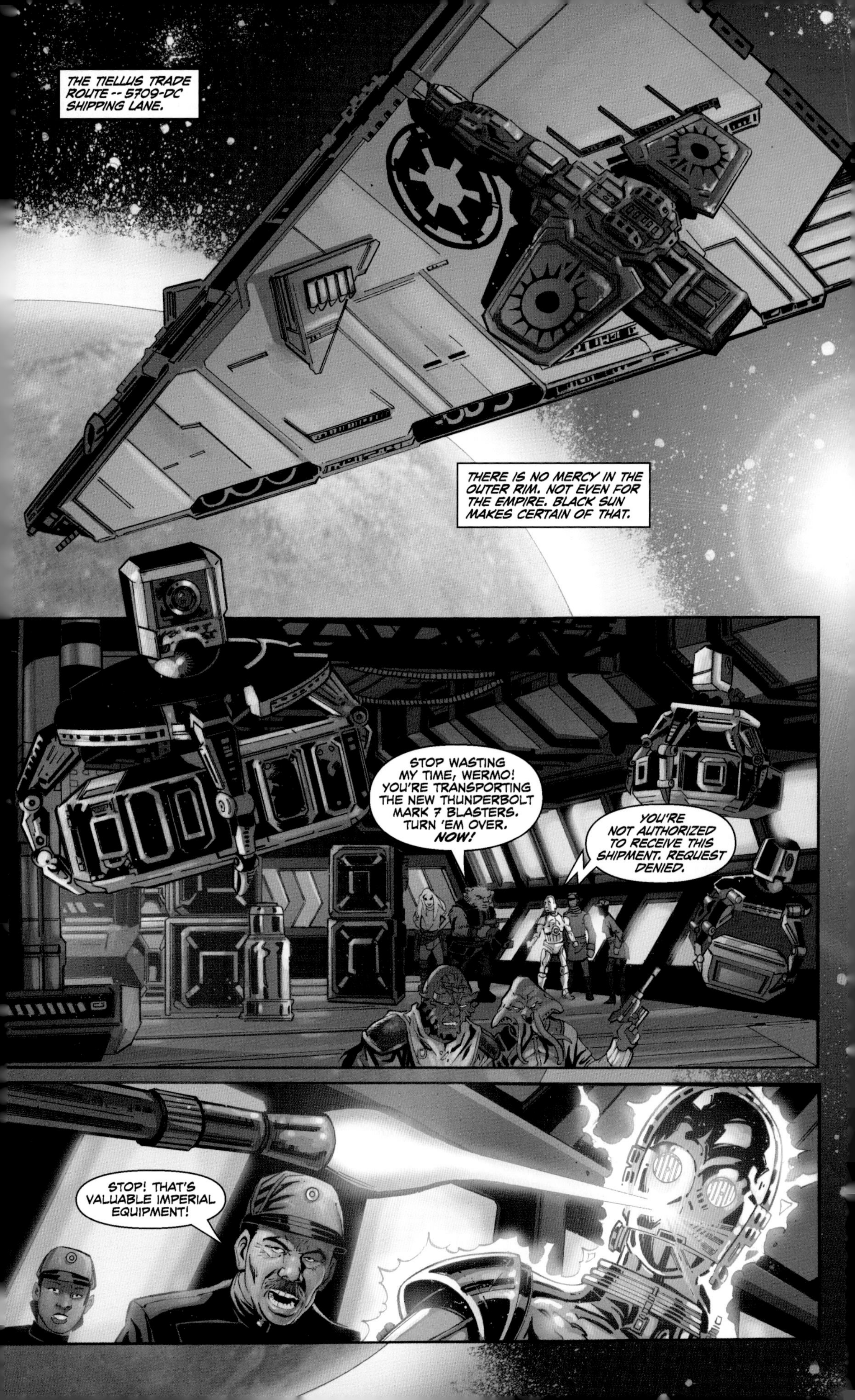
THE TIELLUS TRADE ROUTE -- 5709-DC SHIPPING LANE.
THERE IS NO MERCY IN THE OUTER RIM. NOT EVEN FOR THE EMPIRE. BLACK SUN MAKES CERTAIN OF THAT.
STOP WASTING MY TIME, WERMO! YOU'RE TRANSPORTING THE NEW THUNDERBOLT MARK 7 BLASTERS. TURN 'EM OVER. NOW!
YOU'RE NOT AUTHORIZED TO RECEIVE THIS SHIPMENT. REQUEST DENIED.
STOP! THAT'S VALUABLE IMPERIAL EQUIPMENT!

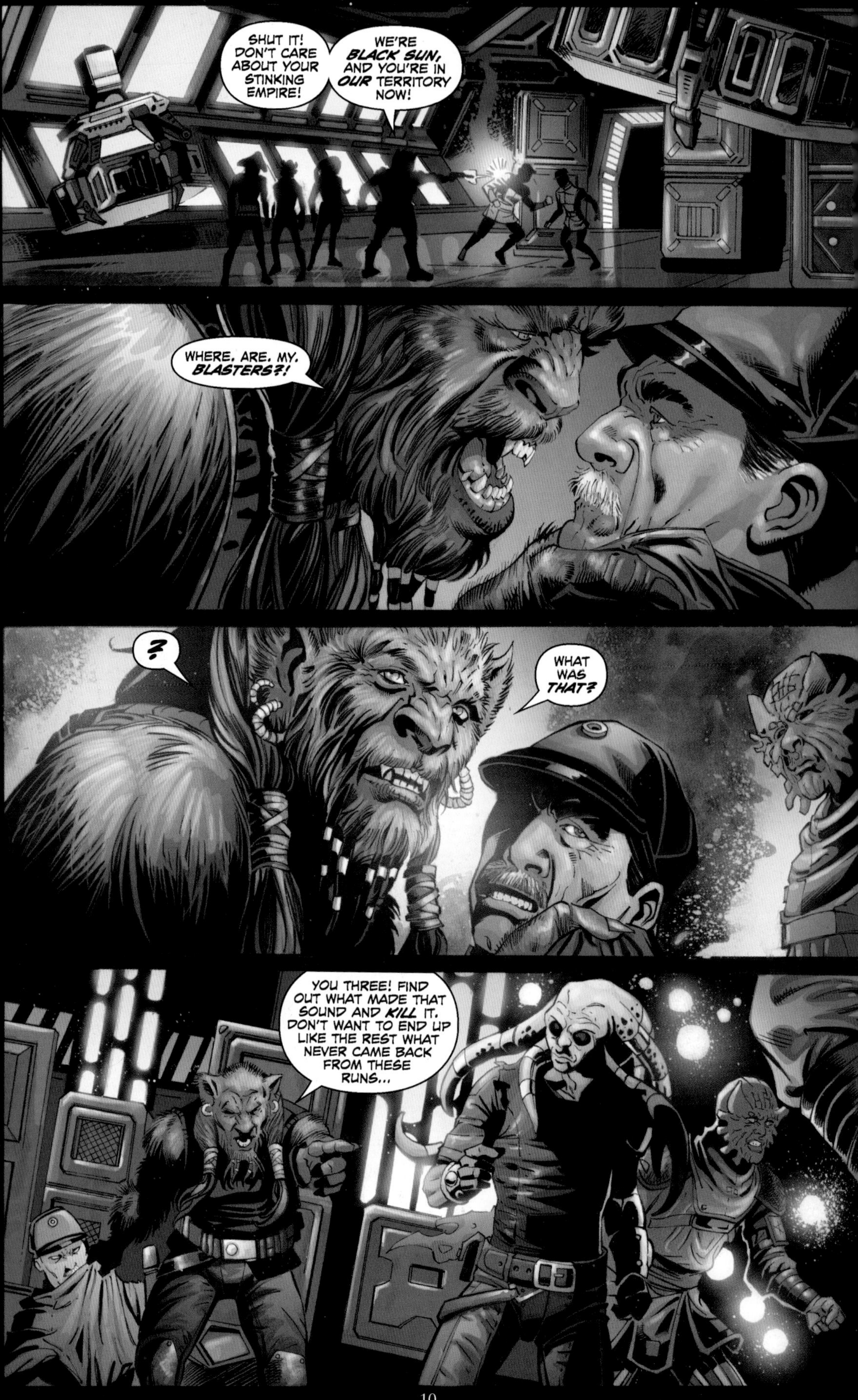
SHUT IT! DON'T CARE ABOUT YOUR STINKING EMPIRE!
WE'RE BLACK SUN, AND YOU'RE IN OUR TERRITORY NOW!
WHERE. ARE. MY. BLASTERS?!
?
WHAT WAS THAT?
YOU THREE! FIND OUT WHAT MADE THAT SOUND AND KILL IT. DON'T WANT TO END UP LIKE THE REST WHAT NEVER CAME BACK FROM THESE RUNS...

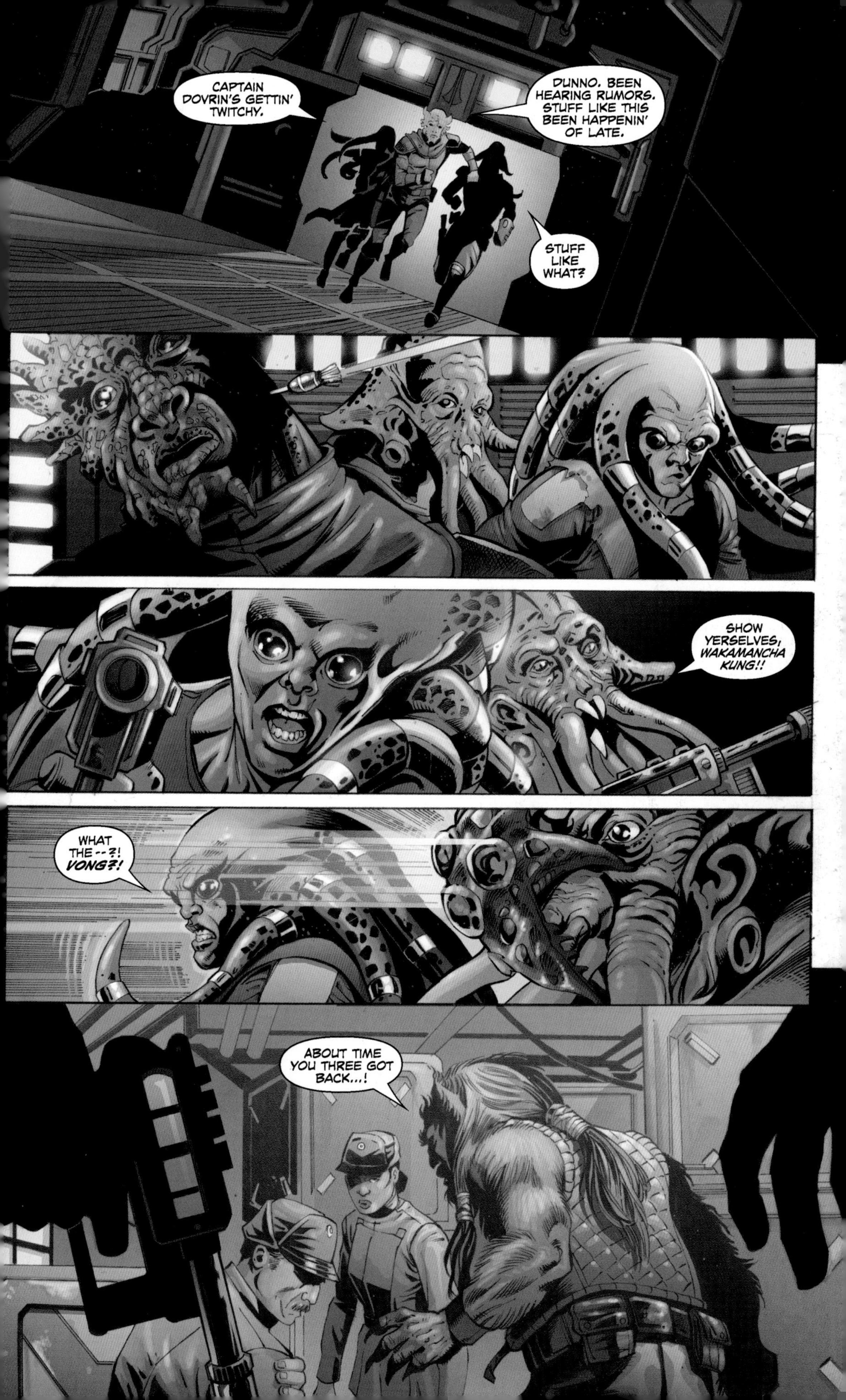
CAPTAIN DOVRIN'S GETTIN' TWITCHY.
DUNNO. BEEN HEARING RUMORS. STUFF LIKE THIS BEEN HAPPENIN' OF LATE.
STUFF LIKE WHAT?
SHOW YERSELVES, WAKAMANCHA KUNG!!
WHAT THE--?! VONG?!
ABOUT TIME YOU THREE GOT BACK...!

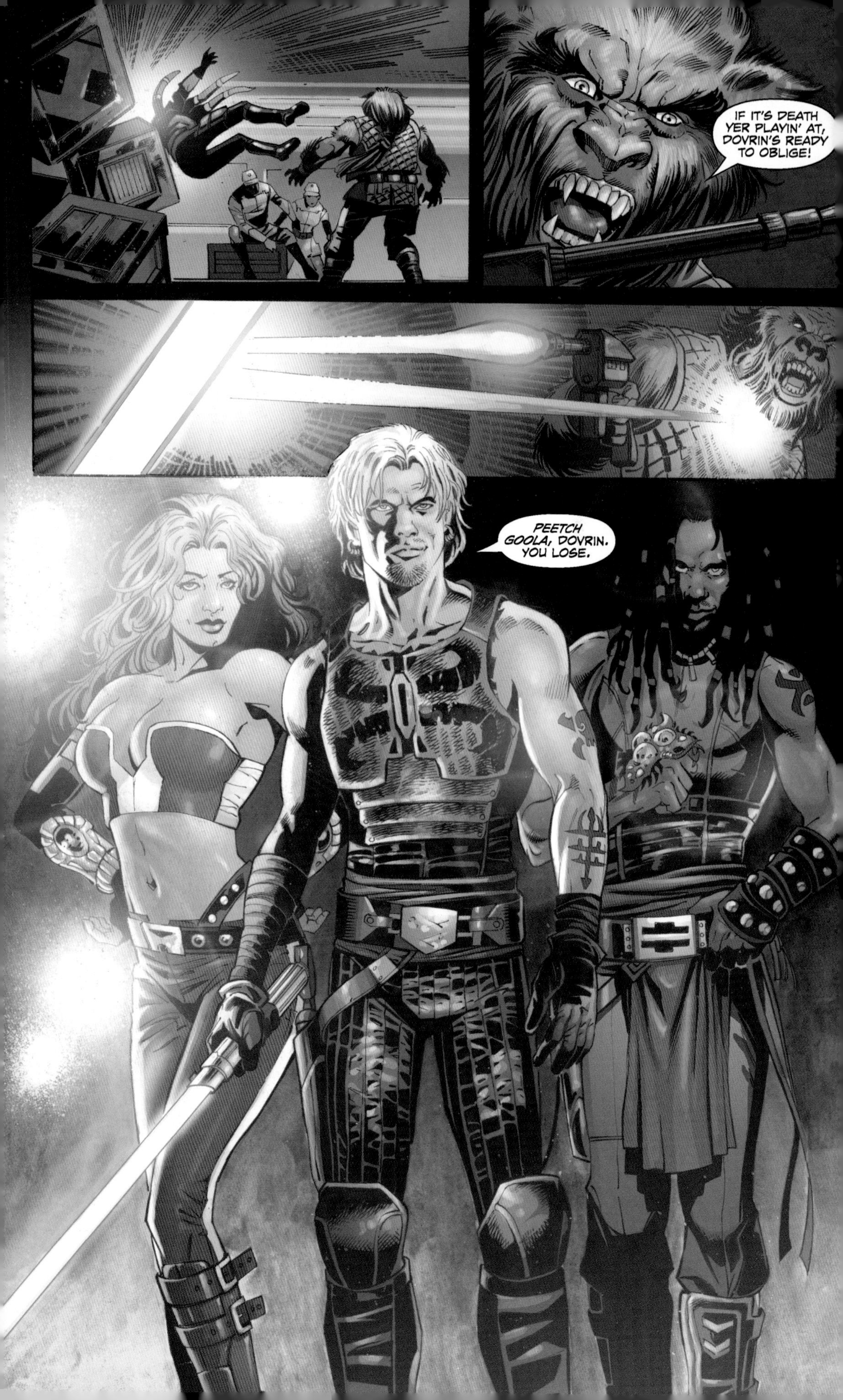
IF IT'S DEATH YER PLAYIN' AT, DOVRIN'S READY TO OBLIGE!
PEETCH GOOLA, DOVRIN. YOU LOSE.

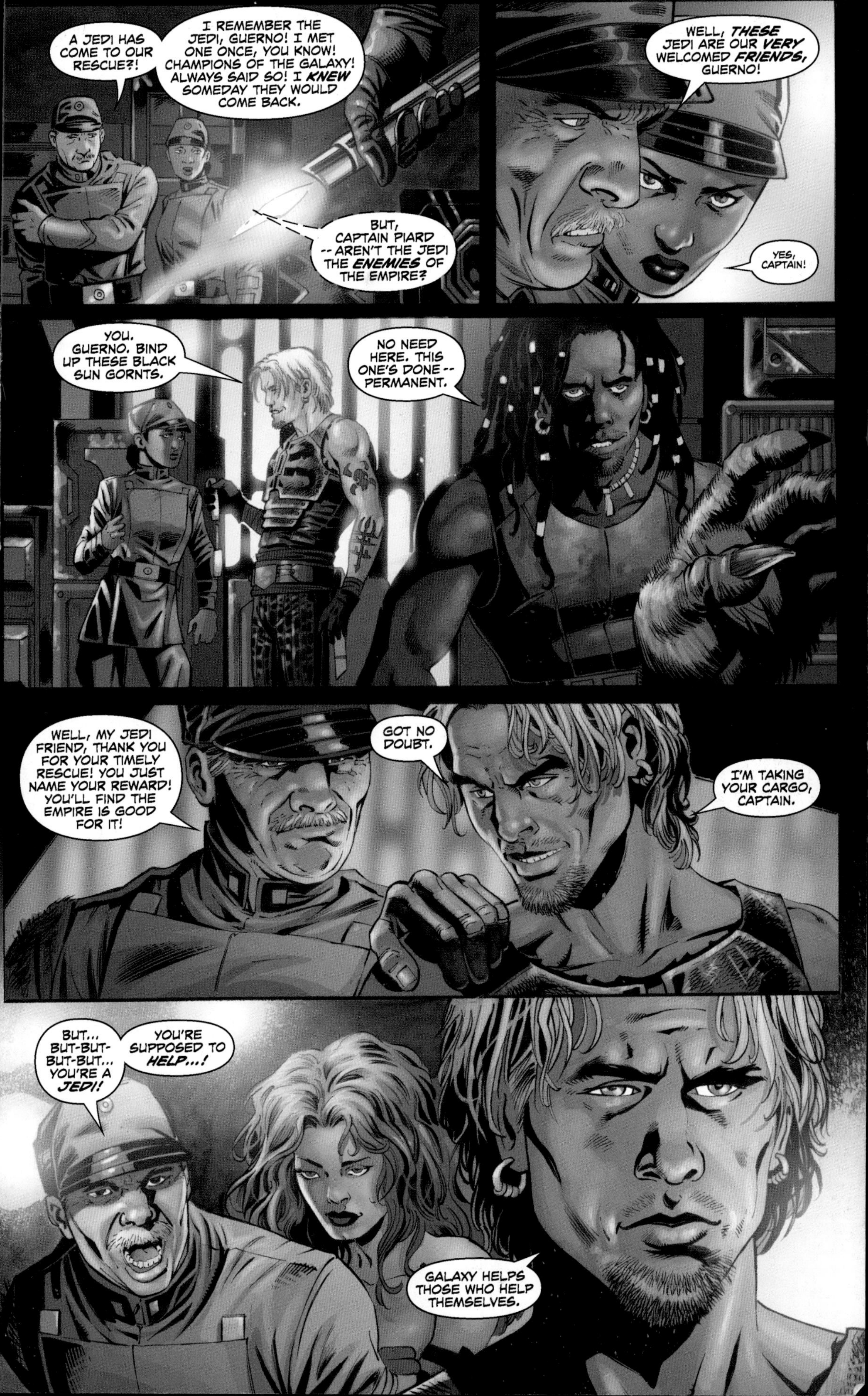
A JEDI HAS COME TO OUR RESCUE?!
I REMEMBER THE JEDI, GUERNO! I MET ONE ONCE, YOU KNOW! CHAMPIONS OF THE GALAXY! ALWAYS SAID SO! I KNEW SOMEDAY THEY WOULD COME BACK.
BUT, CAPTAIN PIARD -- AREN'T THE JEDI THE ENEMIES OF THE EMPIRE?
WELL, THESE JEDI ARE OUR VERY WELCOMED FRIENDS, GUERNO!
YES, CAPTAIN!
YOU. GUERNO. BIND UP THESE BLACK SUN GORNTS.
NO NEED HERE. THIS ONE'S DONE -- PERMANENT.
WELL, MY JEDI FRIEND, THANK YOU FOR YOUR TIMELY RESCUE! YOU JUST NAME YOUR REWARD! YOU'LL FIND THE EMPIRE IS GOOD FOR IT!
GOT NO DOUBT.
I'M TAKING YOUR CARGO, CAPTAIN.
BUT... BUT-BUT-BUT-BUT... YOU'RE A JEDI!
YOU'RE SUPPOSED TO HELP...!
GALAXY HELPS THOSE WHO HELP THEMSELVES.

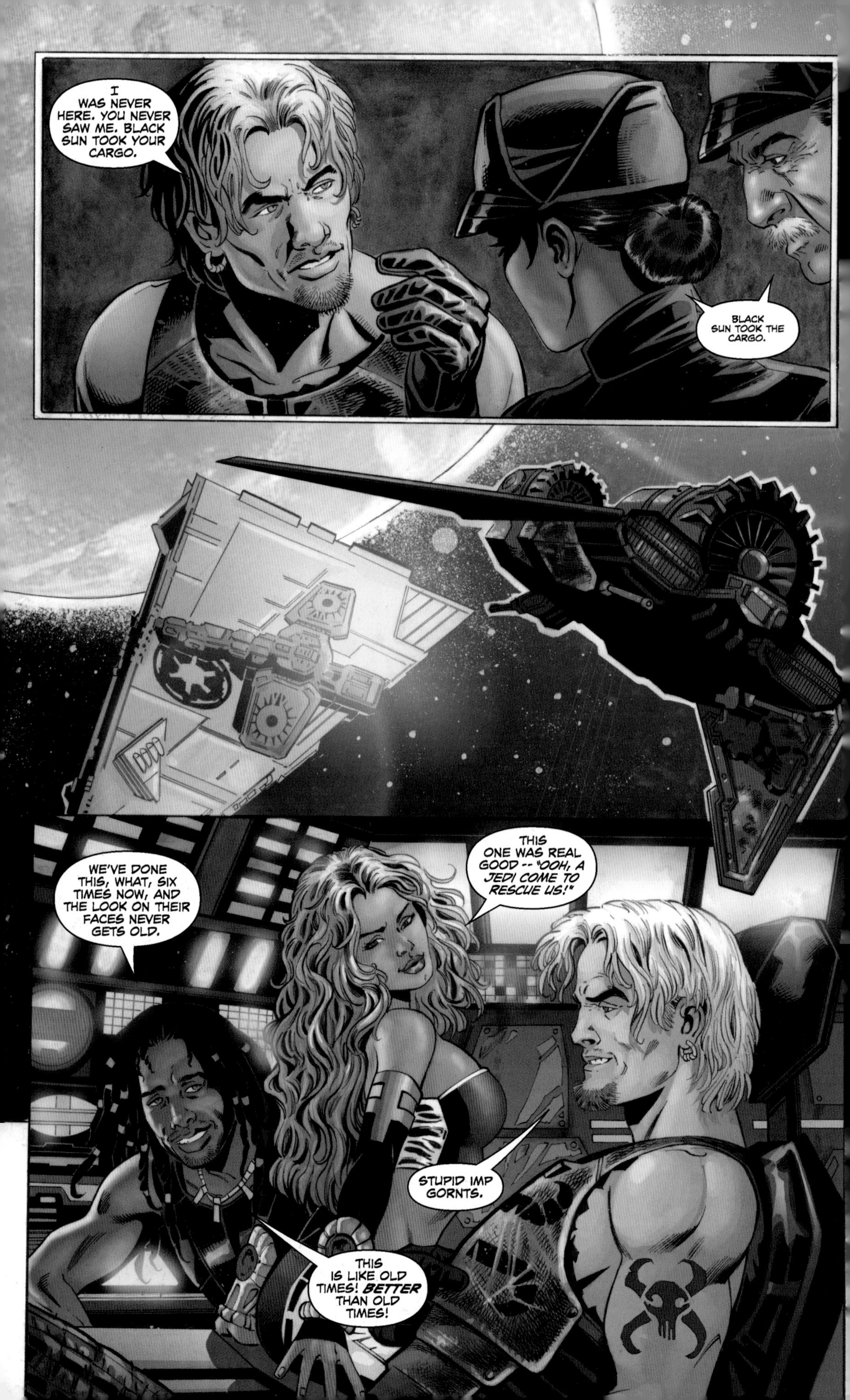
I WAS NEVER HERE. YOU NEVER SAW ME. BLACK SUN TOOK YOUR CARGO.
BLACK SUN TOOK THE CARGO.
WE'VE DONE THIS, WHAT, SIX TIMES NOW, AND THE LOOK ON THEIR FACES NEVER GETS OLD.
THIS ONE WAS REAL GOOD -- "OOH, A JEDI COME TO RESCUE US!"
STUPID IMP GORNTS.
THIS IS LIKE OLD TIMES! BETTER THAN OLD TIMES!

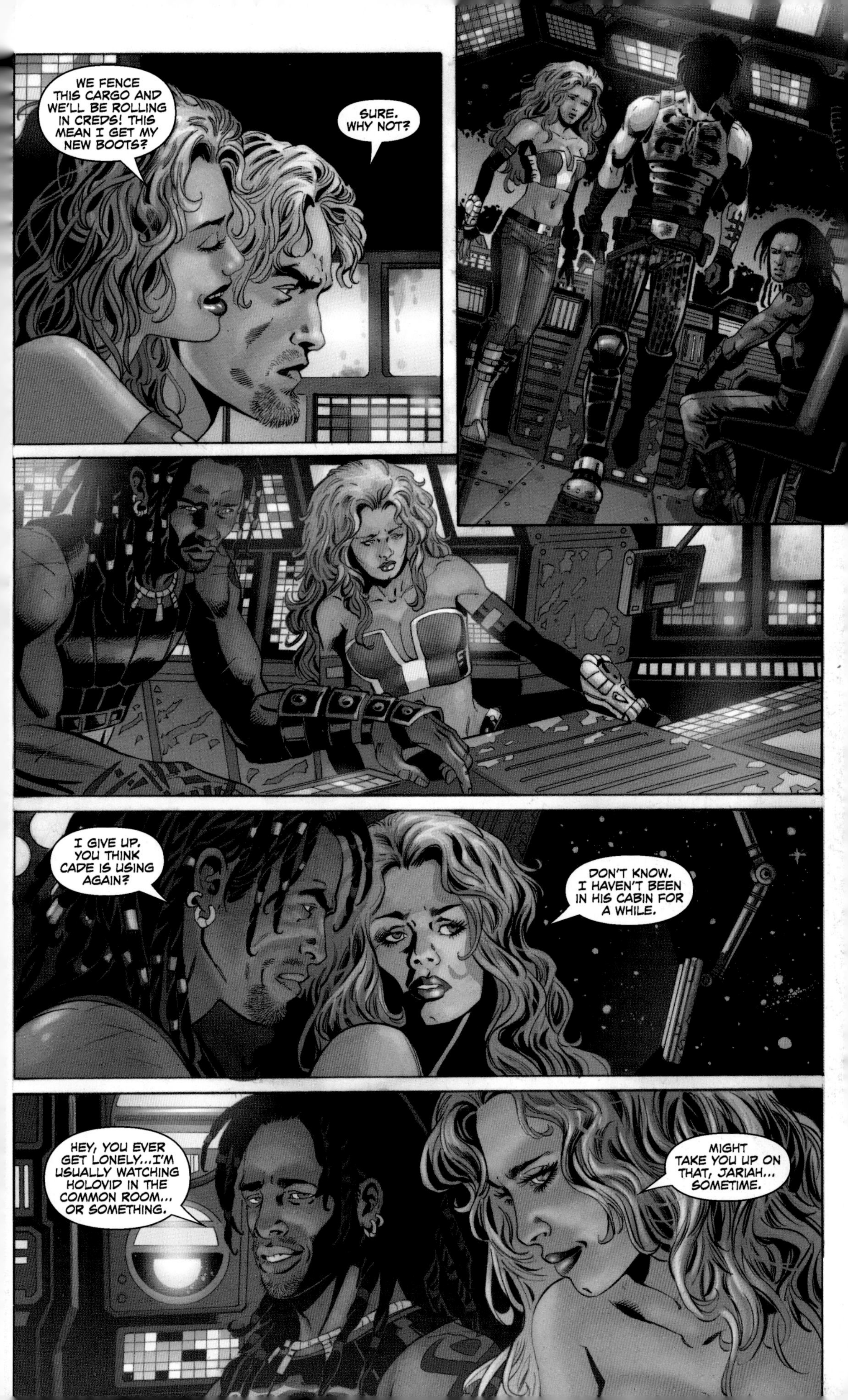
WE FENCE THIS CARGO AND WE'LL BE ROLLING IN CREDS! THIS MEAN I GET MY NEW BOOTS?
SURE. WHY NOT?
I GIVE UP. YOU THINK CADE IS USING AGAIN?
DON'T KNOW. I HAVEN'T BEEN IN HIS CABIN FOR A WHILE.
HEY, YOU EVER GET LONELY...I'M USUALLY WATCHING HOLOVID IN THE COMMON ROOM... OR SOMETHING.
MIGHT TAKE YOU UP ON THAT, JARIAH... SOMETIME.

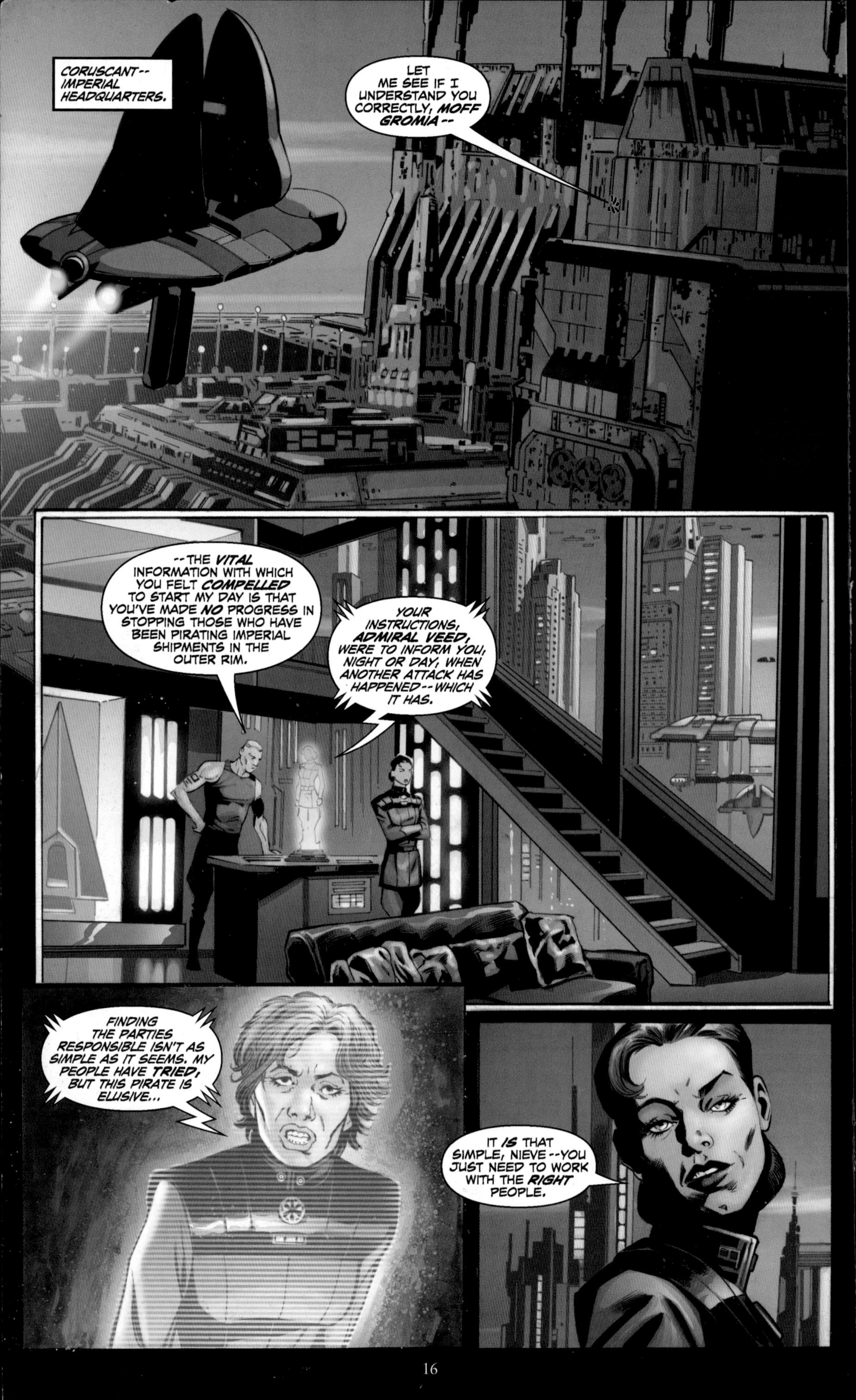
CORUSCANT--
IMPERIAL
HEADQUARTERS.
LET ME SEE IF I UNDERSTAND YOU CORRECTLY, MOFF GROMIA--
--THE VITAL INFORMATION WITH WHICH YOU FELT COMPELLED TO START MY DAY IS THAT YOU'VE MADE NO PROGRESS IN STOPPING THOSE WHO HAVE BEEN PIRATING IMPERIAL SHIPMENTS IN THE OUTER RIM.
YOUR INSTRUCTIONS, ADMIRAL VEED, WERE TO INFORM YOU, NIGHT OR DAY, WHEN ANOTHER ATTACK HAS HAPPENED--WHICH IT HAS.
FINDING THE PARTIES RESPONSIBLE ISN'T AS SIMPLE AS IT SEEMS. MY PEOPLE HAVE TRIED, BUT THIS PIRATE IS ELUSIVE...
IT IS THAT SIMPLE, NIEVE--YOU JUST NEED TO WORK WITH THE RIGHT PEOPLE.

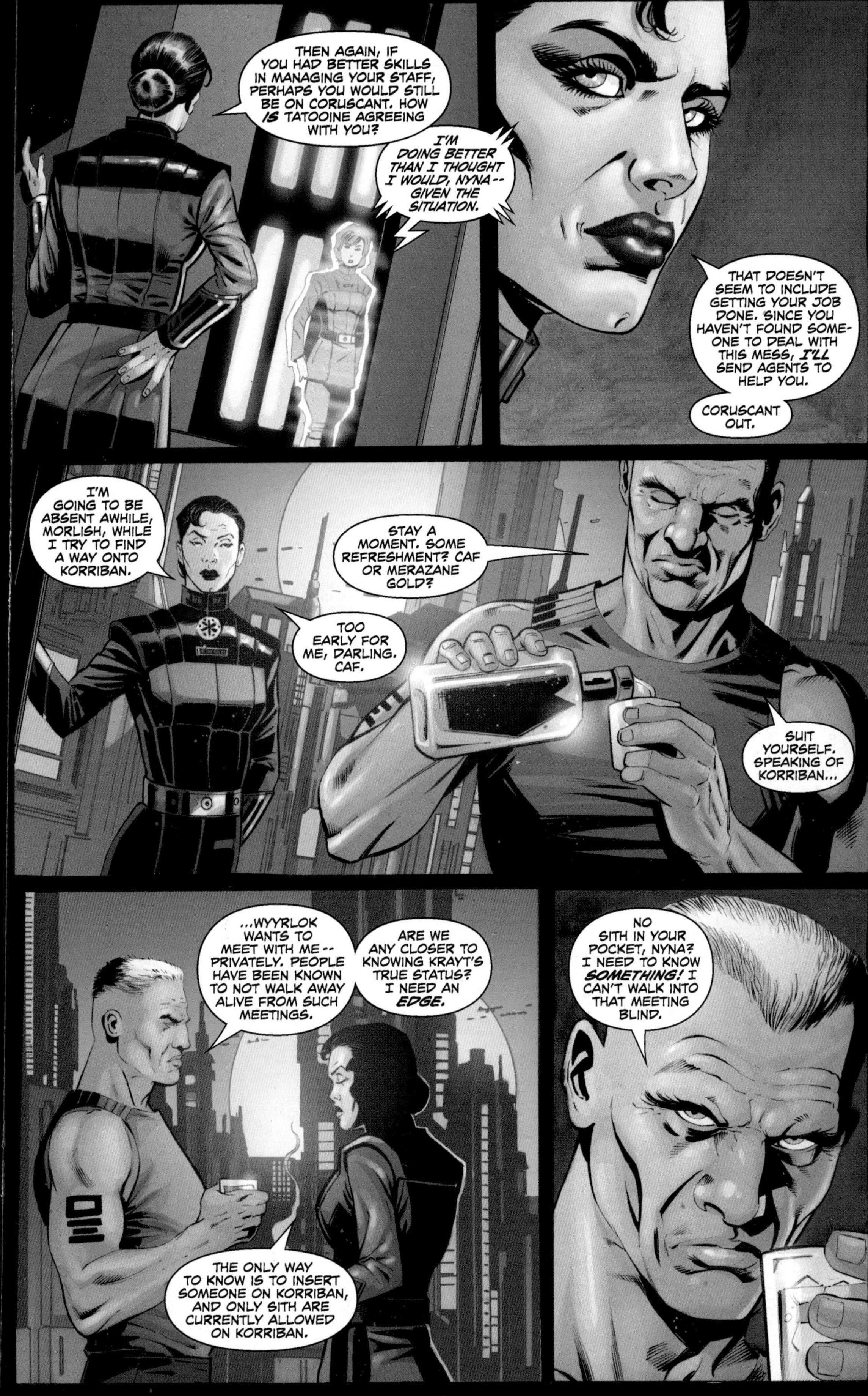
THEN AGAIN, IF YOU HAD BETTER SKILLS IN MANAGING YOUR STAFF, PERHAPS YOU WOULD STILL BE ON CORUSCANT. HOW *IS* TATOOINE AGREEING WITH YOU?
I'M DOING BETTER THAN I THOUGHT I WOULD, NYNA-- GIVEN THE SITUATION.
THAT DOESN'T SEEM TO INCLUDE GETTING YOUR JOB DONE. SINCE YOU HAVEN'T FOUND SOMEONE TO DEAL WITH THIS MESS, *I'LL* SEND AGENTS TO HELP YOU.
CORUSCANT OUT.
I'M GOING TO BE ABSENT AWHILE, MORLISH, WHILE I TRY TO FIND A WAY ONTO KORRIBAN.
STAY A MOMENT. SOME REFRESHMENT? CAF OR MERAZANE GOLD?
TOO EARLY FOR ME, DARLING. CAF.
SUIT YOURSELF. SPEAKING OF KORRIBAN...
...WYYRLOK WANTS TO MEET WITH ME--PRIVATELY. PEOPLE HAVE BEEN KNOWN TO NOT WALK AWAY ALIVE FROM SUCH MEETINGS.
ARE WE ANY CLOSER TO KNOWING KRAYT'S TRUE STATUS? I NEED AN *EDGE.*
THE ONLY WAY TO KNOW IS TO INSERT SOMEONE ON KORRIBAN, AND ONLY SITH ARE CURRENTLY ALLOWED ON KORRIBAN.
NO SITH IN YOUR POCKET, NYNA? I NEED TO KNOW *SOMETHING!* I CAN'T WALK INTO THAT MEETING BLIND.

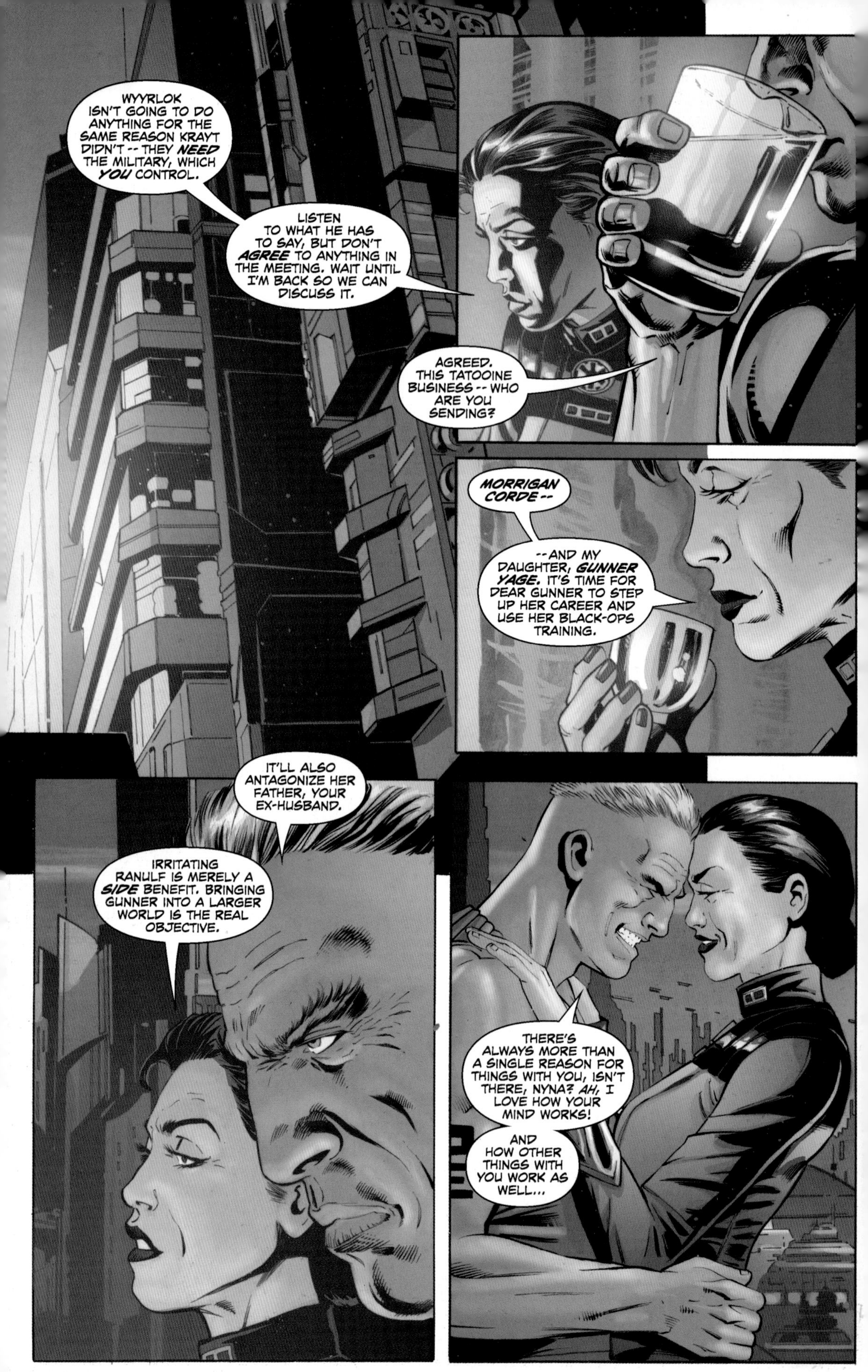
WYYRLOK ISN'T GOING TO DO ANYTHING FOR THE SAME REASON KRAYT DIDN'T -- THEY NEED THE MILITARY, WHICH YOU CONTROL.
LISTEN TO WHAT HE HAS TO SAY, BUT DON'T AGREE TO ANYTHING IN THE MEETING. WAIT UNTIL I'M BACK SO WE CAN DISCUSS IT.
AGREED. THIS TATOOINE BUSINESS -- WHO ARE YOU SENDING?
MORRIGAN CORDE --
-- AND MY DAUGHTER, GUNNER YAGE. IT'S TIME FOR DEAR GUNNER TO STEP UP HER CAREER AND USE HER BLACK-OPS TRAINING.
IT'LL ALSO ANTAGONIZE HER FATHER, YOUR EX-HUSBAND.
IRRITATING RANULF IS MERELY A SIDE BENEFIT. BRINGING GUNNER INTO A LARGER WORLD IS THE REAL OBJECTIVE.
THERE'S ALWAYS MORE THAN A SINGLE REASON FOR THINGS WITH YOU, ISN'T THERE, NYNA? AH, I LOVE HOW YOUR MIND WORKS!
AND HOW OTHER THINGS WITH YOU WORK AS WELL...

ARKANIS SECTOR, THE SISKEEN SYSTEM, THE GAS GIANT KAER.

ONCE, THIS WAS A TIBANNA-GAS-MINING PLATFORM. NOW IT BELONGS TO THE CRIMINAL ORGANIZATION KNOWN AS *BLACK SUN.*

THE SECTOR'S VIGO, *LUN RASK,* HAS MADE IT HIS BASE AND FORTRESS.

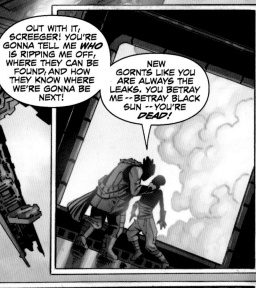

OUT WITH IT, SCREEGER! YOU'RE GONNA TELL ME *WHO* IS RIPPING ME OFF, WHERE THEY CAN BE FOUND, AND HOW THEY KNOW WHERE WE'RE GONNA BE NEXT!

NEW GORNTS LIKE YOU ARE ALWAYS THE LEAKS. YOU BETRAY ME -- BETRAY BLACK SUN -- YOU'RE *DEAD!*

CAN'T LEAK WHAT I WAS NEVER *TOLD,* BOSS! I AIN'T EARNED YER-- WHADDYA CALL IT--YER *CONFIDENCE* LIKE THAT YET!

HEY, SOMEONE MUSTA TIPPED *YOU* OFF ABOUT THEM IMP SHIPMENTS, AM I RIGHT?

NONE OF YER BUSINESS, WERMO.

JUS' SAYIN' A LEAK COULD COME FROM THE *OTHER* END, KNOW WHAT I MEAN? THEY COULD BE, WHADDYA CALL IT, DOUBLE-DEALING, RIGHT?

MAYBE.

YOU'RE THE INFORMATION BROKER, SCREEGER... FIND THE PIRATES RIPPING ME OFF, AND MAYBE I WON'T TEAR YOUR LUNGS OUT.

ON IT! RIGHT AWAY! YOU BET, BOSS! YOU BET!

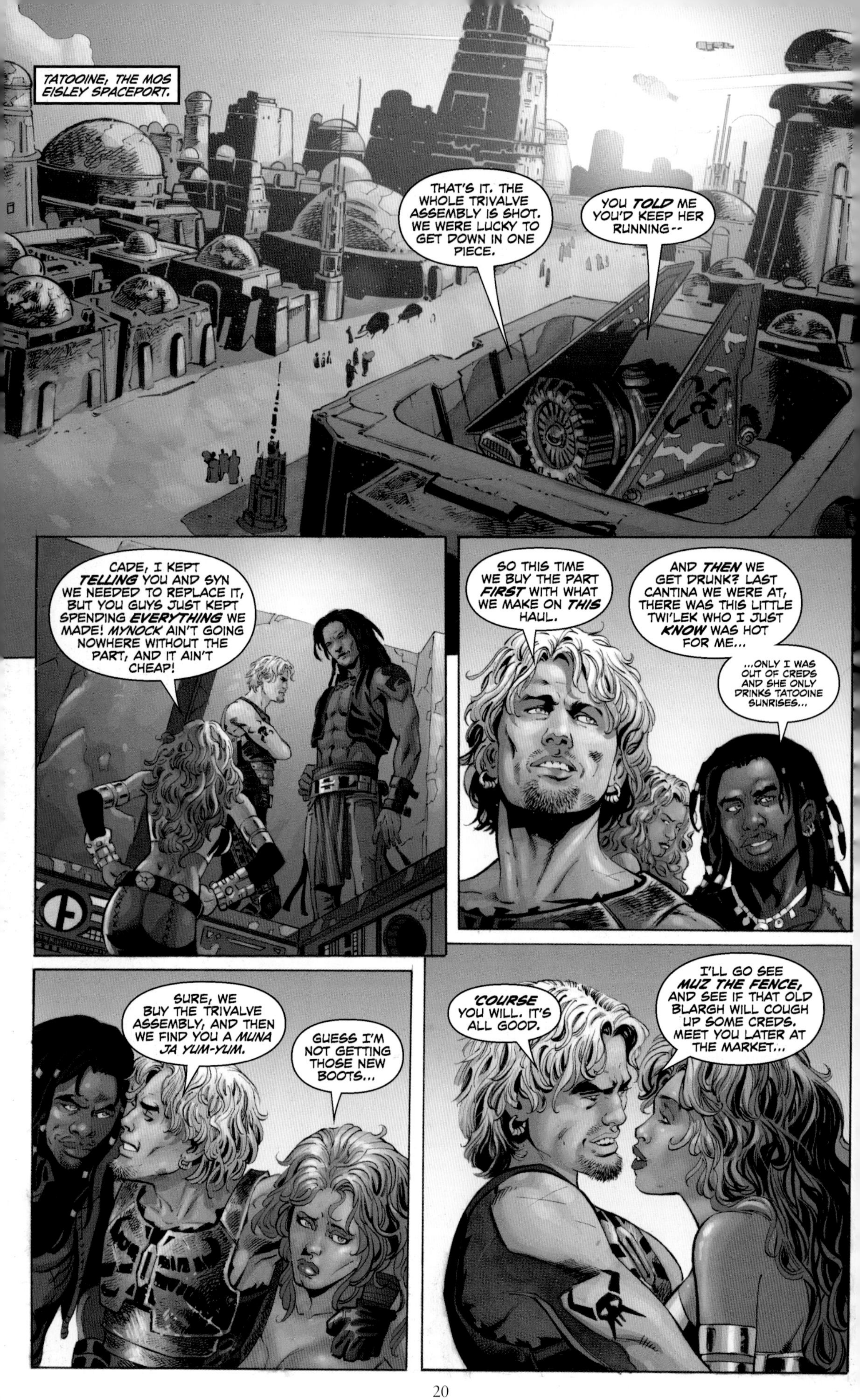
TATOOINE, THE MOS EISLEY SPACEPORT.
THAT'S IT. THE WHOLE TRIVALVE ASSEMBLY IS SHOT. WE WERE LUCKY TO GET DOWN IN ONE PIECE.
YOU TOLD ME YOU'D KEEP HER RUNNING--
CADE, I KEPT TELLING YOU AND SYN WE NEEDED TO REPLACE IT, BUT YOU GUYS JUST KEPT SPENDING EVERYTHING WE MADE! MYNOCK AIN'T GOING NOWHERE WITHOUT THE PART, AND IT AIN'T CHEAP!
SO THIS TIME WE BUY THE PART FIRST WITH WHAT WE MAKE ON THIS HAUL.
AND THEN WE GET DRUNK? LAST CANTINA WE WERE AT, THERE WAS THIS LITTLE TWI'LEK WHO I JUST KNOW WAS HOT FOR ME...
...ONLY I WAS OUT OF CREDS AND SHE ONLY DRINKS TATOOINE SUNRISES...
SURE, WE BUY THE TRIVALVE ASSEMBLY, AND THEN WE FIND YOU A MUNA JA YUM-YUM.
GUESS I'M NOT GETTING THOSE NEW BOOTS...
'COURSE YOU WILL. IT'S ALL GOOD.
I'LL GO SEE MUZ THE FENCE, AND SEE IF THAT OLD BLARGH WILL COUGH UP SOME CREDS. MEET YOU LATER AT THE MARKET...

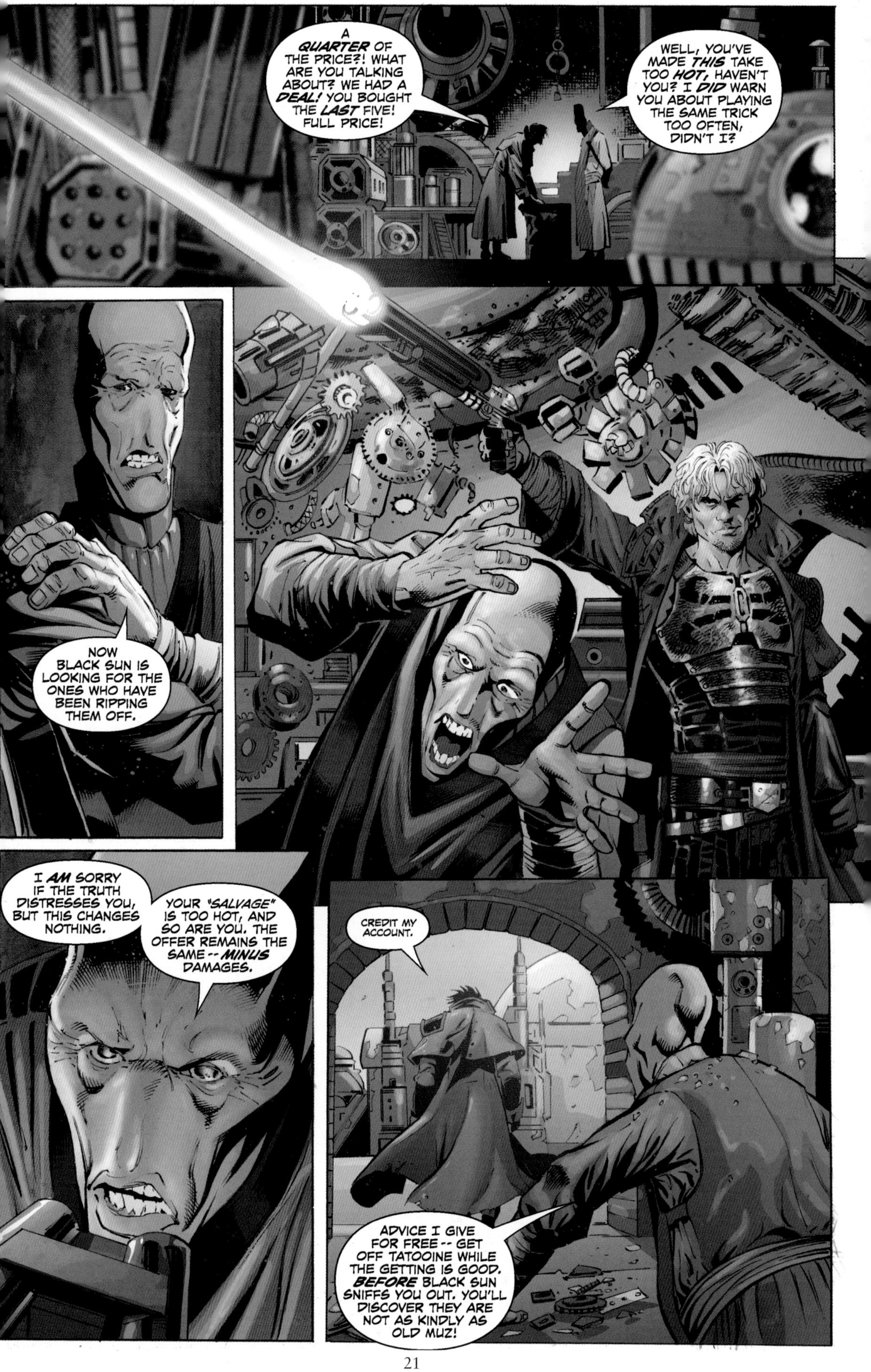
A QUARTER OF THE PRICE?! WHAT ARE YOU TALKING ABOUT? WE HAD A DEAL! YOU BOUGHT THE LAST FIVE! FULL PRICE!
WELL, YOU'VE MADE THIS TAKE TOO HOT, HAVEN'T YOU? I DID WARN YOU ABOUT PLAYING THE SAME TRICK TOO OFTEN, DIDN'T I?
NOW BLACK SUN IS LOOKING FOR THE ONES WHO HAVE BEEN RIPPING THEM OFF.
I AM SORRY IF THE TRUTH DISTRESSES YOU, BUT THIS CHANGES NOTHING.
YOUR "SALVAGE" IS TOO HOT, AND SO ARE YOU. THE OFFER REMAINS THE SAME -- MINUS DAMAGES.
CREDIT MY ACCOUNT.
ADVICE I GIVE FOR FREE -- GET OFF TATOOINE WHILE THE GETTING IS GOOD. BEFORE BLACK SUN SNIFFS YOU OUT. YOU'LL DISCOVER THEY ARE NOT AS KINDLY AS OLD MUZ!

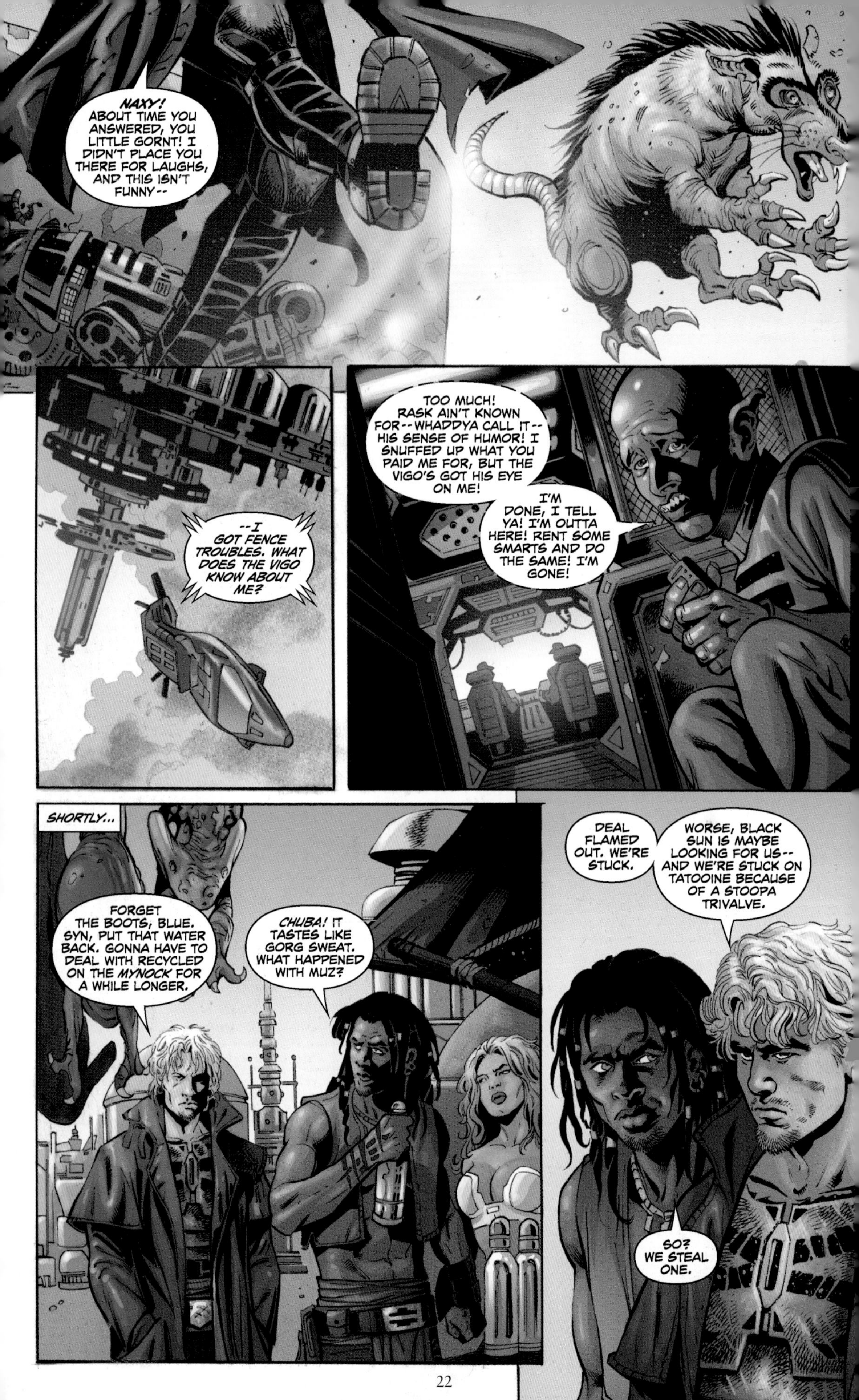
NAXY! ABOUT TIME YOU ANSWERED, YOU LITTLE GORNT! I DIDN'T PLACE YOU THERE FOR LAUGHS, AND THIS ISN'T FUNNY--
--I GOT FENCE TROUBLES. WHAT DOES THE VIGO KNOW ABOUT ME?
TOO MUCH! RASK AIN'T KNOWN FOR--WHADDYA CALL IT--HIS SENSE OF HUMOR! I SNUFFED UP WHAT YOU PAID ME FOR, BUT THE VIGO'S GOT HIS EYE ON ME!
I'M DONE, I TELL YA! I'M OUTTA HERE! RENT SOME SMARTS AND DO THE SAME! I'M GONE!
SHORTLY...
FORGET THE BOOTS, BLUE. SYN, PUT THAT WATER BACK. GONNA HAVE TO DEAL WITH RECYCLED ON THE MYNOCK FOR A WHILE LONGER.
CHUBA! IT TASTES LIKE GORG SWEAT. WHAT HAPPENED WITH MUZ?
DEAL FLAMED OUT. WE'RE STUCK.
WORSE, BLACK SUN IS MAYBE LOOKING FOR US--AND WE'RE STUCK ON TATOOINE BECAUSE OF A STOOPA TRIVALVE.
SO? WE STEAL ONE.

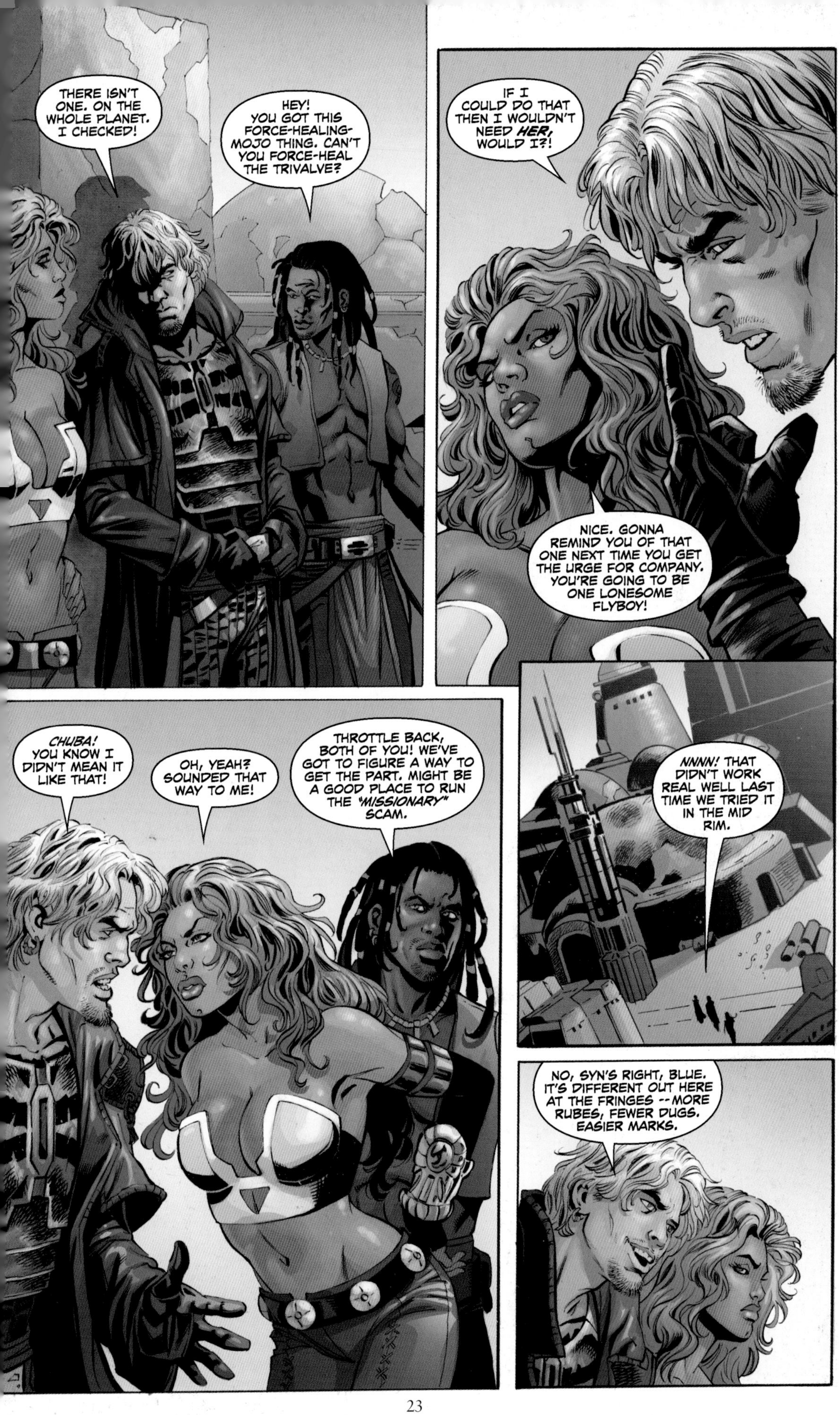
THERE ISN'T ONE. ON THE WHOLE PLANET. I CHECKED!
HEY! YOU GOT THIS FORCE-HEALING-MOJO THING. CAN'T YOU FORCE-HEAL THE TRIVALVE?
IF I COULD DO THAT THEN I WOULDN'T NEED *HER*, WOULD I?!
NICE. GONNA REMIND YOU OF THAT ONE NEXT TIME YOU GET THE URGE FOR COMPANY. YOU'RE GOING TO BE ONE LONESOME FLYBOY!
CHUBA! YOU KNOW I DIDN'T MEAN IT LIKE THAT!
OH, YEAH? SOUNDED THAT WAY TO ME!
THROTTLE BACK, BOTH OF YOU! WE'VE GOT TO FIGURE A WAY TO GET THE PART. MIGHT BE A GOOD PLACE TO RUN THE *"MISSIONARY"* SCAM.
NNNN! THAT DIDN'T WORK REAL WELL LAST TIME WE TRIED IT IN THE MID RIM.
NO, SYN'S RIGHT, BLUE. IT'S DIFFERENT OUT HERE AT THE FRINGES --MORE RUBES, FEWER DUGS. EASIER MARKS.

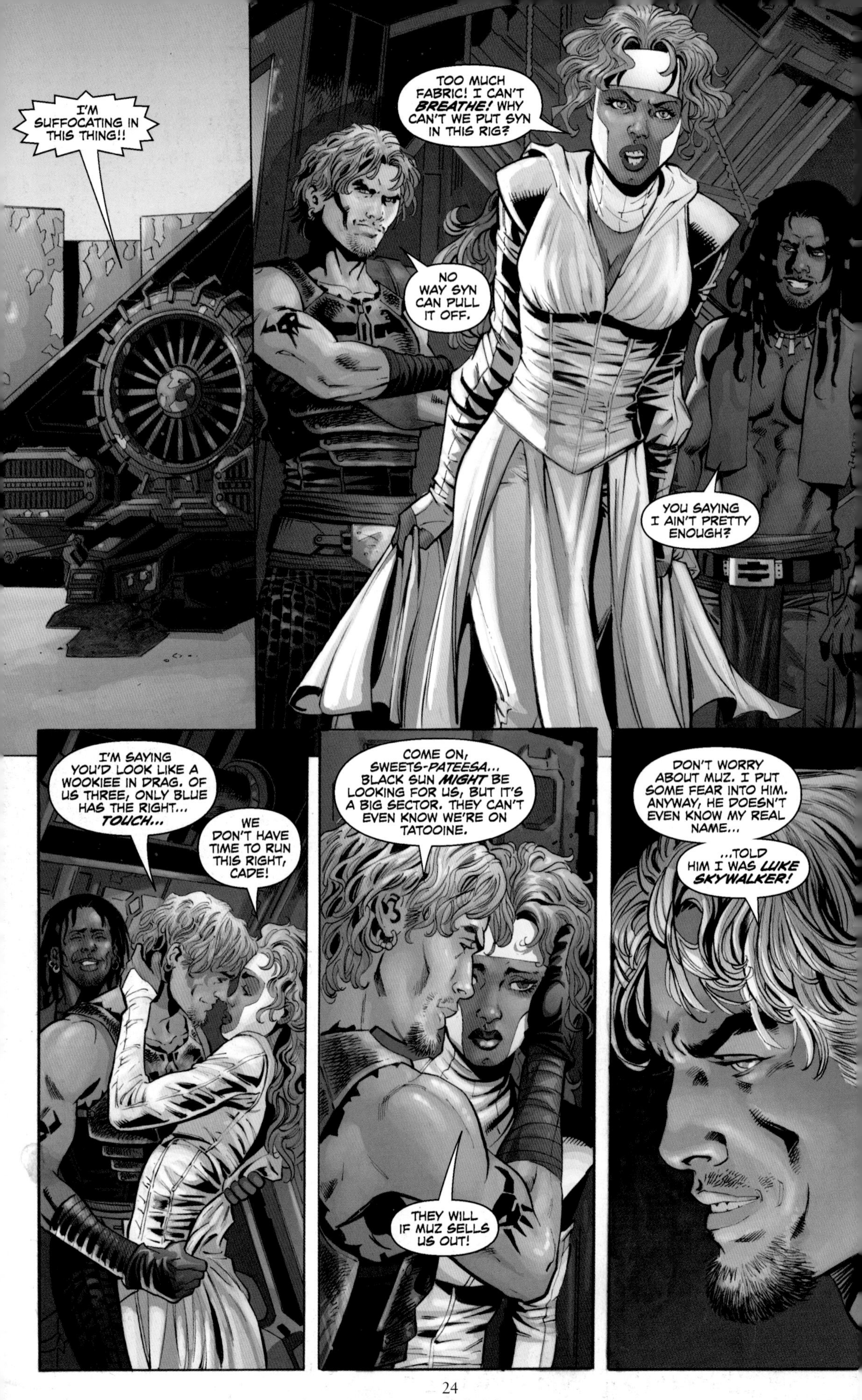
I'M SUFFOCATING IN THIS THING!!
TOO MUCH FABRIC! I CAN'T BREATHE! WHY CAN'T WE PUT SYN IN THIS RIG?
NO WAY SYN CAN PULL IT OFF.
YOU SAYING I AIN'T PRETTY ENOUGH?
I'M SAYING YOU'D LOOK LIKE A WOOKIEE IN DRAG. OF US THREE, ONLY BLUE HAS THE RIGHT... TOUCH...
WE DON'T HAVE TIME TO RUN THIS RIGHT, CADE!
COME ON, SWEETS-PATEESA... BLACK SUN MIGHT BE LOOKING FOR US, BUT IT'S A BIG SECTOR. THEY CAN'T EVEN KNOW WE'RE ON TATOOINE.
THEY WILL IF MUZ SELLS US OUT!
DON'T WORRY ABOUT MUZ. I PUT SOME FEAR INTO HIM. ANYWAY, HE DOESN'T EVEN KNOW MY REAL NAME...
...TOLD HIM I WAS LUKE SKYWALKER!

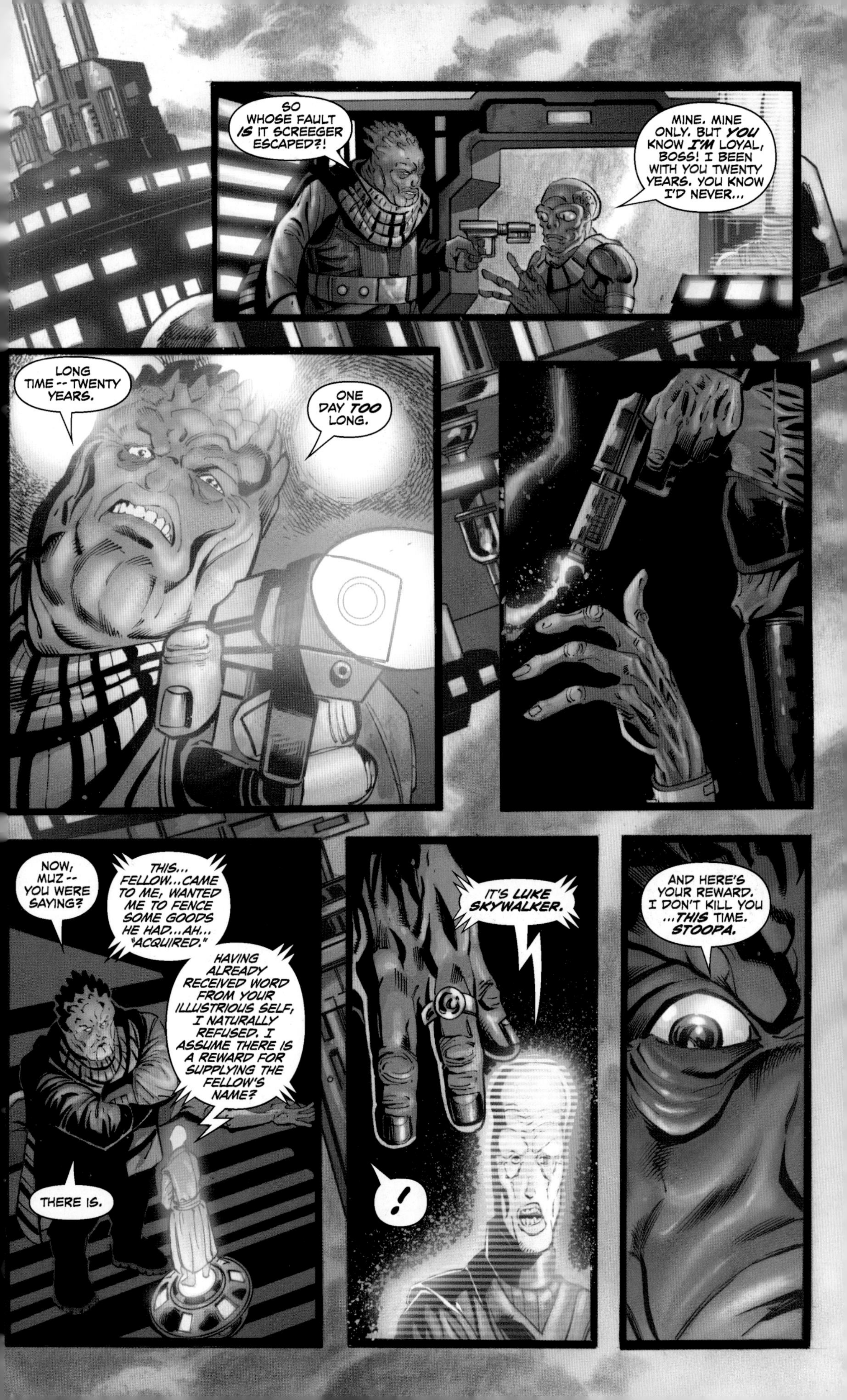
SO WHOSE FAULT IS IT SCREEGER ESCAPED?!
MINE. MINE ONLY. BUT YOU KNOW I'M LOYAL, BOSS! I BEEN WITH YOU TWENTY YEARS. YOU KNOW I'D NEVER...
LONG TIME -- TWENTY YEARS.
ONE DAY TOO LONG.
NOW, MUZ -- YOU WERE SAYING?
THIS... FELLOW...CAME TO ME, WANTED ME TO FENCE SOME GOODS HE HAD...AH... "ACQUIRED."
HAVING ALREADY RECEIVED WORD FROM YOUR ILLUSTRIOUS SELF, I NATURALLY REFUSED. I ASSUME THERE IS A REWARD FOR SUPPLYING THE FELLOW'S NAME?
THERE IS.
IT'S LUKE SKYWALKER.
!
AND HERE'S YOUR REWARD. I DON'T KILL YOU ...THIS TIME. STOOPA.

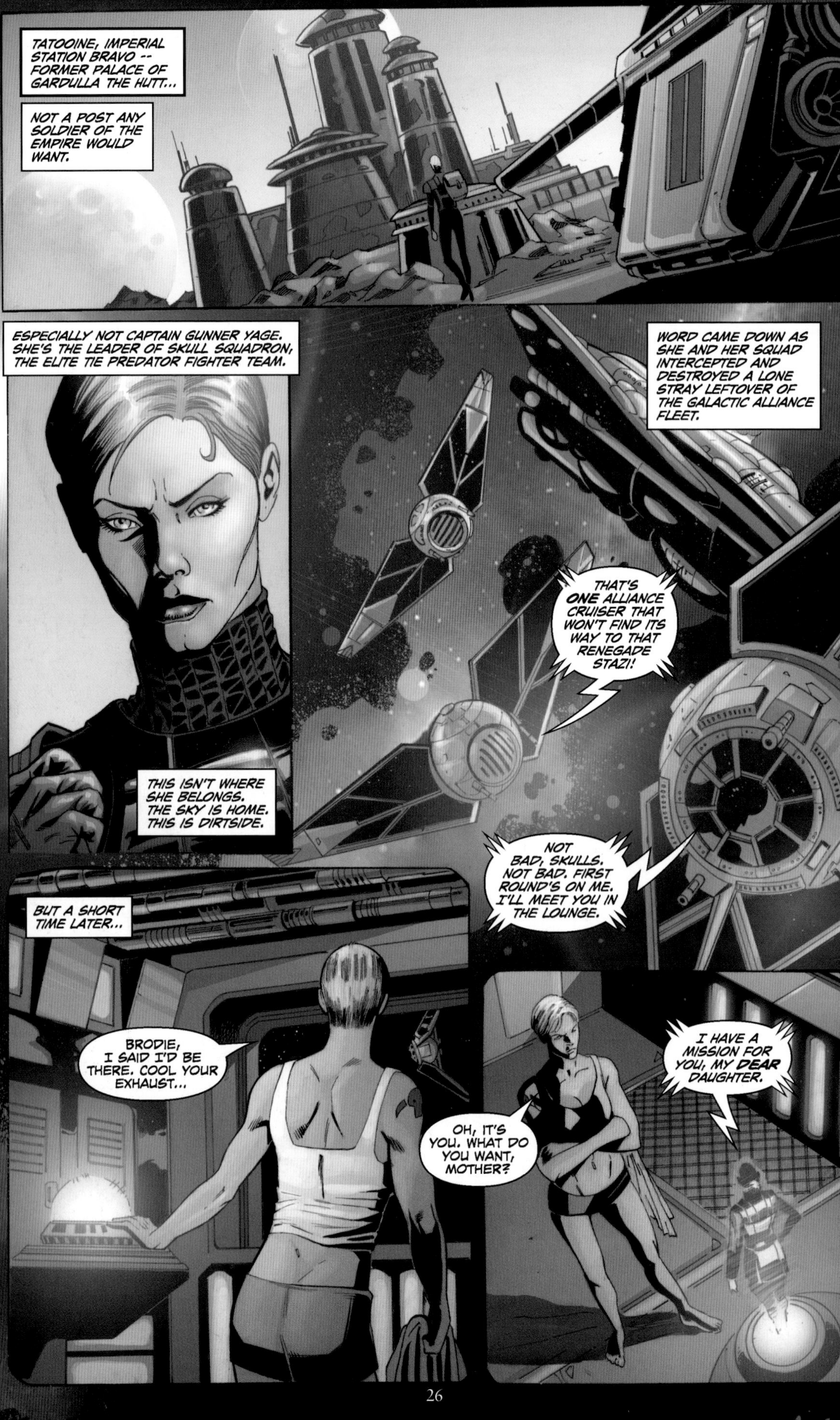
TATOOINE, IMPERIAL STATION BRAVO -- FORMER PALACE OF GARDULLA THE HUTT...
NOT A POST ANY SOLDIER OF THE EMPIRE WOULD WANT.
ESPECIALLY NOT CAPTAIN GUNNER YAGE. SHE'S THE LEADER OF SKULL SQUADRON, THE ELITE TIE PREDATOR FIGHTER TEAM.
THIS ISN'T WHERE SHE BELONGS. THE SKY IS HOME. THIS IS DIRTSIDE.
WORD CAME DOWN AS SHE AND HER SQUAD INTERCEPTED AND DESTROYED A LONE STRAY LEFTOVER OF THE GALACTIC ALLIANCE FLEET.
THAT'S ONE ALLIANCE CRUISER THAT WON'T FIND ITS WAY TO THAT RENEGADE STAZI!
NOT BAD, SKULLS. NOT BAD. FIRST ROUND'S ON ME. I'LL MEET YOU IN THE LOUNGE.
BUT A SHORT TIME LATER...
BRODIE, I SAID I'D BE THERE. COOL YOUR EXHAUST...
OH, IT'S YOU. WHAT DO YOU WANT, MOTHER?
I HAVE A MISSION FOR YOU, MY DEAR DAUGHTER.

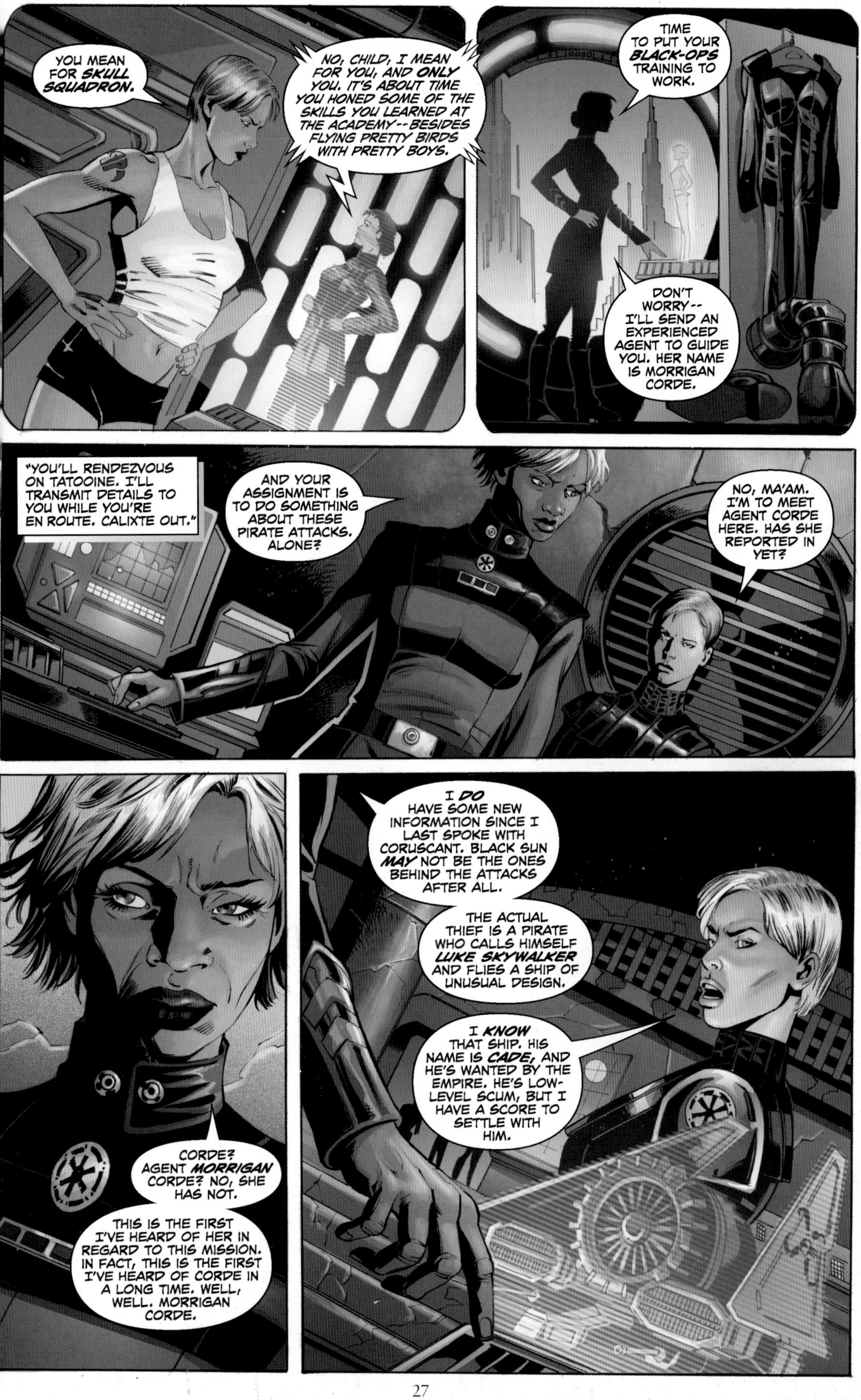
YOU MEAN FOR SKULL SQUADRON.
NO, CHILD, I MEAN FOR YOU, AND ONLY YOU. IT'S ABOUT TIME YOU HONED SOME OF THE SKILLS YOU LEARNED AT THE ACADEMY--BESIDES FLYING PRETTY BIRDS WITH PRETTY BOYS.
TIME TO PUT YOUR BLACK-OPS TRAINING TO WORK.
DON'T WORRY-- I'LL SEND AN EXPERIENCED AGENT TO GUIDE YOU. HER NAME IS MORRIGAN CORDE.
"YOU'LL RENDEZVOUS ON TATOOINE. I'LL TRANSMIT DETAILS TO YOU WHILE YOU'RE EN ROUTE. CALIXTE OUT."
AND YOUR ASSIGNMENT IS TO DO SOMETHING ABOUT THESE PIRATE ATTACKS. ALONE?
NO, MA'AM. I'M TO MEET AGENT CORDE HERE. HAS SHE REPORTED IN YET?
CORDE? AGENT MORRIGAN CORDE? NO, SHE HAS NOT.
THIS IS THE FIRST I'VE HEARD OF HER IN REGARD TO THIS MISSION. IN FACT, THIS IS THE FIRST I'VE HEARD OF CORDE IN A LONG TIME. WELL, WELL. MORRIGAN CORDE.
I DO HAVE SOME NEW INFORMATION SINCE I LAST SPOKE WITH CORUSCANT. BLACK SUN MAY NOT BE THE ONES BEHIND THE ATTACKS AFTER ALL.
THE ACTUAL THIEF IS A PIRATE WHO CALLS HIMSELF LUKE SKYWALKER AND FLIES A SHIP OF UNUSUAL DESIGN.
I KNOW THAT SHIP. HIS NAME IS CADE, AND HE'S WANTED BY THE EMPIRE. HE'S LOW-LEVEL SCUM, BUT I HAVE A SCORE TO SETTLE WITH HIM.

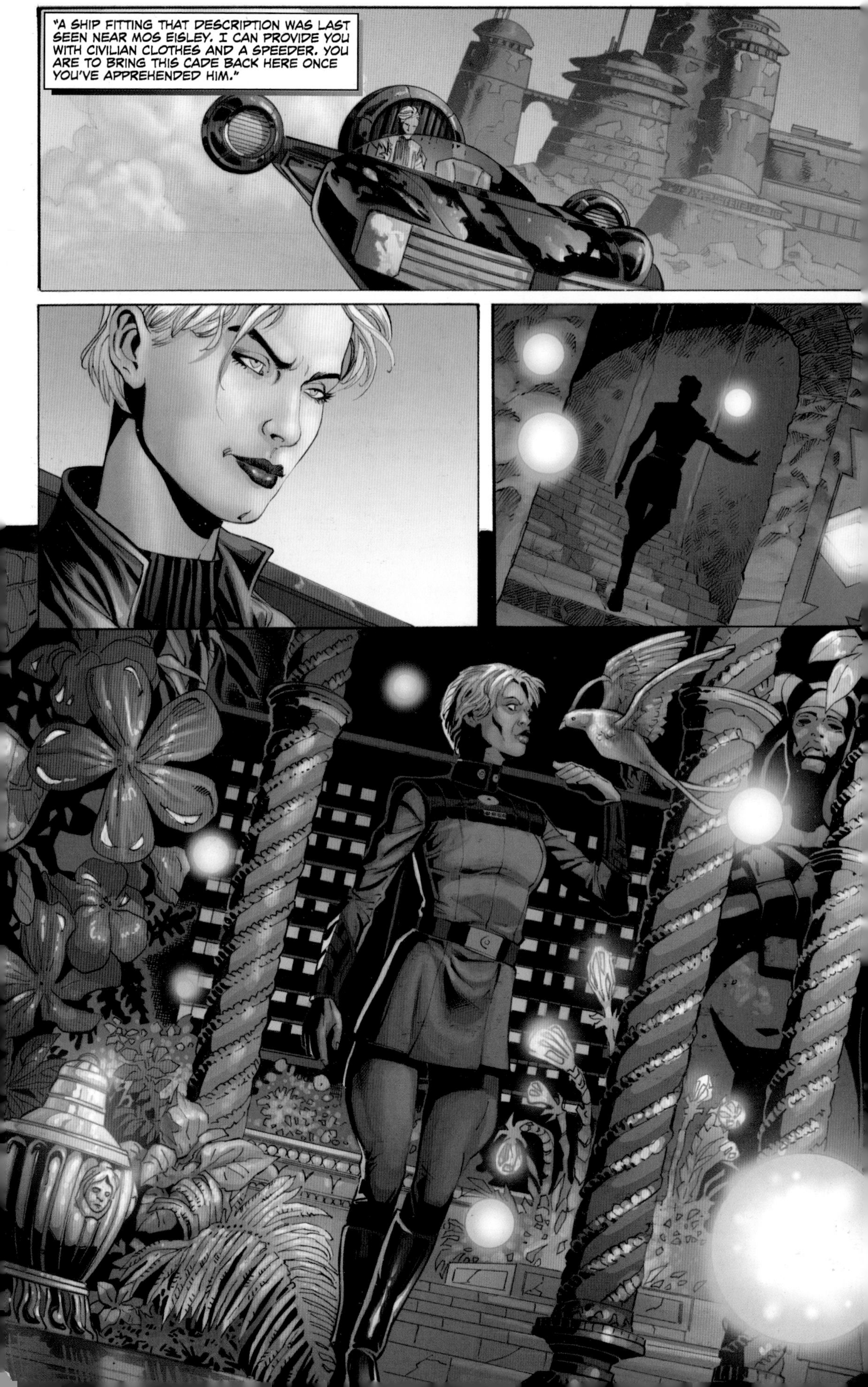
"A SHIP FITTING THAT DESCRIPTION WAS LAST SEEN NEAR MOS EISLEY. I CAN PROVIDE YOU WITH CIVILIAN CLOTHES AND A SPEEDER. YOU ARE TO BRING THIS CADE BACK HERE ONCE YOU'VE APPREHENDED HIM."

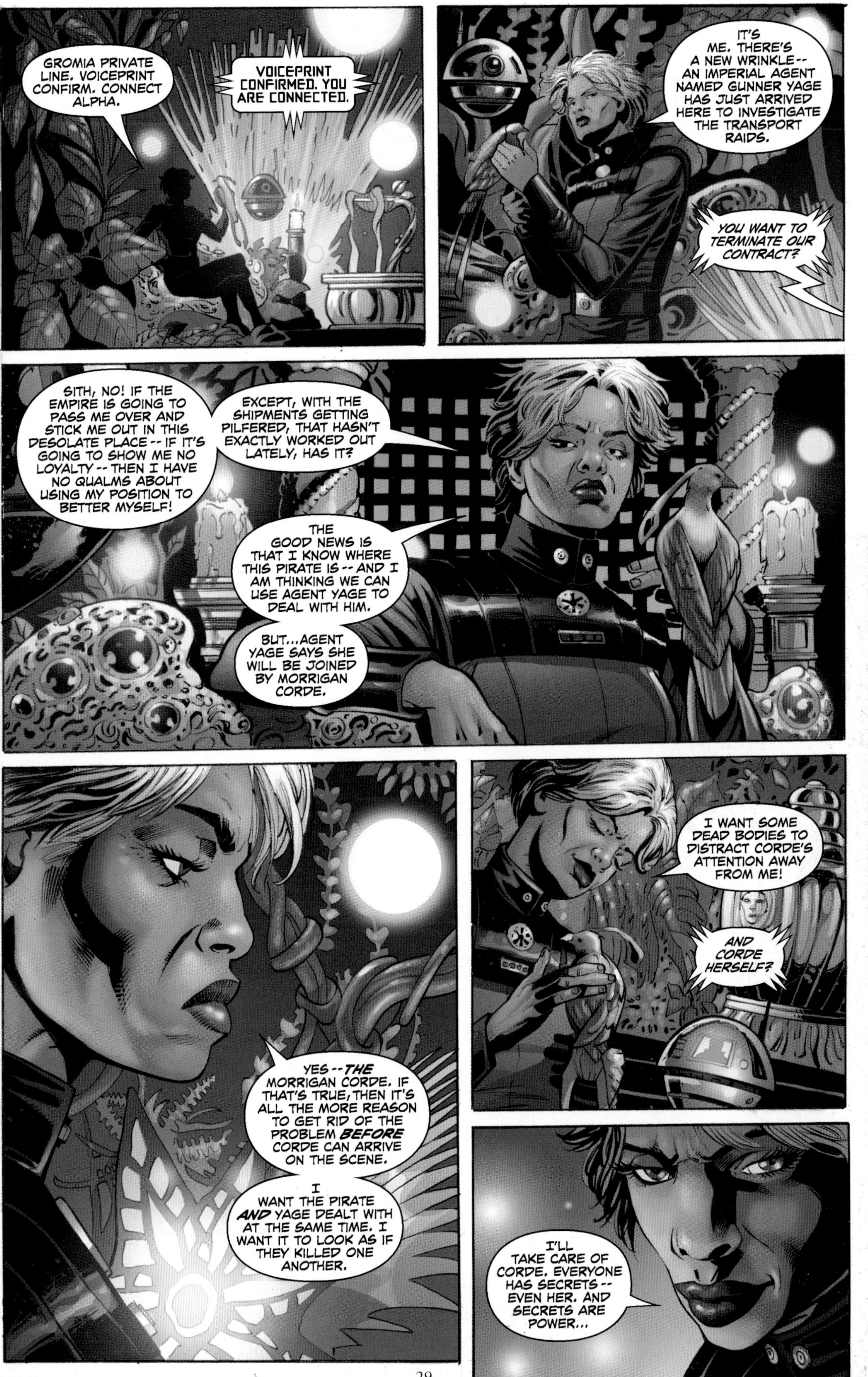

GROMIA PRIVATE LINE. VOICEPRINT CONFIRM. CONNECT ALPHA.
VOICEPRINT CONFIRMED. YOU ARE CONNECTED.
IT'S ME. THERE'S A NEW WRINKLE-- AN IMPERIAL AGENT NAMED GUNNER YAGE HAS JUST ARRIVED HERE TO INVESTIGATE THE TRANSPORT RAIDS.
YOU WANT TO TERMINATE OUR CONTRACT?
SITH, NO! IF THE EMPIRE IS GOING TO PASS ME OVER AND STICK ME OUT IN THIS DESOLATE PLACE -- IF IT'S GOING TO SHOW ME NO LOYALTY -- THEN I HAVE NO QUALMS ABOUT USING MY POSITION TO BETTER MYSELF!
EXCEPT, WITH THE SHIPMENTS GETTING PILFERED, THAT HASN'T EXACTLY WORKED OUT LATELY, HAS IT?
THE GOOD NEWS IS THAT I KNOW WHERE THIS PIRATE IS -- AND I AM THINKING WE CAN USE AGENT YAGE TO DEAL WITH HIM.
BUT...AGENT YAGE SAYS SHE WILL BE JOINED BY MORRIGAN CORDE.
YES -- *THE* MORRIGAN CORDE. IF THAT'S TRUE, THEN IT'S ALL THE MORE REASON TO GET RID OF THE PROBLEM *BEFORE* CORDE CAN ARRIVE ON THE SCENE.
I WANT THE PIRATE *AND* YAGE DEALT WITH AT THE SAME TIME. I WANT IT TO LOOK AS IF THEY KILLED ONE ANOTHER.
I WANT SOME DEAD BODIES TO DISTRACT CORDE'S ATTENTION AWAY FROM ME!
AND CORDE HERSELF?
I'LL TAKE CARE OF CORDE. EVERYONE HAS SECRETS -- EVEN HER. AND SECRETS ARE POWER...

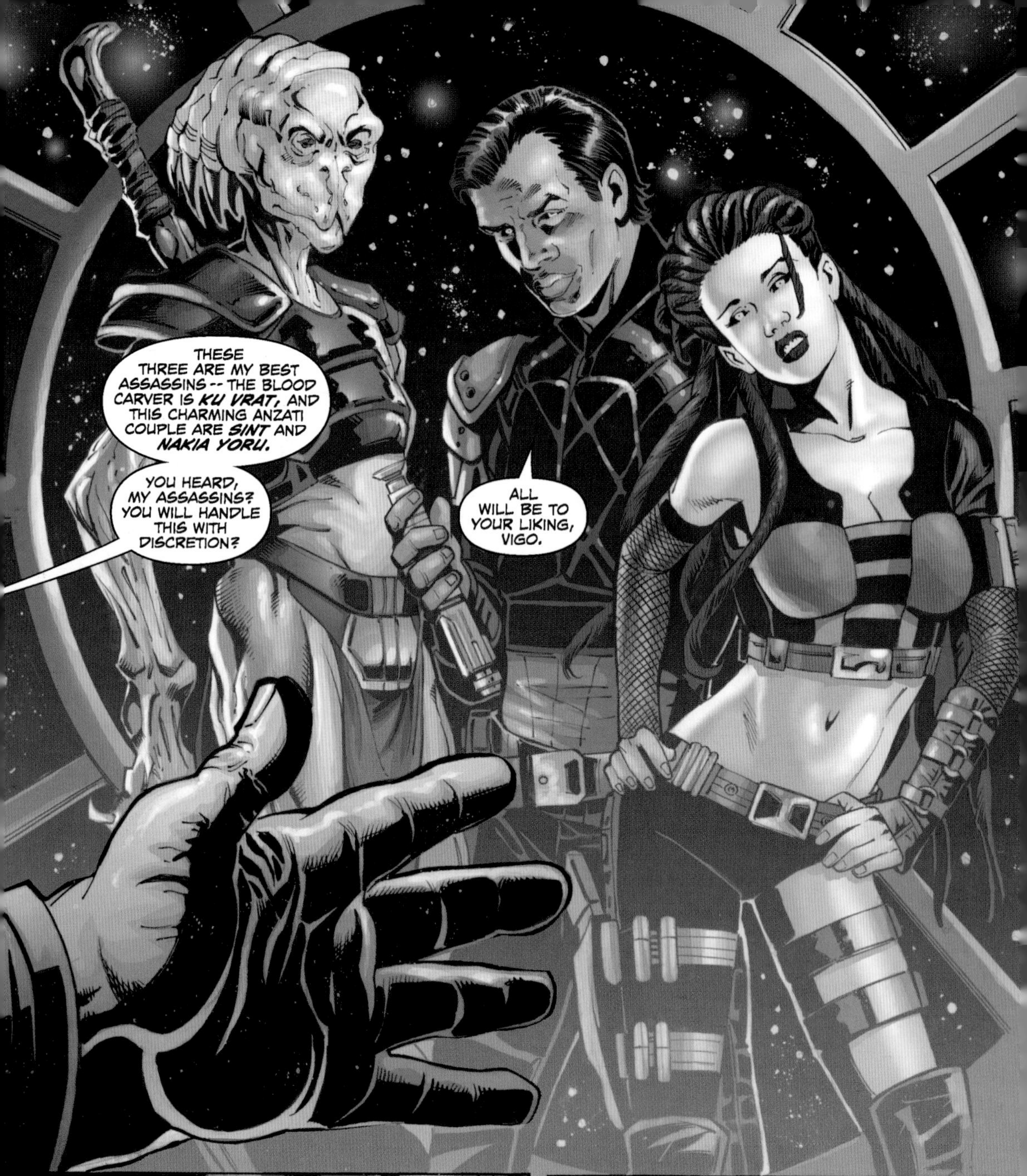
THESE THREE ARE MY BEST ASSASSINS -- THE BLOOD CARVER IS KU VRAT, AND THIS CHARMING ANZATI COUPLE ARE SINT AND NAKIA YORU.
YOU HEARD, MY ASSASSINS? YOU WILL HANDLE THIS WITH DISCRETION?
ALL WILL BE TO YOUR LIKING, VIGO.

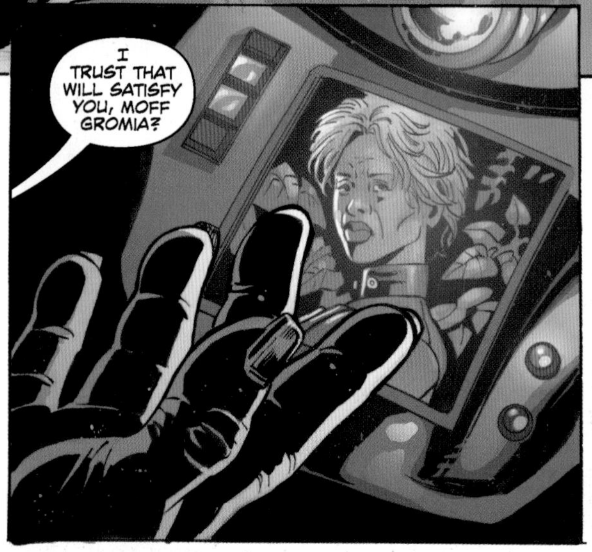
I TRUST THAT WILL SATISFY YOU, MOFF GROMIA?

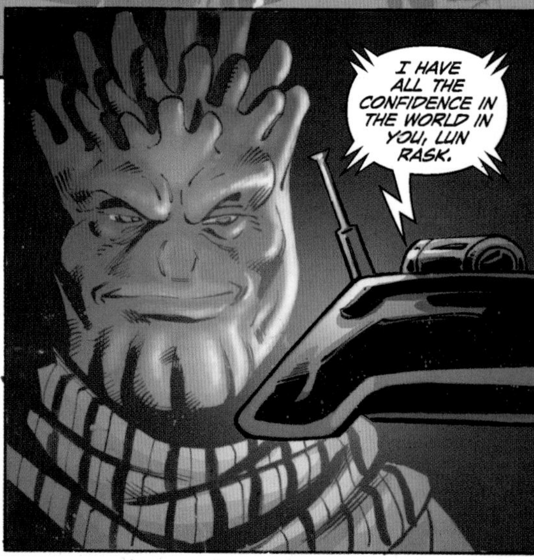
I HAVE ALL THE CONFIDENCE IN THE WORLD IN YOU, LUN RASK.

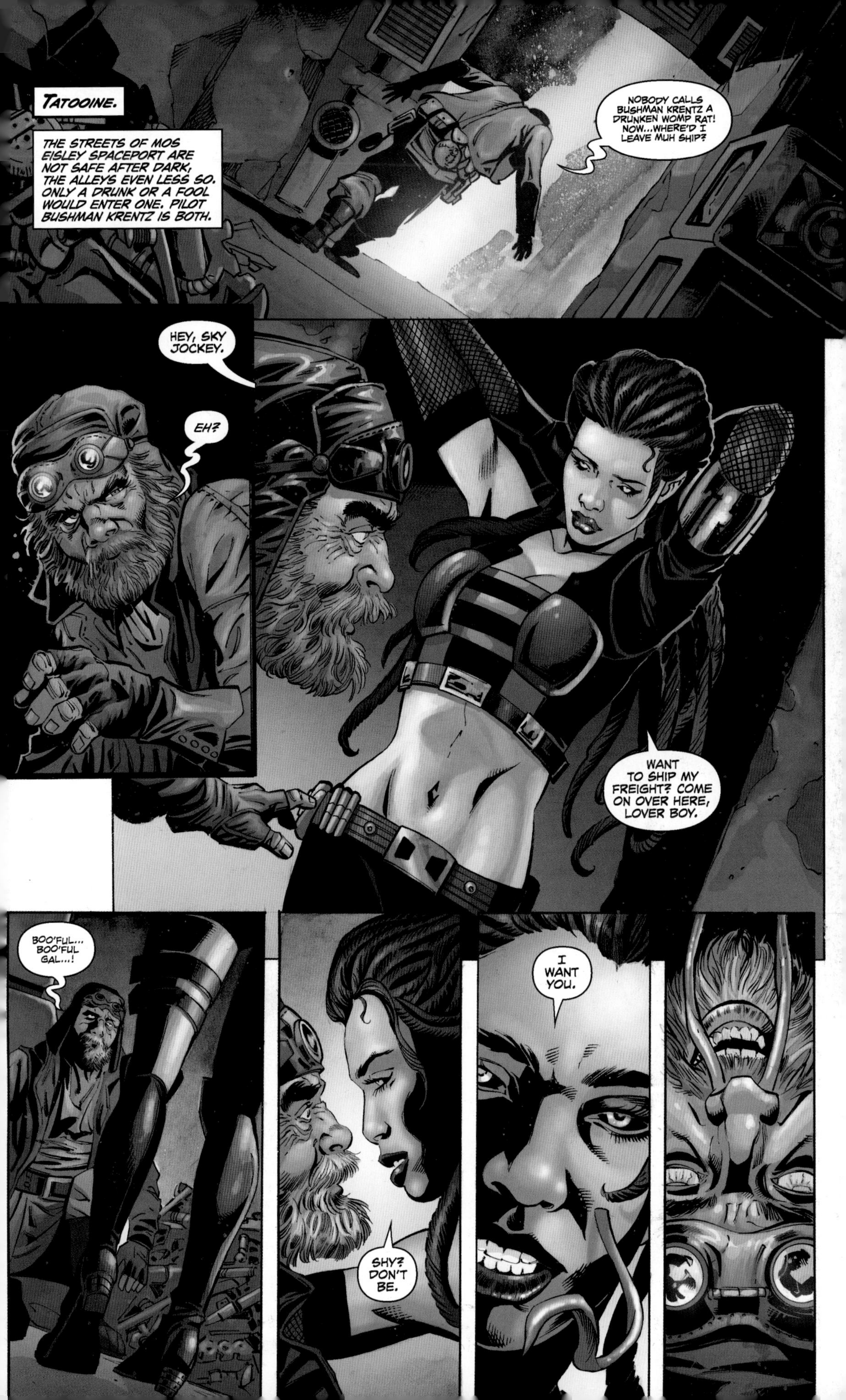
TATOOINE.
THE STREETS OF MOS EISLEY SPACEPORT ARE NOT SAFE AFTER DARK; THE ALLEYS EVEN LESS SO. ONLY A DRUNK OR A FOOL WOULD ENTER ONE. PILOT BUSHMAN KRENTZ IS BOTH.
NOBODY CALLS BUSHMAN KRENTZ A DRUNKEN WOMP RAT! NOW...WHERE'D I LEAVE MUH SHIP?
HEY, SKY JOCKEY.
EH?
WANT TO SHIP MY FREIGHT? COME ON OVER HERE, LOVER BOY.
BOO'FUL... BOO'FUL GAL...!
SHY? DON'T BE.
I WANT YOU.

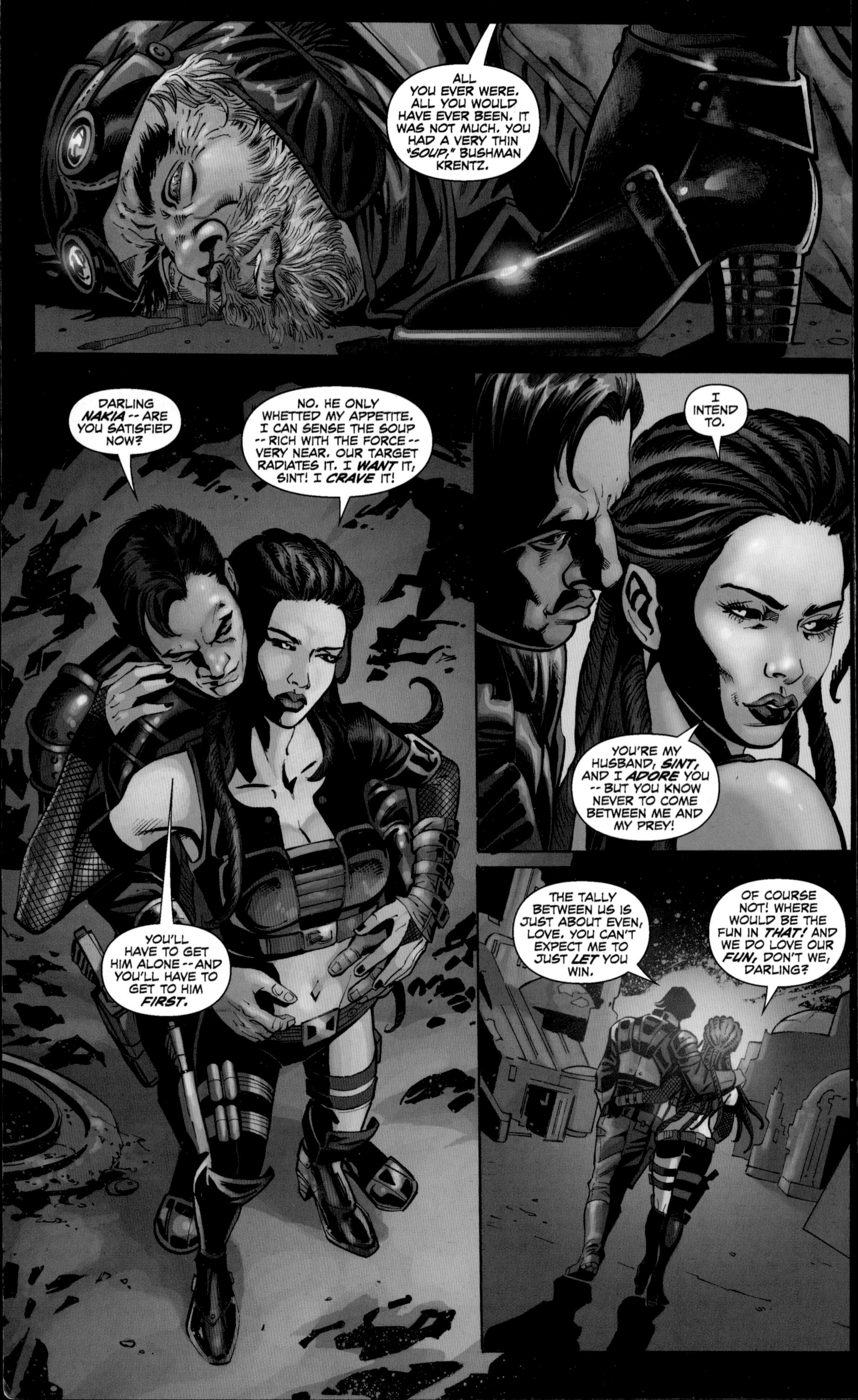
ALL YOU EVER WERE. ALL YOU WOULD HAVE EVER BEEN. IT WAS NOT MUCH. YOU HAD A VERY THIN "SOUP," BUSHMAN KRENTZ.
DARLING NAKIA -- ARE YOU SATISFIED NOW?
NO. HE ONLY WHETTED MY APPETITE. I CAN SENSE THE SOUP -- RICH WITH THE FORCE -- VERY NEAR. OUR TARGET RADIATES IT. I WANT IT, SINT! I CRAVE IT!
YOU'LL HAVE TO GET HIM ALONE -- AND YOU'LL HAVE TO GET TO HIM FIRST.
I INTEND TO.
YOU'RE MY HUSBAND, SINT, AND I ADORE YOU -- BUT YOU KNOW NEVER TO COME BETWEEN ME AND MY PREY!
THE TALLY BETWEEN US IS JUST ABOUT EVEN, LOVE. YOU CAN'T EXPECT ME TO JUST LET YOU WIN.
OF COURSE NOT! WHERE WOULD BE THE FUN IN THAT! AND WE DO LOVE OUR FUN, DON'T WE, DARLING?

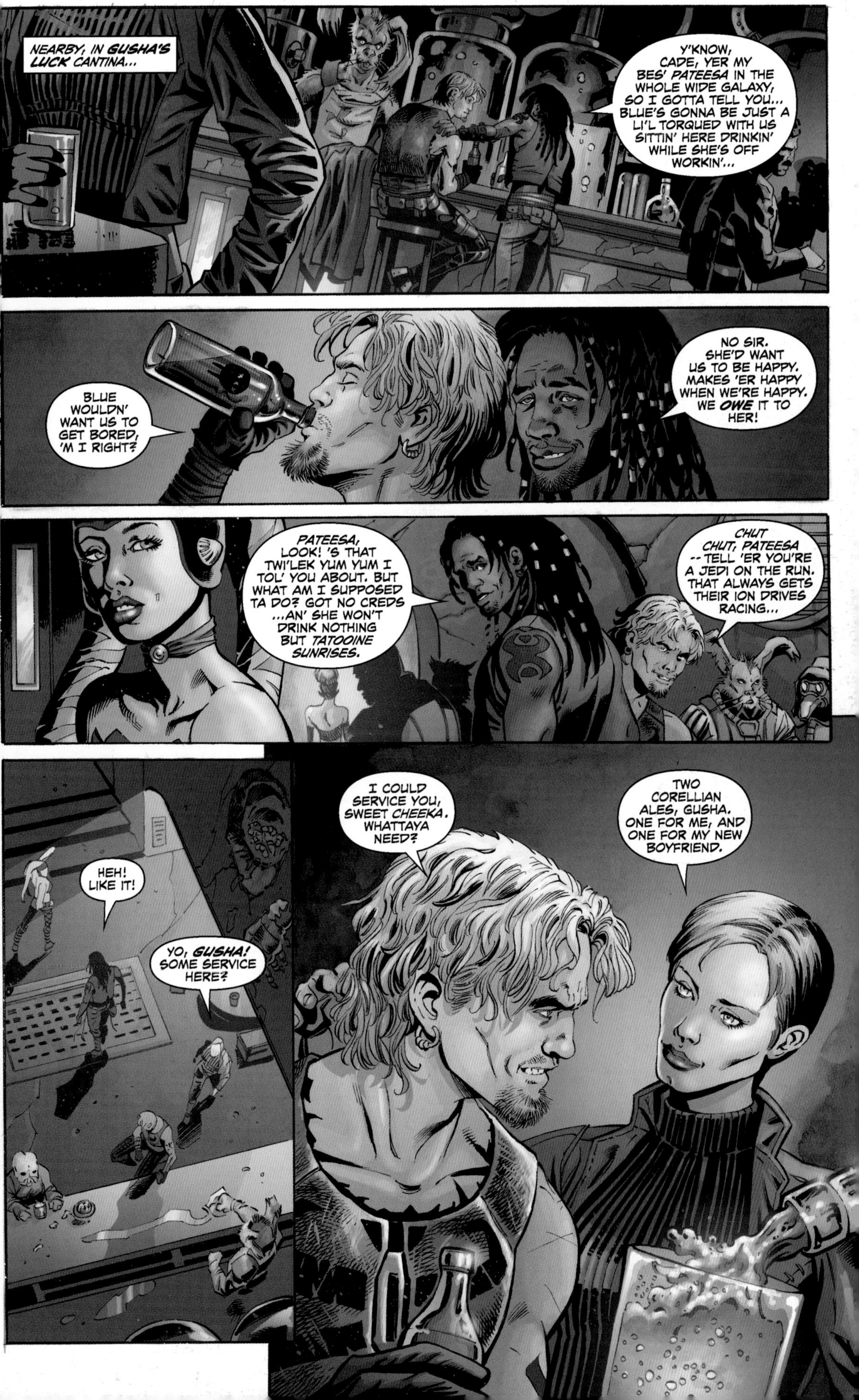
NEARBY, IN GUSHA'S LUCK CANTINA...
Y'KNOW, CADE, YER MY BES' PATEESA IN THE WHOLE WIDE GALAXY, SO I GOTTA TELL YOU... BLUE'S GONNA BE JUST A LI'L TORQUED WITH US SITTIN' HERE DRINKIN' WHILE SHE'S OFF WORKIN'...
BLUE WOULDN' WANT US TO GET BORED, 'M I RIGHT?
NO SIR. SHE'D WANT US TO BE HAPPY. MAKES 'ER HAPPY WHEN WE'RE HAPPY. WE OWE IT TO HER!
PATEESA, LOOK! 'S THAT TWI'LEK YUM YUM I TOL' YOU ABOUT. BUT WHAT AM I SUPPOSED TA DO? GOT NO CREDS ...AN' SHE WON'T DRINK NOTHING BUT TATOOINE SUNRISES.
CHUT CHUT, PATEESA -- TELL 'ER YOU'RE A JEDI ON THE RUN. THAT ALWAYS GETS THEIR ION DRIVES RACING...
HEH! LIKE IT!
YO, GUSHA! SOME SERVICE HERE?
I COULD SERVICE YOU, SWEET CHEEKA. WHATTAYA NEED?
TWO CORELLIAN ALES, GUSHA. ONE FOR ME, AND ONE FOR MY NEW BOYFRIEND.

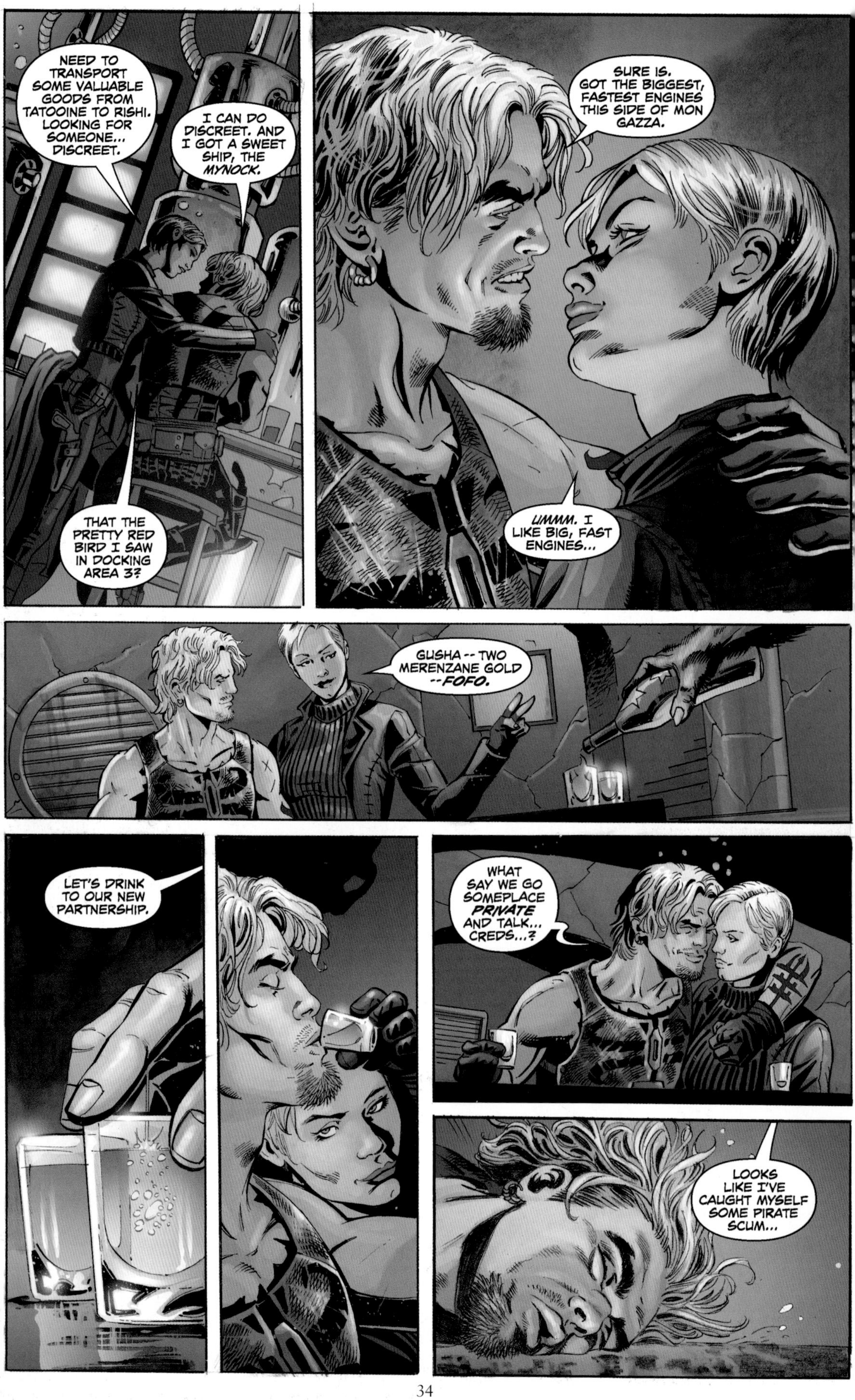
NEED TO TRANSPORT SOME VALUABLE GOODS FROM TATOOINE TO RISHI. LOOKING FOR SOMEONE... DISCREET.
I CAN DO DISCREET. AND I GOT A SWEET SHIP, THE *MYNOCK.*
THAT THE PRETTY RED BIRD I SAW IN DOCKING AREA 3?
SURE IS. GOT THE BIGGEST, FASTEST ENGINES THIS SIDE OF MON GAZZA.
UMMM. I LIKE BIG, FAST ENGINES...
GUSHA -- TWO MERENZANE GOLD -- ***FOFO.***
LET'S DRINK TO OUR NEW PARTNERSHIP.
WHAT SAY WE GO SOMEPLACE ***PRIVATE*** AND TALK... CREDS...?
LOOKS LIKE I'VE CAUGHT MYSELF SOME PIRATE SCUM...

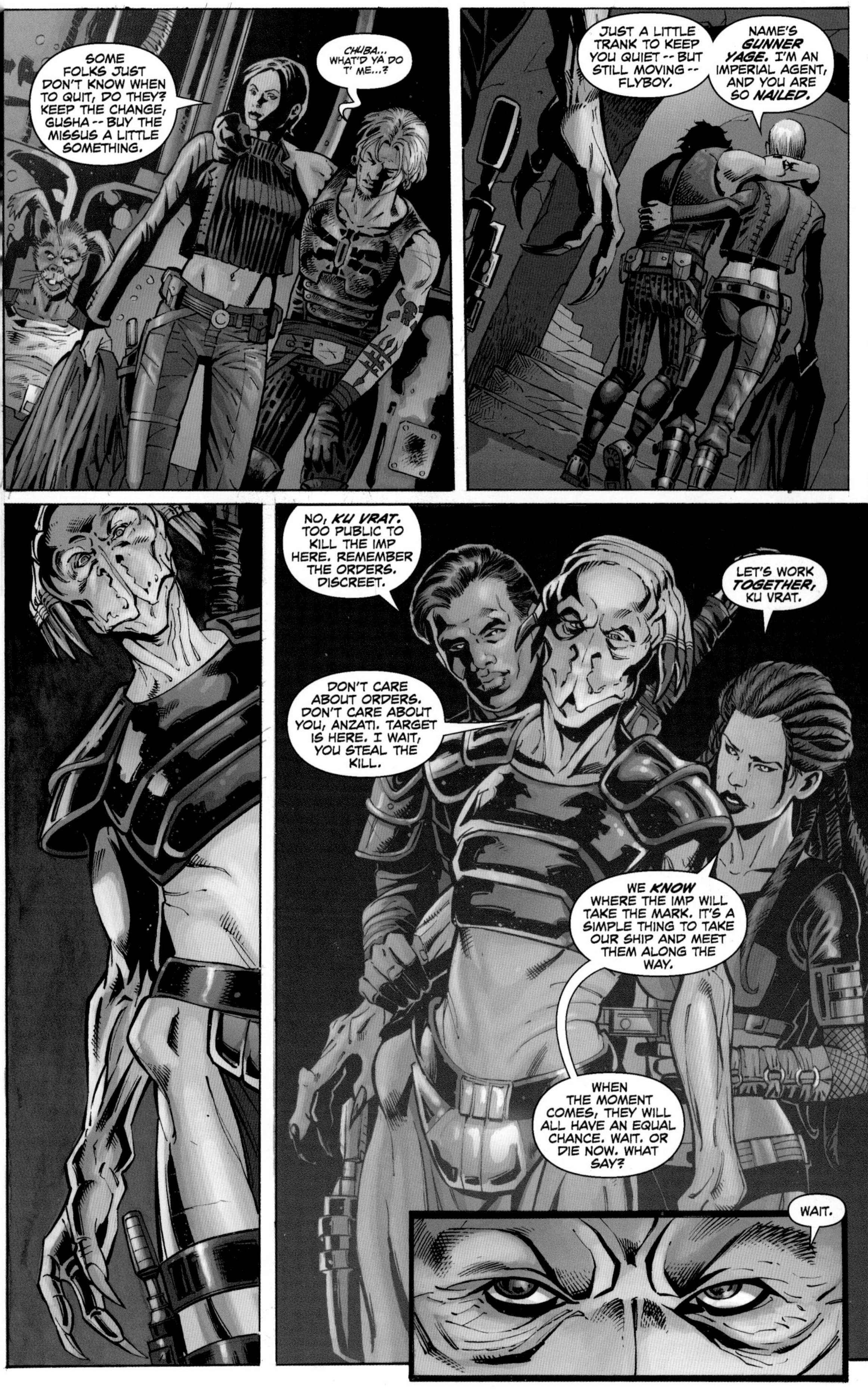
SOME FOLKS JUST DON'T KNOW WHEN TO QUIT, DO THEY? KEEP THE CHANGE, GUSHA -- BUY THE MISSUS A LITTLE SOMETHING.
CHUBA... WHAT'D YA DO T' ME...?
JUST A LITTLE TRANK TO KEEP YOU QUIET -- BUT STILL MOVING -- FLYBOY.
NAME'S GUNNER YAGE. I'M AN IMPERIAL AGENT, AND YOU ARE SO NAILED.
NO, KU VRAT. TOO PUBLIC TO KILL THE IMP HERE. REMEMBER THE ORDERS. DISCREET.
LET'S WORK TOGETHER, KU VRAT.
DON'T CARE ABOUT ORDERS. DON'T CARE ABOUT YOU, ANZATI. TARGET IS HERE. I WAIT, YOU STEAL THE KILL.
WE KNOW WHERE THE IMP WILL TAKE THE MARK. IT'S A SIMPLE THING TO TAKE OUR SHIP AND MEET THEM ALONG THE WAY.
WHEN THE MOMENT COMES, THEY WILL ALL HAVE AN EQUAL CHANCE. WAIT. OR DIE NOW. WHAT SAY?
WAIT.

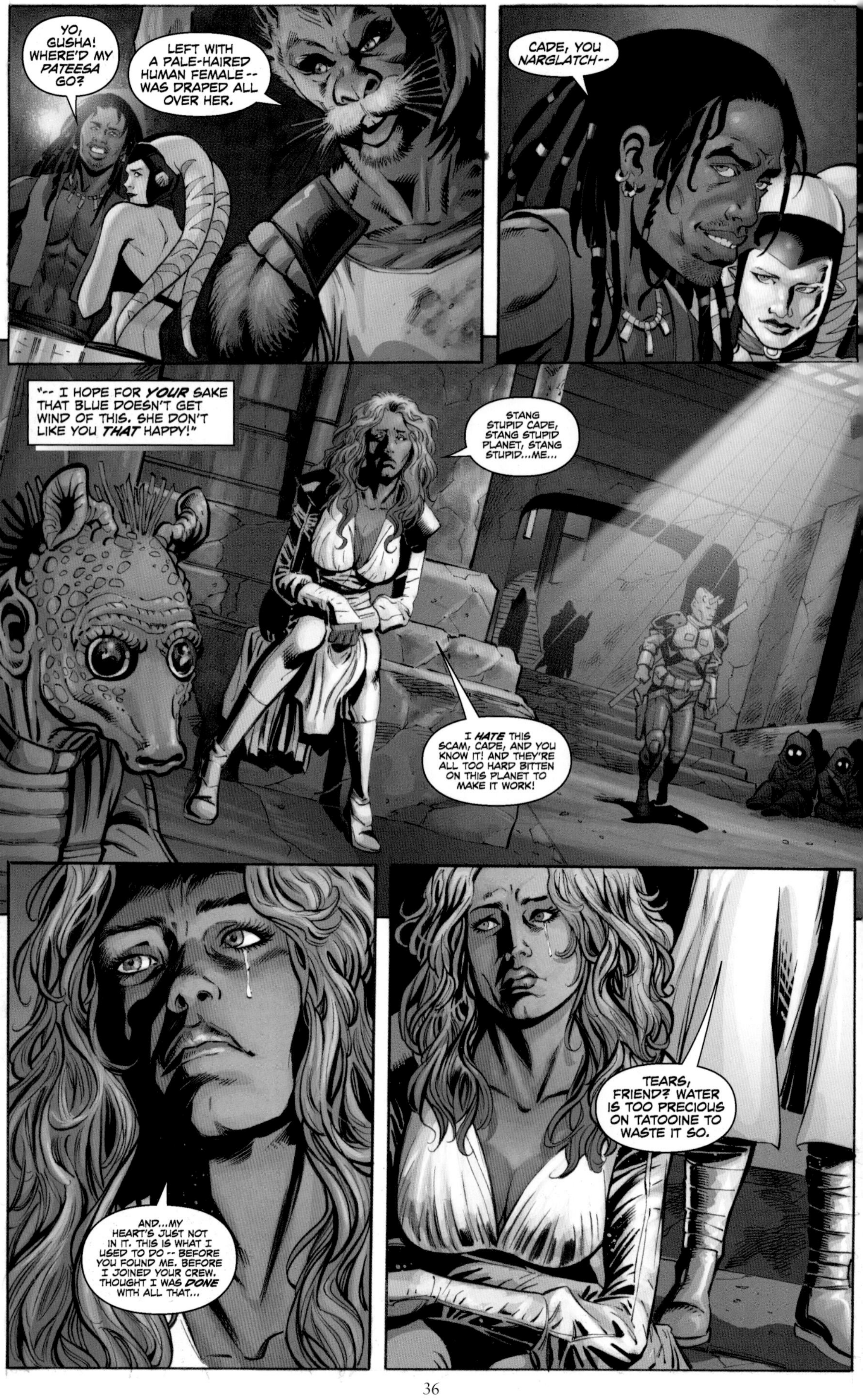
YO, GUSHA! WHERE'D MY *PATEESA* GO?
LEFT WITH A PALE-HAIRED HUMAN FEMALE -- WAS DRAPED ALL OVER HER.
CADE, YOU *NARGLATCH* --
"-- I HOPE FOR ***YOUR*** SAKE THAT BLUE DOESN'T GET WIND OF THIS. SHE DON'T LIKE YOU ***THAT*** HAPPY!"
STANG STUPID CADE, STANG STUPID PLANET, STANG STUPID...ME...
I ***HATE*** THIS SCAM, CADE, AND YOU KNOW IT! AND THEY'RE ALL TOO HARD BITTEN ON THIS PLANET TO MAKE IT WORK!
AND...MY HEART'S JUST NOT IN IT. THIS IS WHAT I USED TO DO -- BEFORE YOU FOUND ME. BEFORE I JOINED YOUR CREW. THOUGHT I WAS ***DONE*** WITH ALL THAT...
TEARS, FRIEND? WATER IS TOO PRECIOUS ON TATOOINE TO WASTE IT SO.

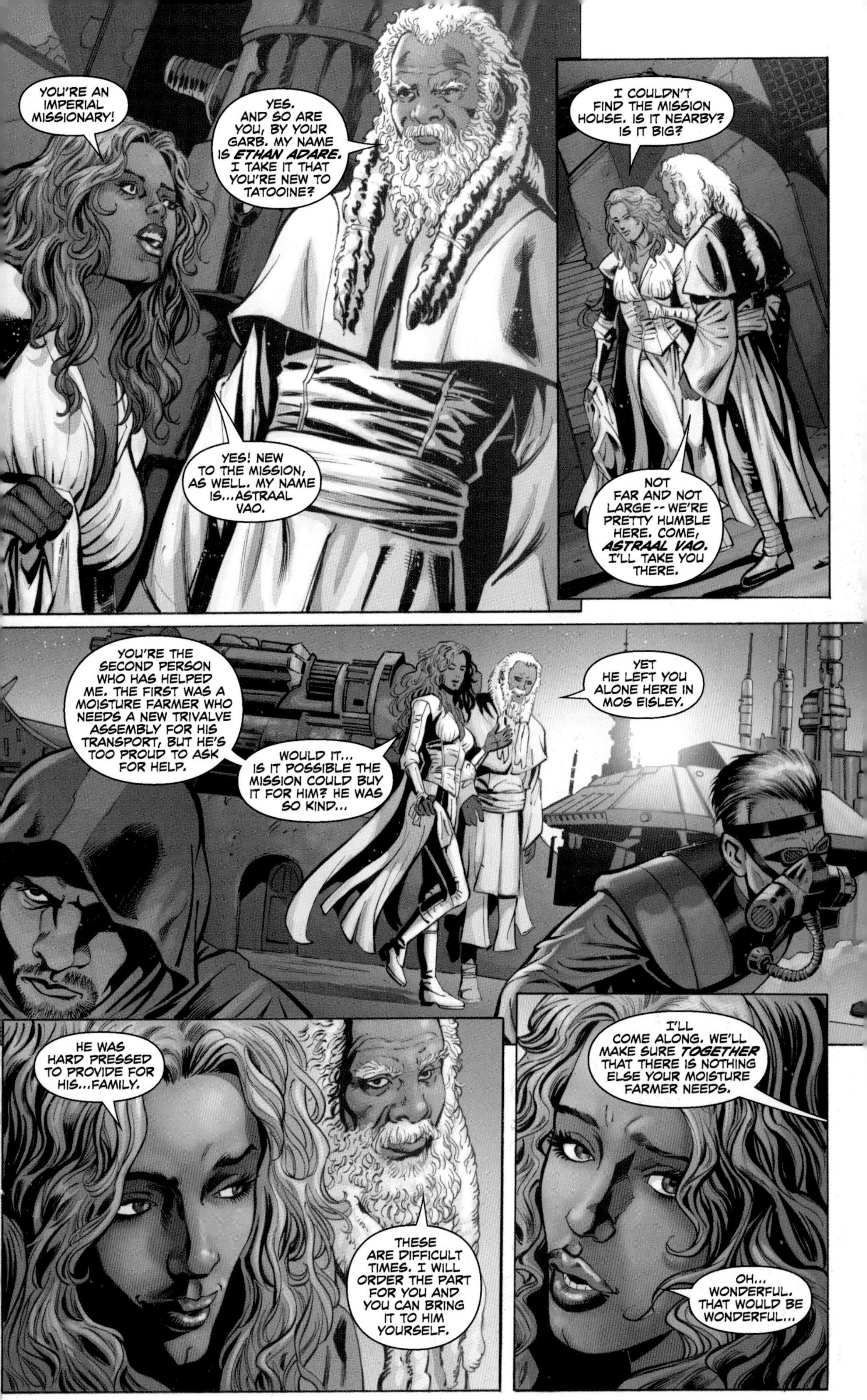
YOU'RE AN IMPERIAL MISSIONARY!
YES. AND SO ARE YOU, BY YOUR GARB. MY NAME IS ETHAN ADARE. I TAKE IT THAT YOU'RE NEW TO TATOOINE?
YES! NEW TO THE MISSION, AS WELL. MY NAME IS...ASTRAAL VAO.
I COULDN'T FIND THE MISSION HOUSE. IS IT NEARBY? IS IT BIG?
NOT FAR AND NOT LARGE -- WE'RE PRETTY HUMBLE HERE. COME, ASTRAAL VAO. I'LL TAKE YOU THERE.
YOU'RE THE SECOND PERSON WHO HAS HELPED ME. THE FIRST WAS A MOISTURE FARMER WHO NEEDS A NEW TRIVALVE ASSEMBLY FOR HIS TRANSPORT, BUT HE'S TOO PROUD TO ASK FOR HELP.
WOULD IT... IS IT POSSIBLE THE MISSION COULD BUY IT FOR HIM? HE WAS SO KIND...
YET HE LEFT YOU ALONE HERE IN MOS EISLEY.
HE WAS HARD PRESSED TO PROVIDE FOR HIS...FAMILY.
THESE ARE DIFFICULT TIMES. I WILL ORDER THE PART FOR YOU AND YOU CAN BRING IT TO HIM YOURSELF.
I'LL COME ALONG. WE'LL MAKE SURE TOGETHER THAT THERE IS NOTHING ELSE YOUR MOISTURE FARMER NEEDS.
OH... WONDERFUL. THAT WOULD BE WONDERFUL...

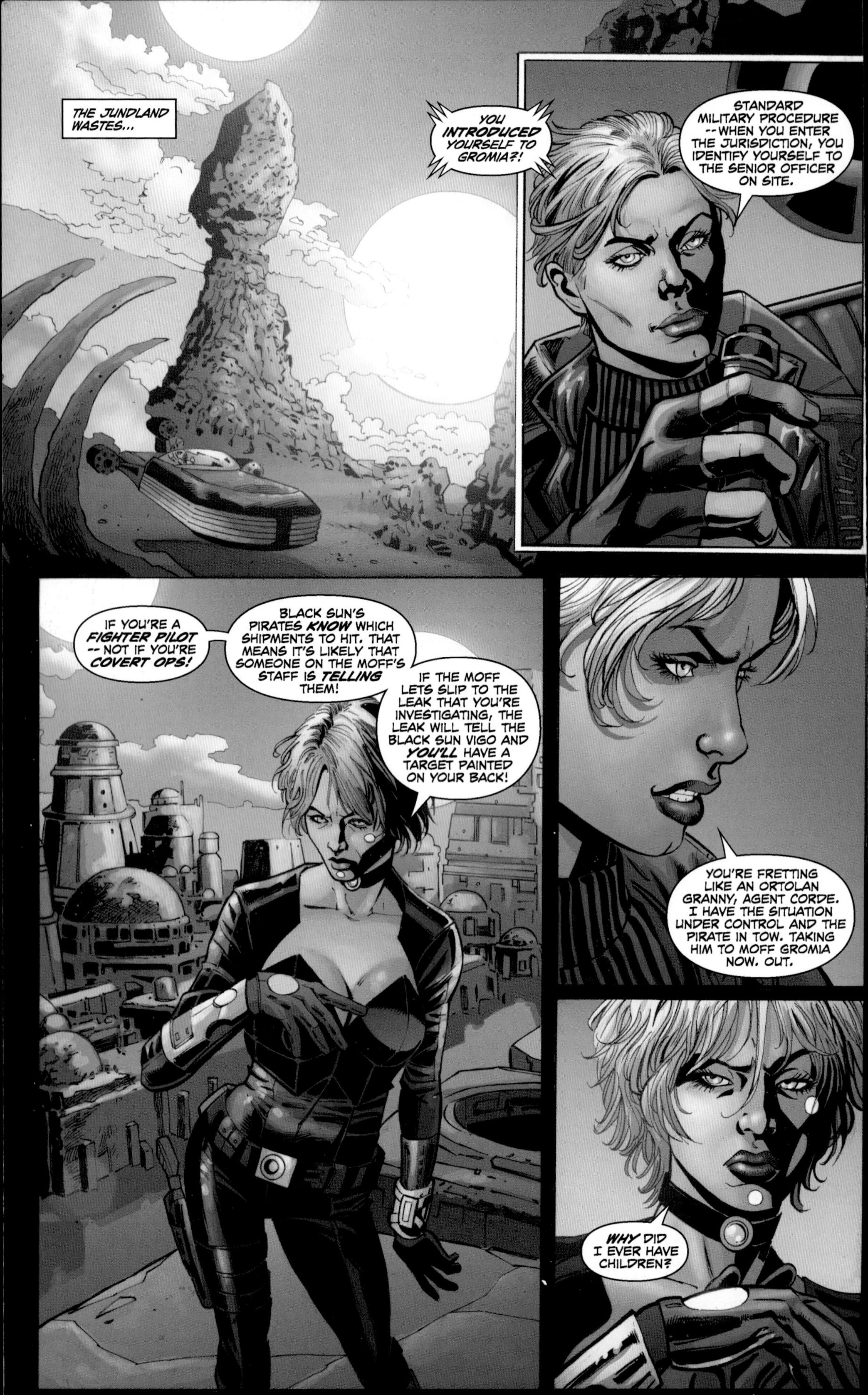

THE JUNDLAND WASTES...
YOU INTRODUCED YOURSELF TO GROMIA?!
STANDARD MILITARY PROCEDURE --WHEN YOU ENTER THE JURISDICTION, YOU IDENTIFY YOURSELF TO THE SENIOR OFFICER ON SITE.
IF YOU'RE A FIGHTER PILOT -- NOT IF YOU'RE COVERT OPS!
BLACK SUN'S PIRATES KNOW WHICH SHIPMENTS TO HIT. THAT MEANS IT'S LIKELY THAT SOMEONE ON THE MOFF'S STAFF IS TELLING THEM!
IF THE MOFF LETS SLIP TO THE LEAK THAT YOU'RE INVESTIGATING, THE LEAK WILL TELL THE BLACK SUN VIGO AND YOU'LL HAVE A TARGET PAINTED ON YOUR BACK!
YOU'RE FRETTING LIKE AN ORTOLAN GRANNY, AGENT CORDE. I HAVE THE SITUATION UNDER CONTROL AND THE PIRATE IN TOW. TAKING HIM TO MOFF GROMIA NOW. OUT.
WHY DID I EVER HAVE CHILDREN?

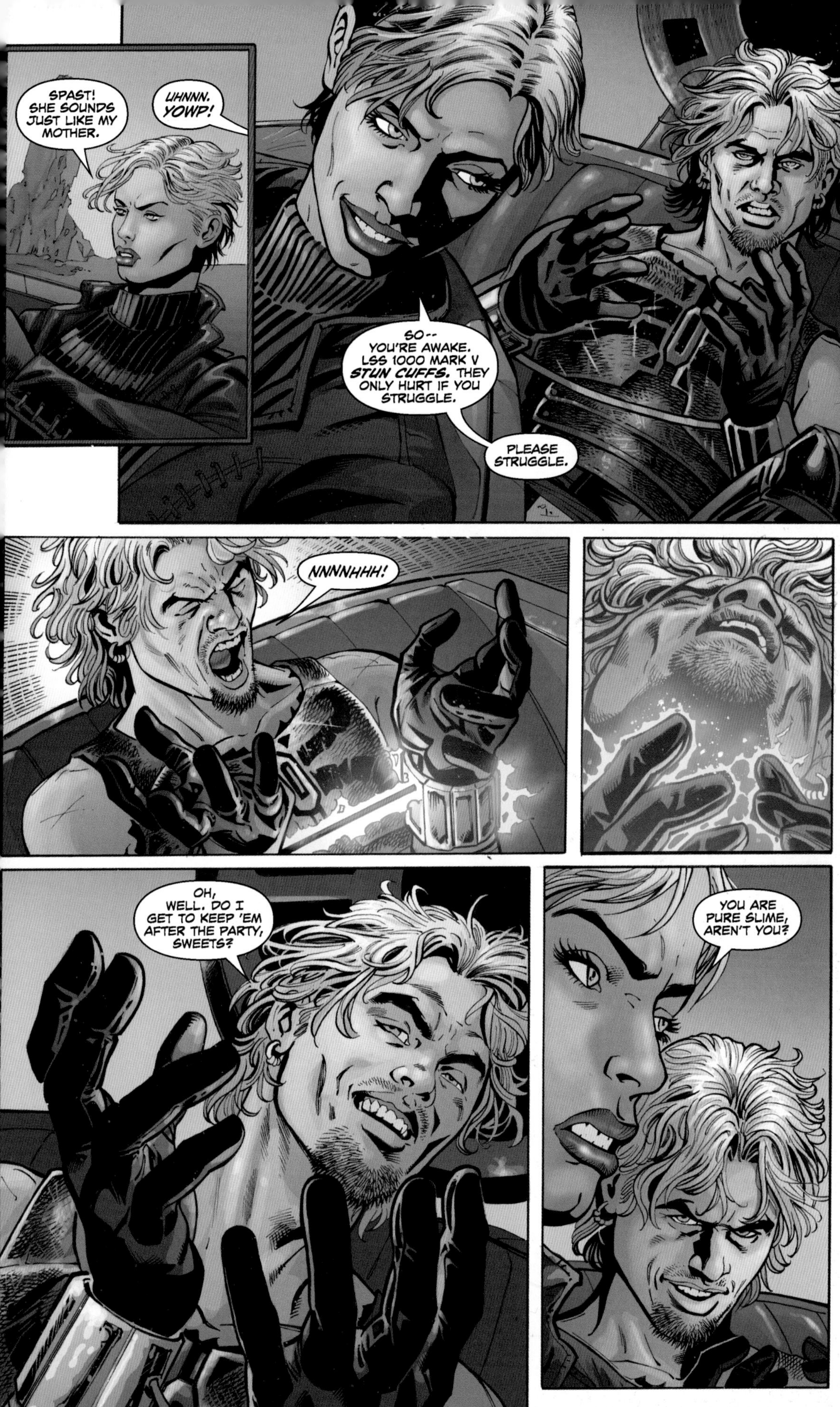
SPAST! SHE SOUNDS JUST LIKE MY MOTHER.
UHNNN. YOWP!
SO-- YOU'RE AWAKE. LSS 1000 MARK V STUN CUFFS. THEY ONLY HURT IF YOU STRUGGLE.
PLEASE STRUGGLE.
NNNNHHH!
OH, WELL. DO I GET TO KEEP 'EM AFTER THE PARTY, SWEETS?
YOU ARE PURE SLIME, AREN'T YOU?

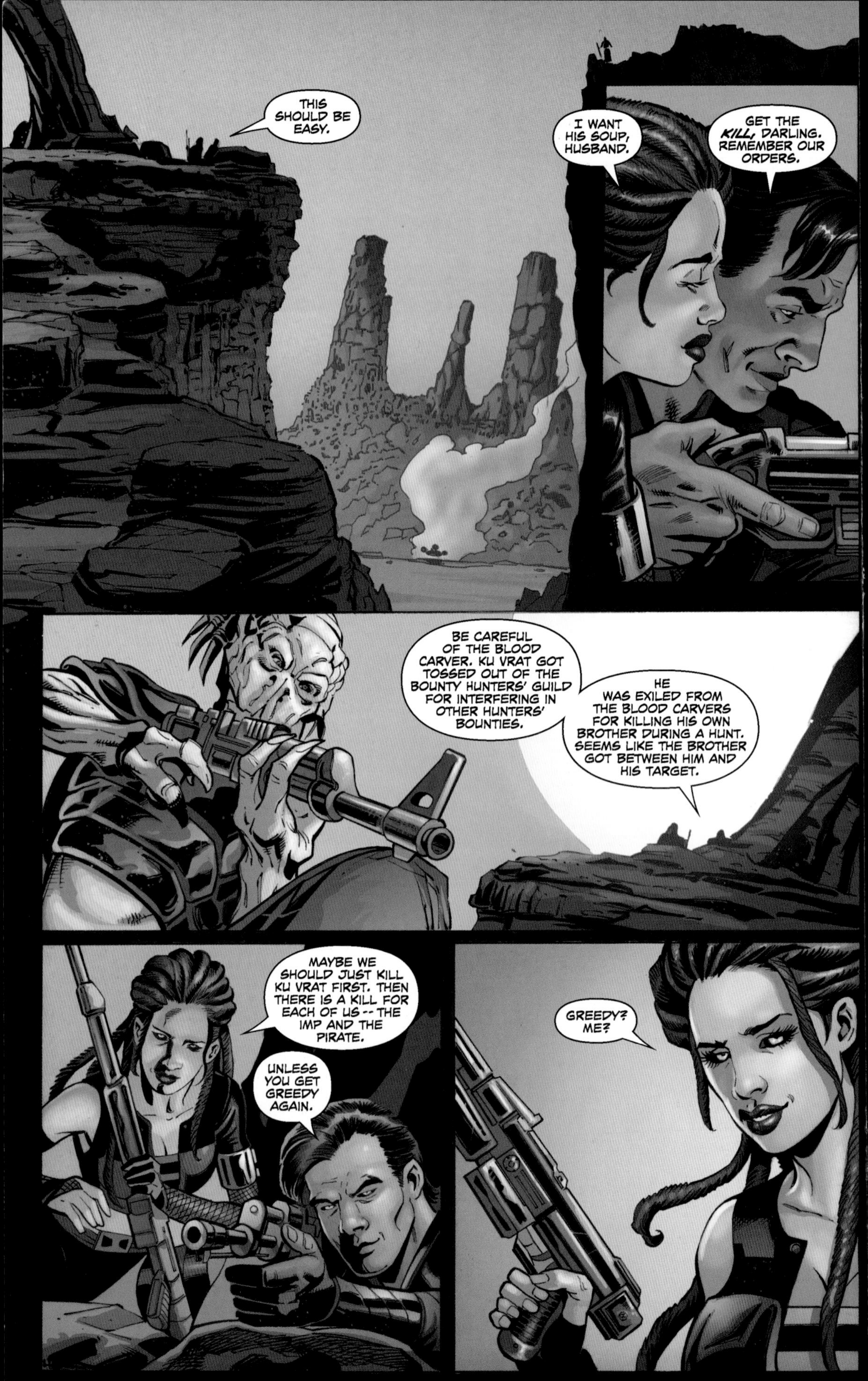
THIS SHOULD BE EASY.
I WANT HIS SOUP, HUSBAND.
GET THE KILL, DARLING. REMEMBER OUR ORDERS.
BE CAREFUL OF THE BLOOD CARVER. KU VRAT GOT TOSSED OUT OF THE BOUNTY HUNTERS' GUILD FOR INTERFERING IN OTHER HUNTERS' BOUNTIES.
HE WAS EXILED FROM THE BLOOD CARVERS FOR KILLING HIS OWN BROTHER DURING A HUNT. SEEMS LIKE THE BROTHER GOT BETWEEN HIM AND HIS TARGET.
MAYBE WE SHOULD JUST KILL KU VRAT FIRST. THEN THERE IS A KILL FOR EACH OF US -- THE IMP AND THE PIRATE.
UNLESS YOU GET GREEDY AGAIN.
GREEDY? ME?

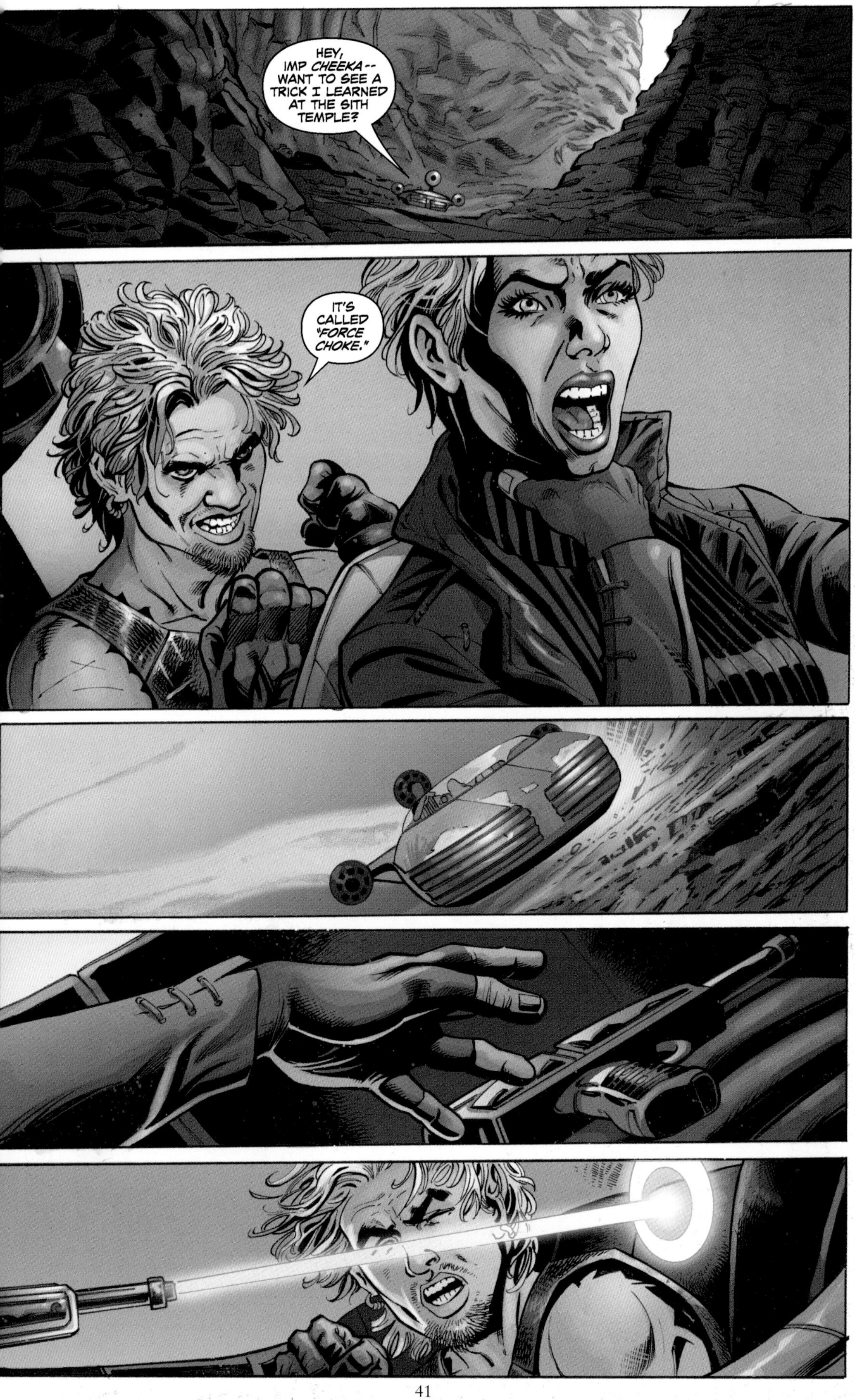
HEY, IMP *CHEEKA*-- WANT TO SEE A TRICK I LEARNED AT THE SITH TEMPLE?
IT'S CALLED *"FORCE CHOKE."*

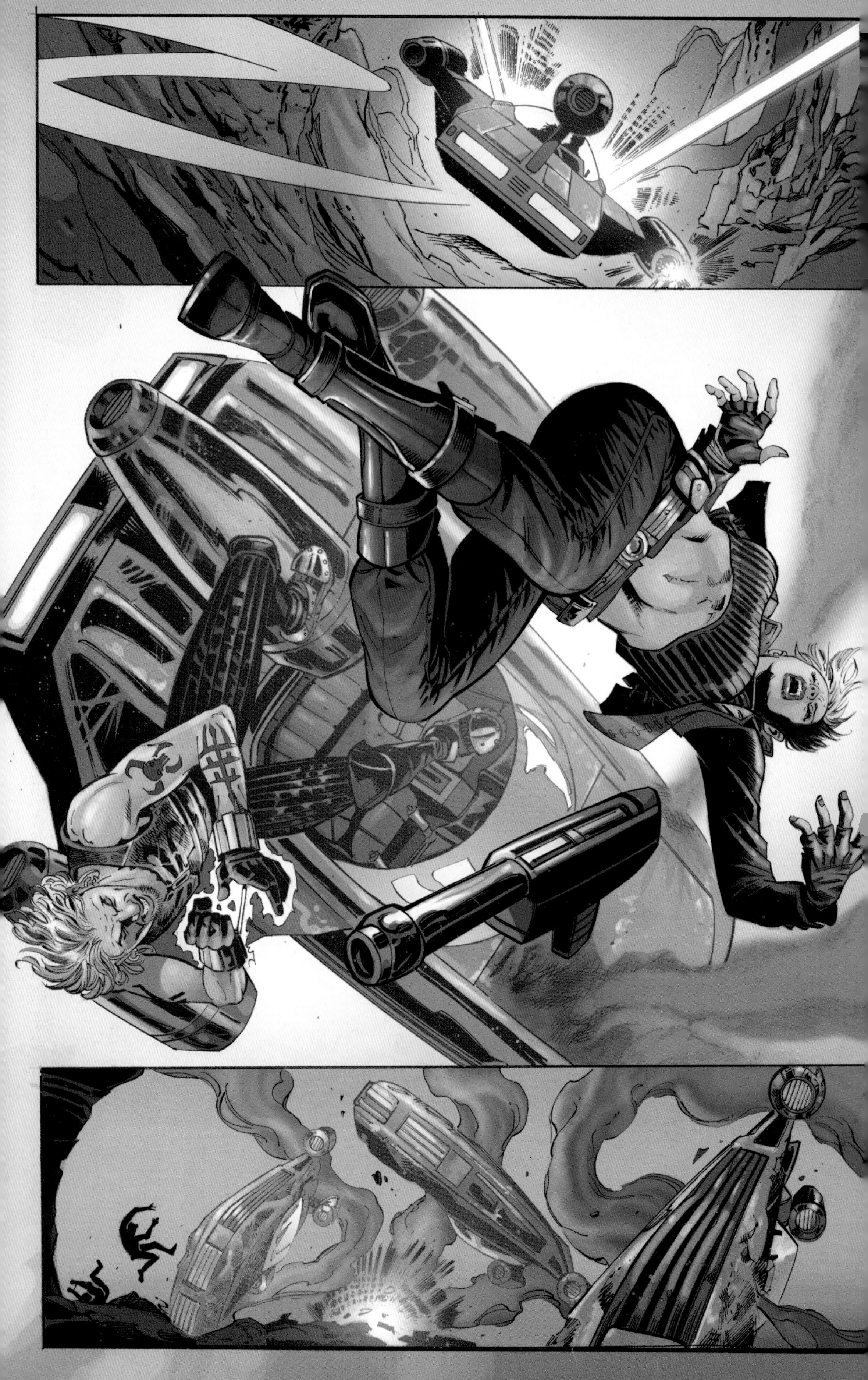

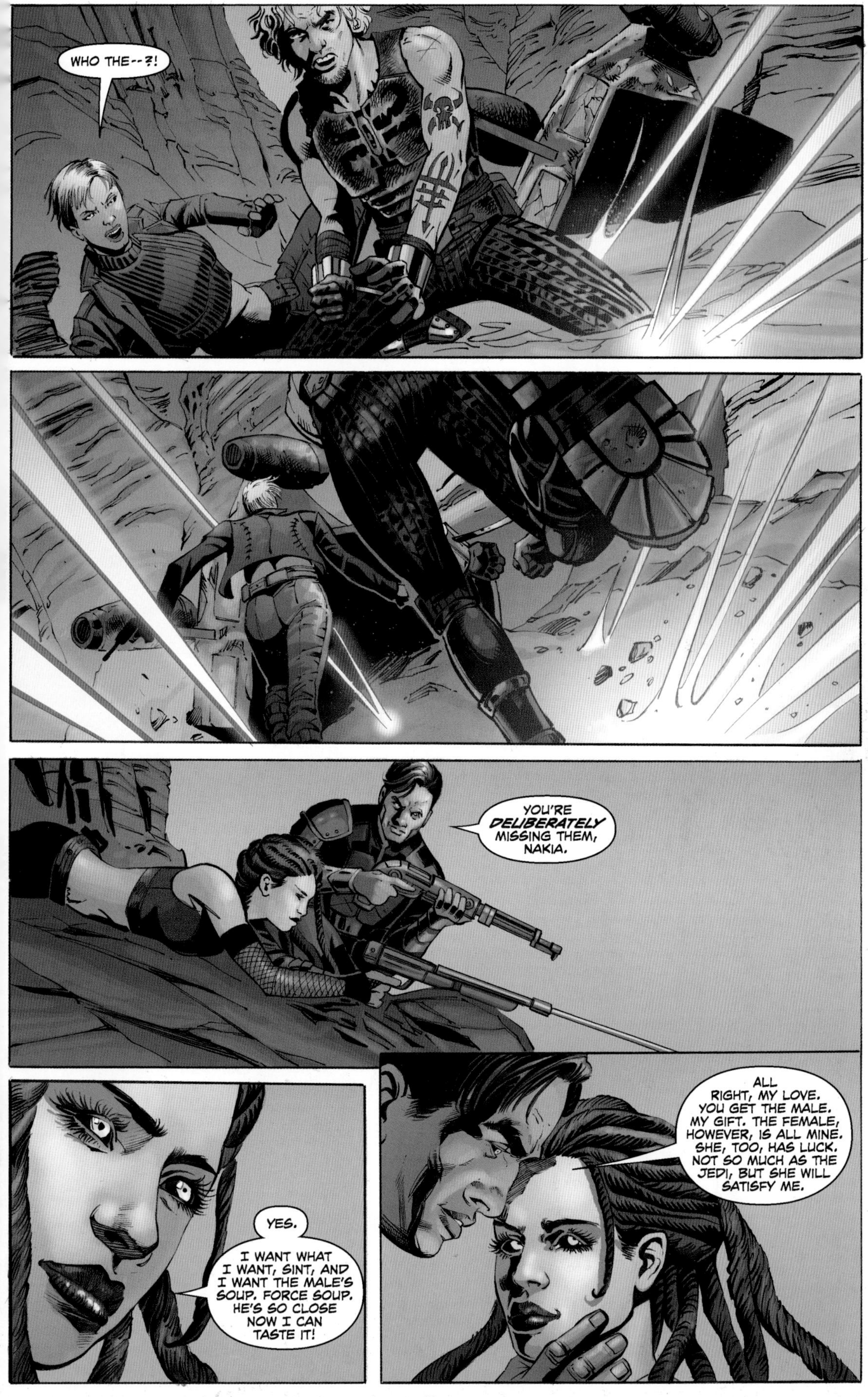
WHO THE--?!
YOU'RE *DELIBERATELY* MISSING THEM, NAKIA.
YES.
I WANT WHAT I WANT, SINT, AND I WANT THE MALE'S SOUP. FORCE SOUP. HE'S SO CLOSE NOW I CAN TASTE IT!
ALL RIGHT, MY LOVE. YOU GET THE MALE. MY GIFT. THE FEMALE, HOWEVER, IS ALL MINE. SHE, TOO, HAS LUCK. NOT SO MUCH AS THE JEDI, BUT SHE WILL SATISFY ME.

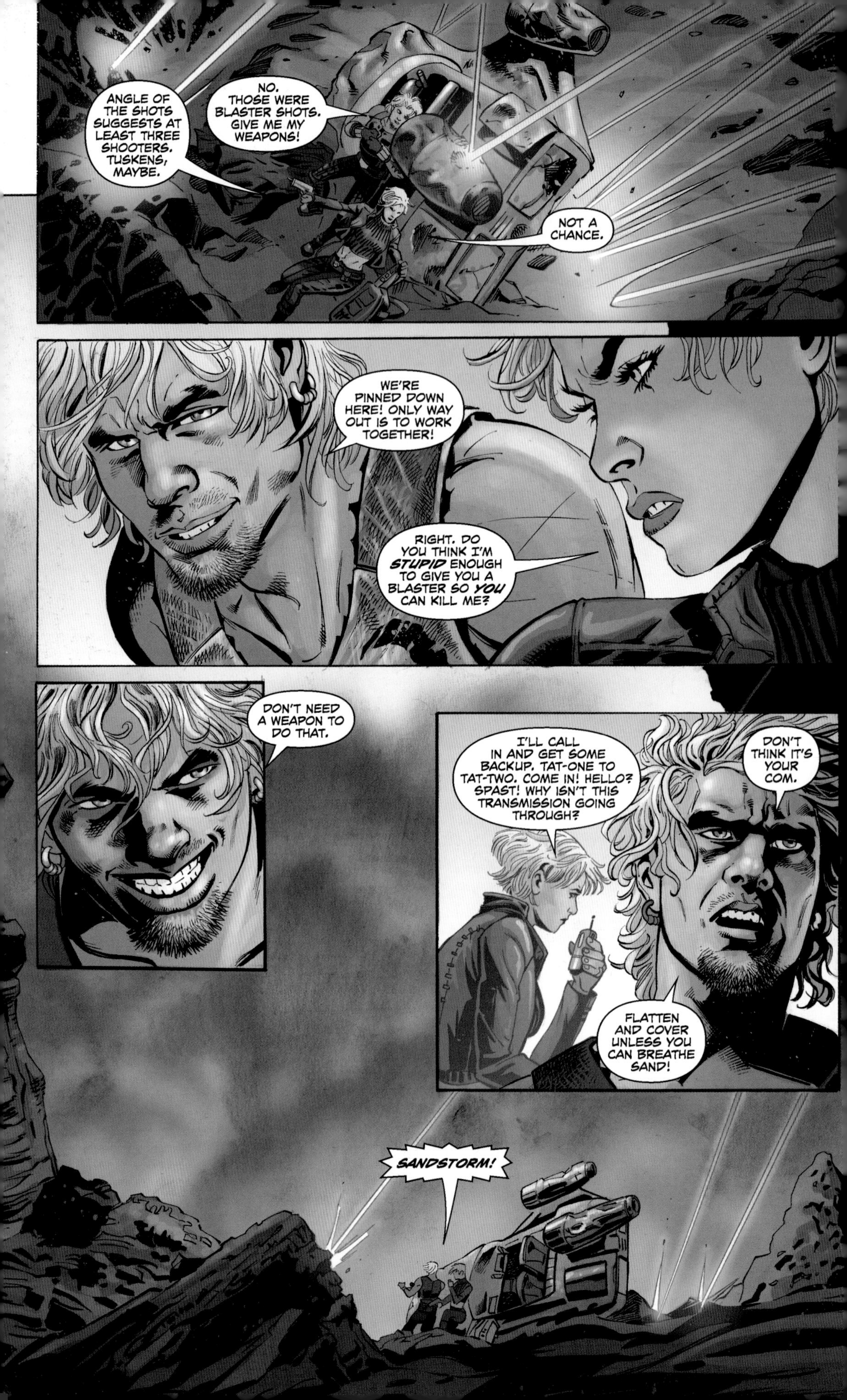
ANGLE OF THE SHOTS SUGGESTS AT LEAST THREE SHOOTERS. TUSKENS, MAYBE.
NO. THOSE WERE BLASTER SHOTS. GIVE ME MY WEAPONS!
NOT A CHANCE.
WE'RE PINNED DOWN HERE! ONLY WAY OUT IS TO WORK TOGETHER!
RIGHT. DO YOU THINK I'M STUPID ENOUGH TO GIVE YOU A BLASTER SO YOU CAN KILL ME?
DON'T NEED A WEAPON TO DO THAT.
I'LL CALL IN AND GET SOME BACKUP. TAT-ONE TO TAT-TWO. COME IN! HELLO? SPAST! WHY ISN'T THIS TRANSMISSION GOING THROUGH?
DON'T THINK IT'S YOUR COM.
FLATTEN AND COVER UNLESS YOU CAN BREATHE SAND!
SANDSTORM!

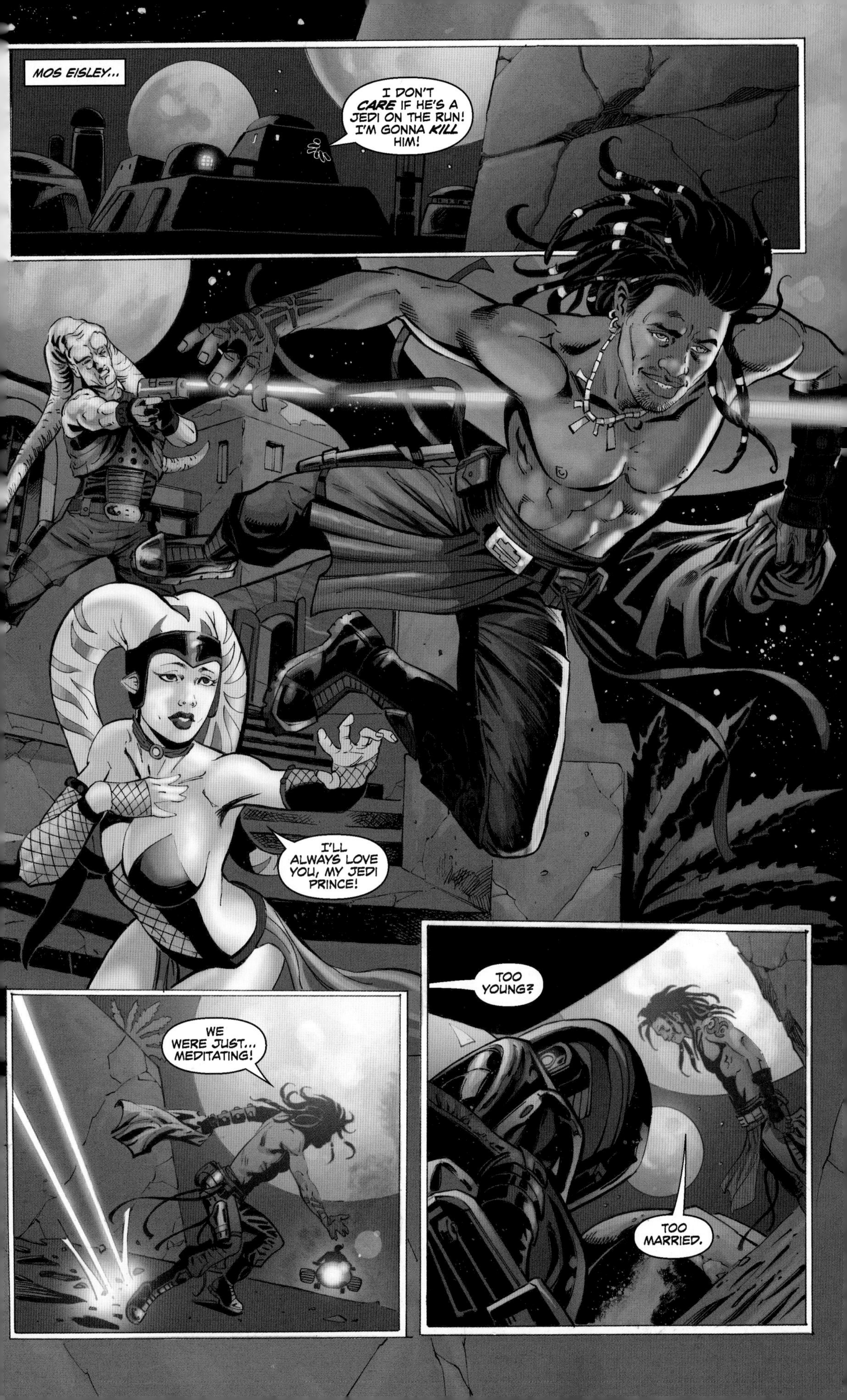
MOS EISLEY...
I DON'T CARE IF HE'S A JEDI ON THE RUN! I'M GONNA KILL HIM!
I'LL ALWAYS LOVE YOU, MY JEDI PRINCE!
WE WERE JUST... MEDITATING!
TOO YOUNG?
TOO MARRIED.

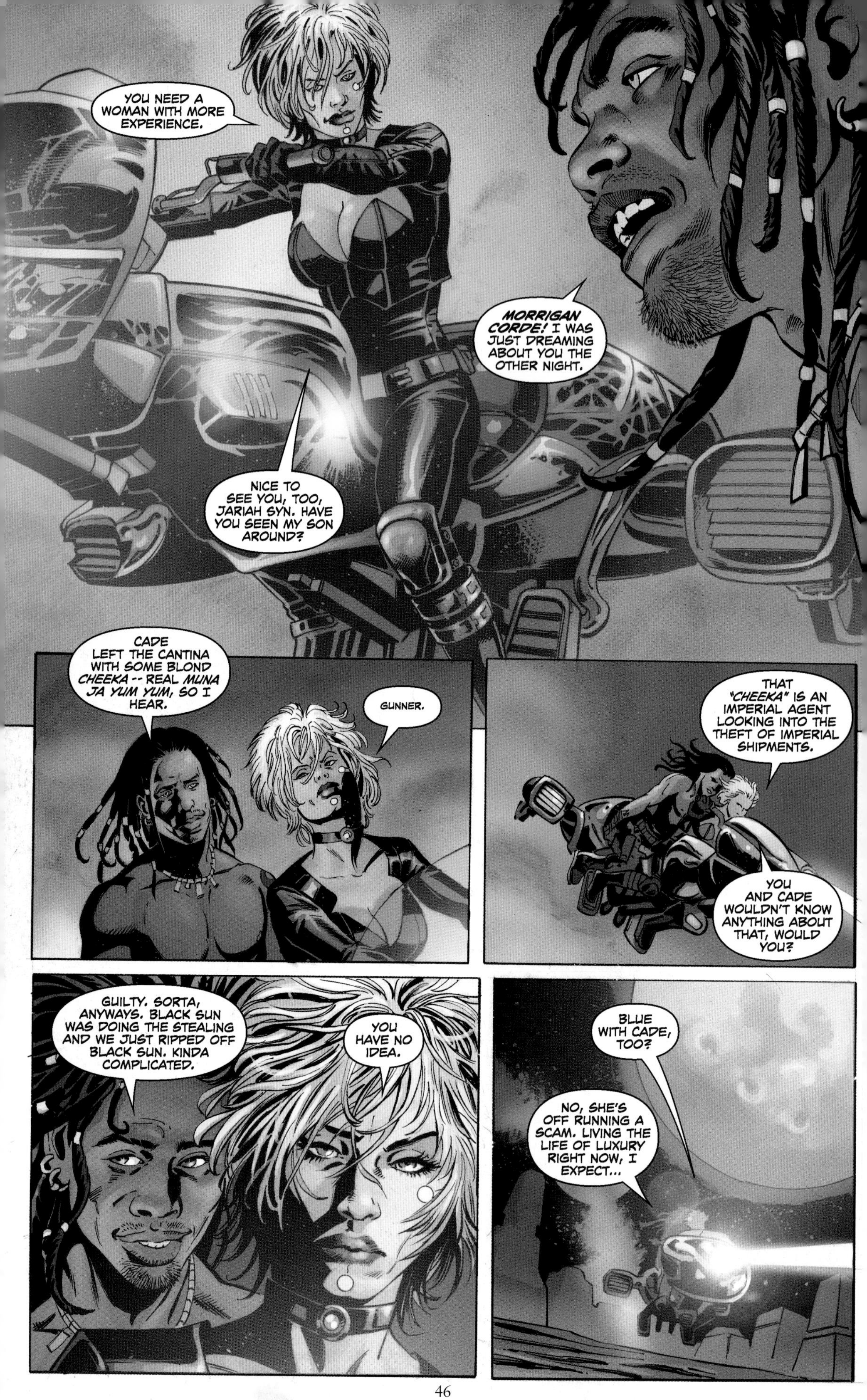

YOU NEED A WOMAN WITH MORE EXPERIENCE.
MORRIGAN CORDE! I WAS JUST DREAMING ABOUT YOU THE OTHER NIGHT.
NICE TO SEE YOU, TOO, JARIAH SYN. HAVE YOU SEEN MY SON AROUND?
CADE LEFT THE CANTINA WITH SOME BLOND CHEEKA -- REAL MUNA JA YUM YUM, SO I HEAR.
GUNNER.
THAT "CHEEKA" IS AN IMPERIAL AGENT LOOKING INTO THE THEFT OF IMPERIAL SHIPMENTS.
YOU AND CADE WOULDN'T KNOW ANYTHING ABOUT THAT, WOULD YOU?
GUILTY. SORTA, ANYWAYS. BLACK SUN WAS DOING THE STEALING AND WE JUST RIPPED OFF BLACK SUN. KINDA COMPLICATED.
YOU HAVE NO IDEA.
BLUE WITH CADE, TOO?
NO, SHE'S OFF RUNNING A SCAM. LIVING THE LIFE OF LUXURY RIGHT NOW, I EXPECT...

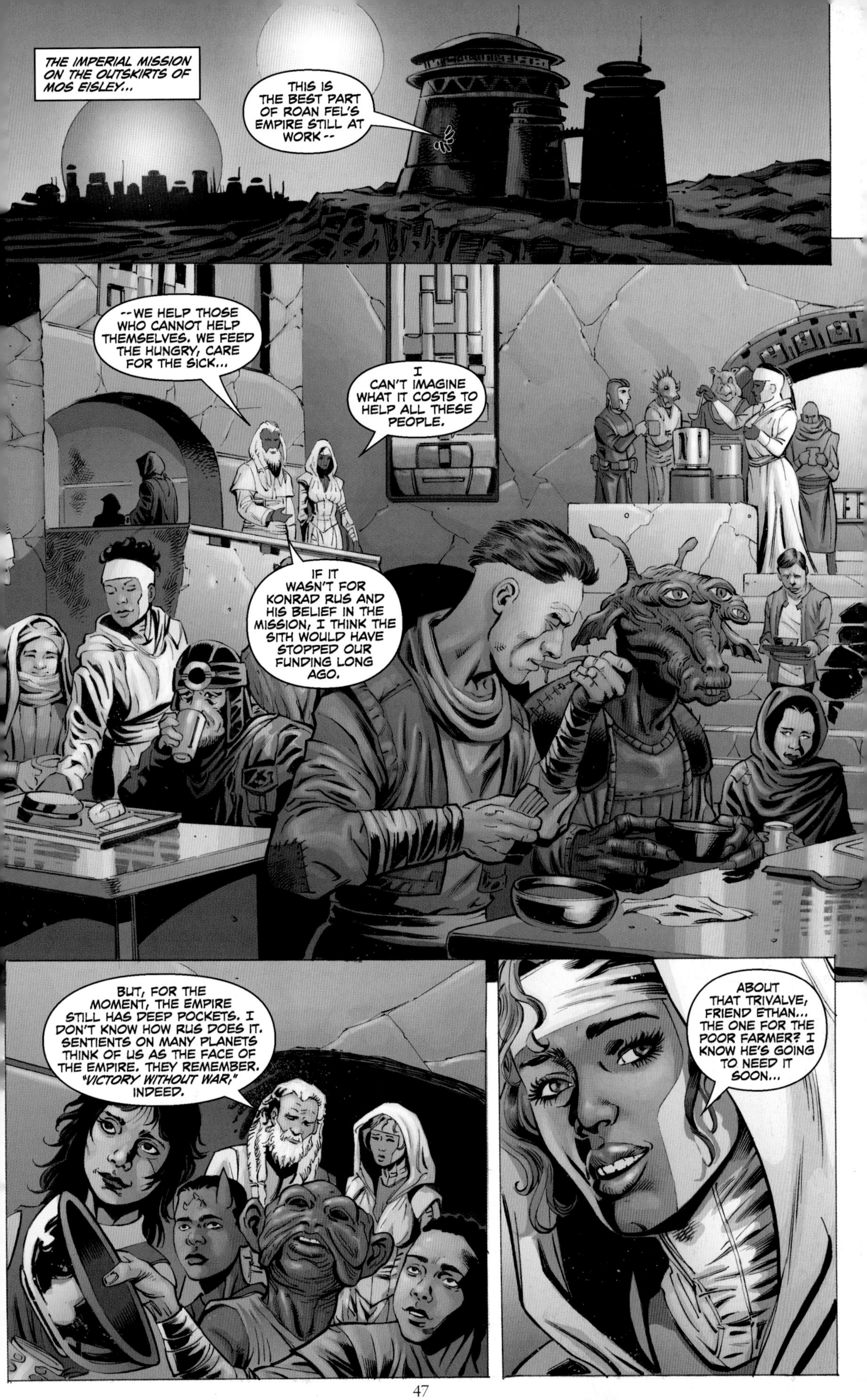
THE IMPERIAL MISSION ON THE OUTSKIRTS OF MOS EISLEY...
THIS IS THE BEST PART OF ROAN FEL'S EMPIRE STILL AT WORK--
--WE HELP THOSE WHO CANNOT HELP THEMSELVES. WE FEED THE HUNGRY, CARE FOR THE SICK...
I CAN'T IMAGINE WHAT IT COSTS TO HELP ALL THESE PEOPLE.
IF IT WASN'T FOR KONRAD RUS AND HIS BELIEF IN THE MISSION, I THINK THE SITH WOULD HAVE STOPPED OUR FUNDING LONG AGO.
BUT, FOR THE MOMENT, THE EMPIRE STILL HAS DEEP POCKETS. I DON'T KNOW HOW RUS DOES IT. SENTIENTS ON MANY PLANETS THINK OF US AS THE FACE OF THE EMPIRE. THEY REMEMBER. "VICTORY WITHOUT WAR," INDEED.
ABOUT THAT TRIVALVE, FRIEND ETHAN... THE ONE FOR THE POOR FARMER? I KNOW HE'S GOING TO NEED IT SOON...

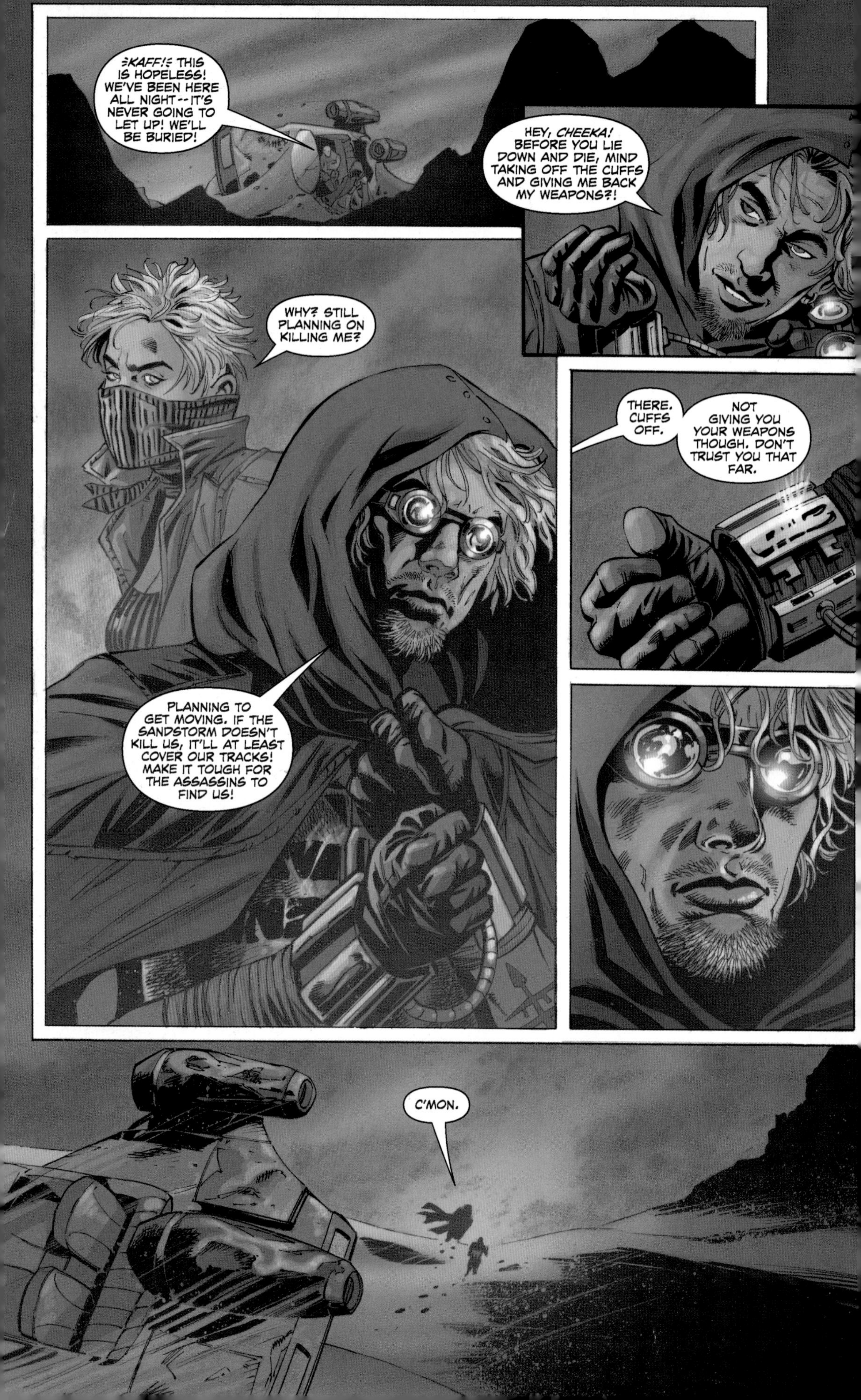

≡KAFF!≡ THIS IS HOPELESS! WE'VE BEEN HERE ALL NIGHT--IT'S NEVER GOING TO LET UP! WE'LL BE BURIED!
HEY, *CHEEKA!* BEFORE YOU LIE DOWN AND DIE, MIND TAKING OFF THE CUFFS AND GIVING ME BACK MY WEAPONS?!
WHY? STILL PLANNING ON KILLING ME?
PLANNING TO GET MOVING. IF THE SANDSTORM DOESN'T KILL US, IT'LL AT LEAST COVER OUR TRACKS! MAKE IT TOUGH FOR THE ASSASSINS TO FIND US!
THERE. CUFFS OFF.
NOT GIVING YOU YOUR WEAPONS THOUGH. DON'T TRUST YOU THAT FAR.
C'MON.

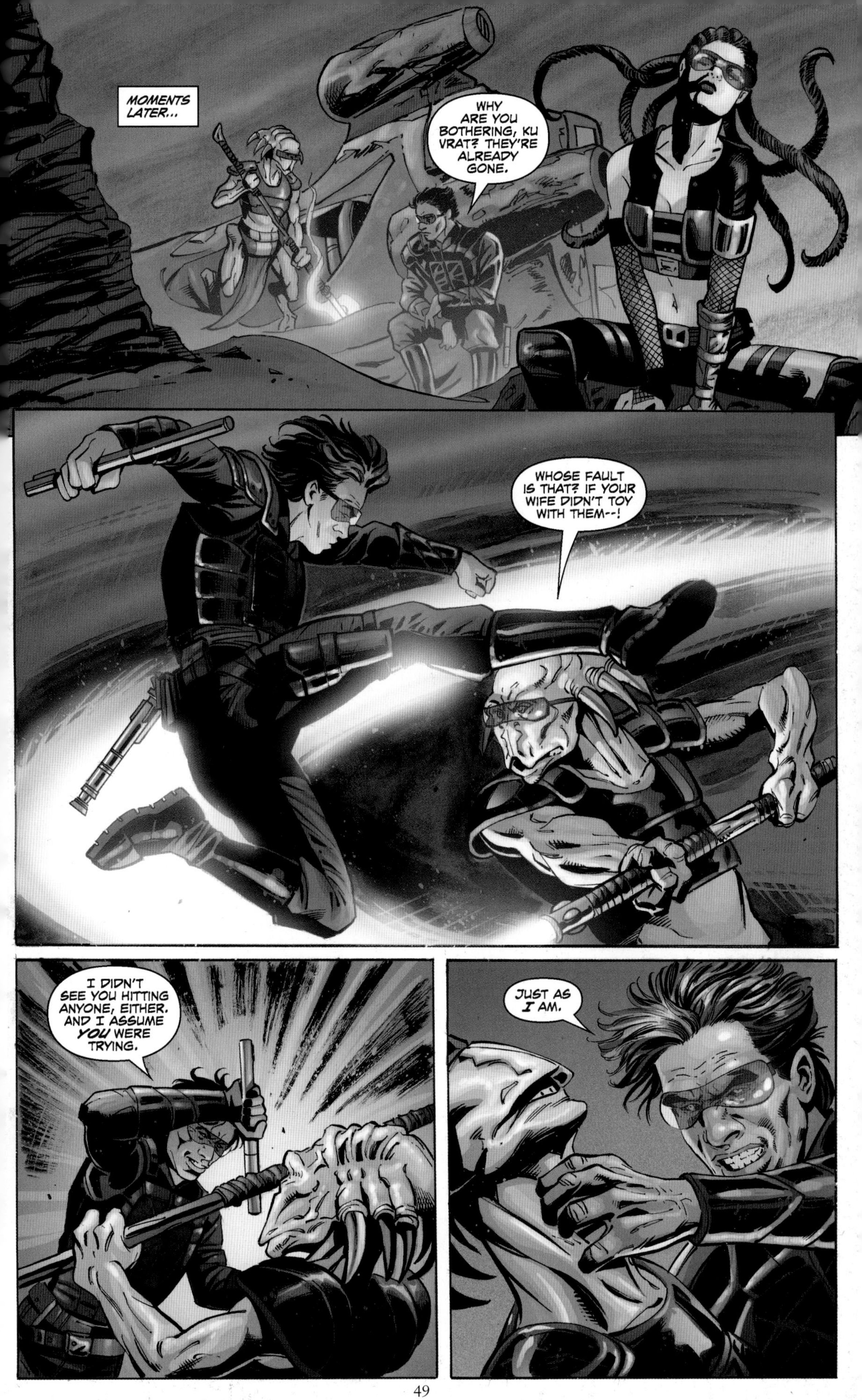
MOMENTS LATER...
WHY ARE YOU BOTHERING, KU VRAT? THEY'RE ALREADY GONE.
WHOSE FAULT IS THAT? IF YOUR WIFE DIDN'T TOY WITH THEM--!
I DIDN'T SEE YOU HITTING ANYONE, EITHER. AND I ASSUME YOU WERE TRYING.
JUST AS I AM.

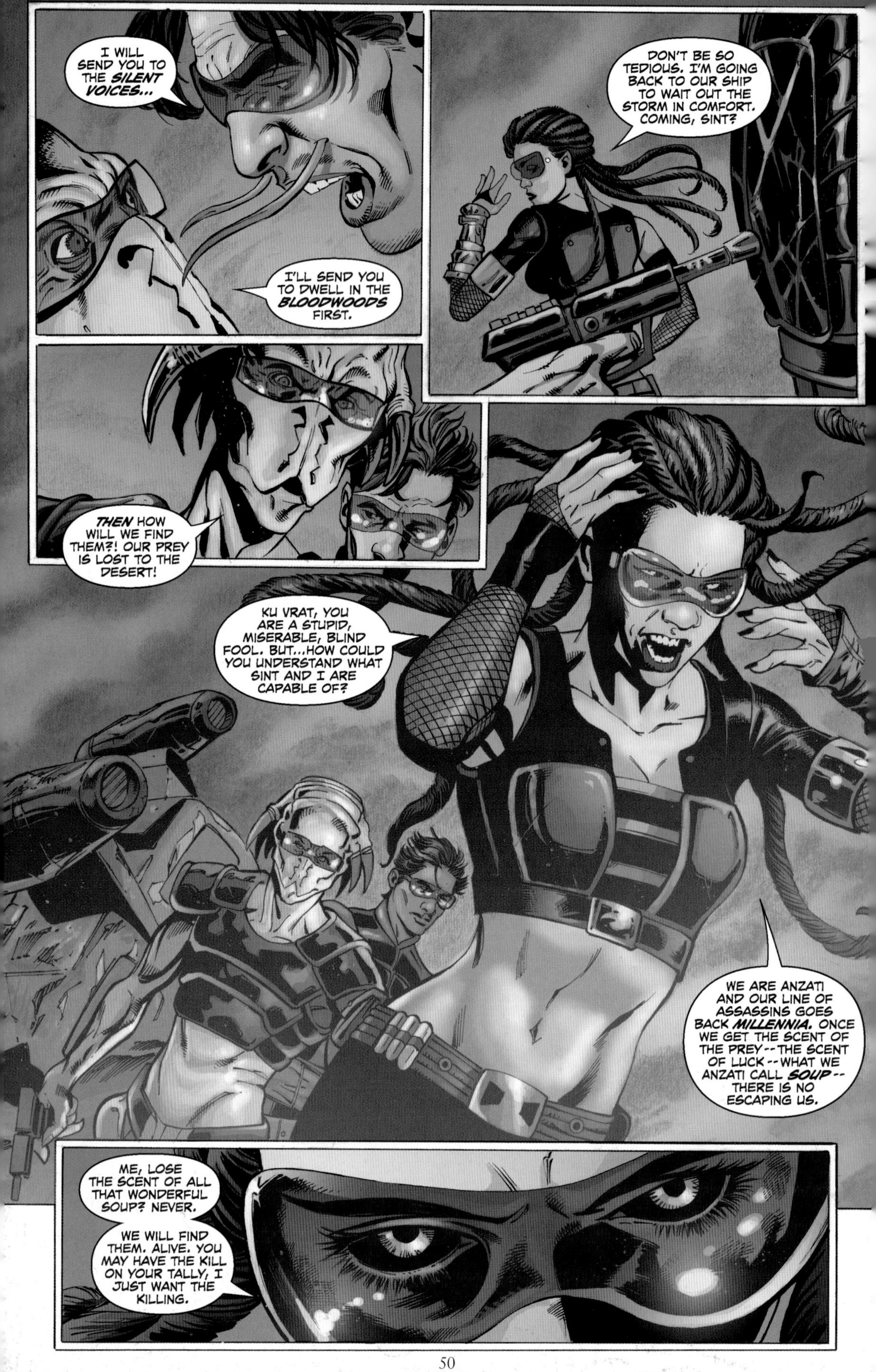
I WILL SEND YOU TO THE SILENT VOICES...
I'LL SEND YOU TO DWELL IN THE BLOODWOODS FIRST.
DON'T BE SO TEDIOUS. I'M GOING BACK TO OUR SHIP TO WAIT OUT THE STORM IN COMFORT. COMING, SINT?
THEN HOW WILL WE FIND THEM?! OUR PREY IS LOST TO THE DESERT!
KU VRAT, YOU ARE A STUPID, MISERABLE, BLIND FOOL. BUT...HOW COULD YOU UNDERSTAND WHAT SINT AND I ARE CAPABLE OF?
WE ARE ANZATI AND OUR LINE OF ASSASSINS GOES BACK MILLENNIA. ONCE WE GET THE SCENT OF THE PREY--THE SCENT OF LUCK--WHAT WE ANZATI CALL SOUP--THERE IS NO ESCAPING US.
ME, LOSE THE SCENT OF ALL THAT WONDERFUL SOUP? NEVER.
WE WILL FIND THEM. ALIVE. YOU MAY HAVE THE KILL ON YOUR TALLY, I JUST WANT THE KILLING.

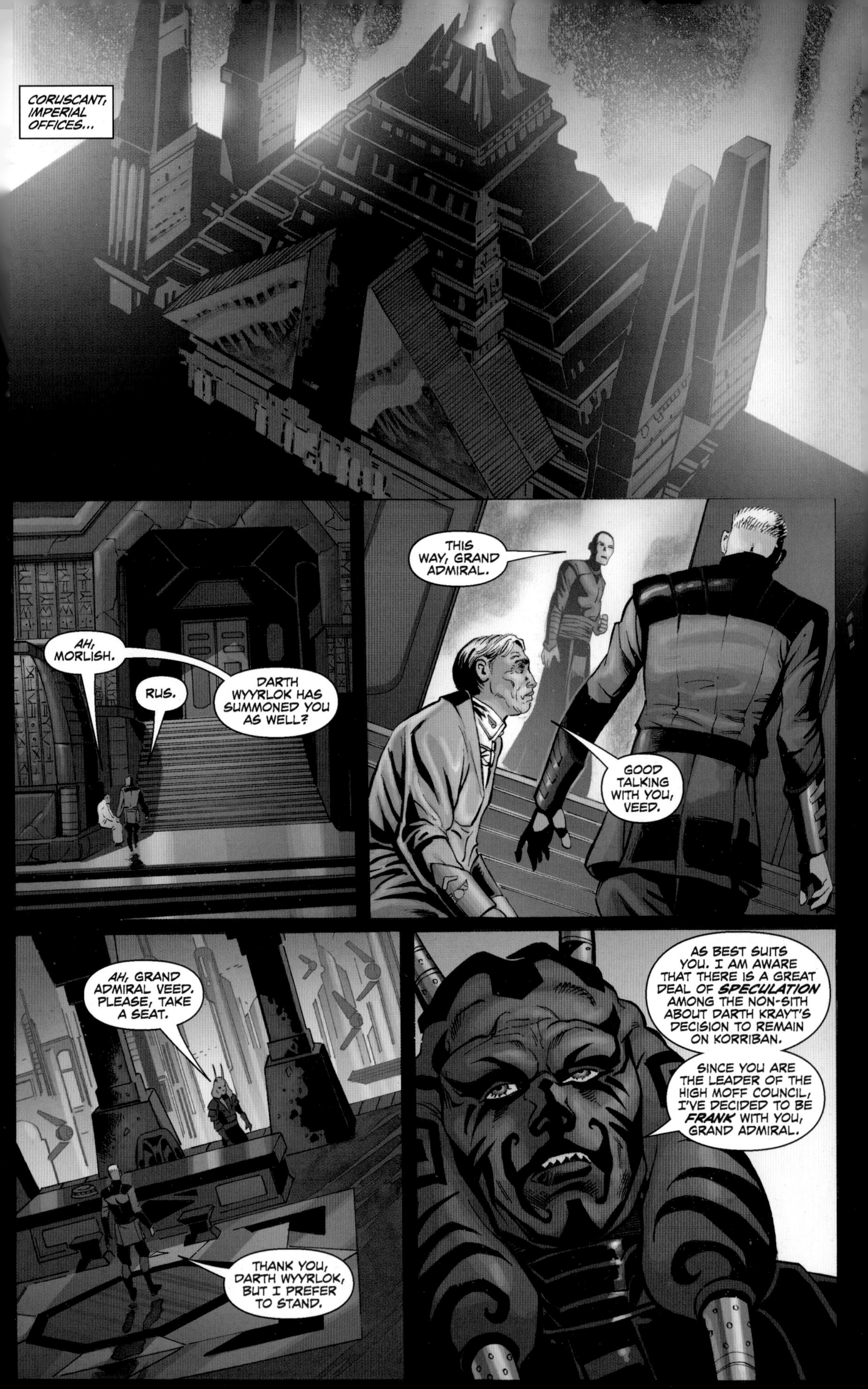
CORUSCANT, IMPERIAL OFFICES...
AH, MORLISH.
RUS.
DARTH WYYRLOK HAS SUMMONED YOU AS WELL?
THIS WAY, GRAND ADMIRAL.
GOOD TALKING WITH YOU, VEED.
AH, GRAND ADMIRAL VEED. PLEASE, TAKE A SEAT.
THANK YOU, DARTH WYYRLOK, BUT I PREFER TO STAND.
AS BEST SUITS YOU. I AM AWARE THAT THERE IS A GREAT DEAL OF SPECULATION AMONG THE NON-SITH ABOUT DARTH KRAYT'S DECISION TO REMAIN ON KORRIBAN.
SINCE YOU ARE THE LEADER OF THE HIGH MOFF COUNCIL, I'VE DECIDED TO BE FRANK WITH YOU, GRAND ADMIRAL.

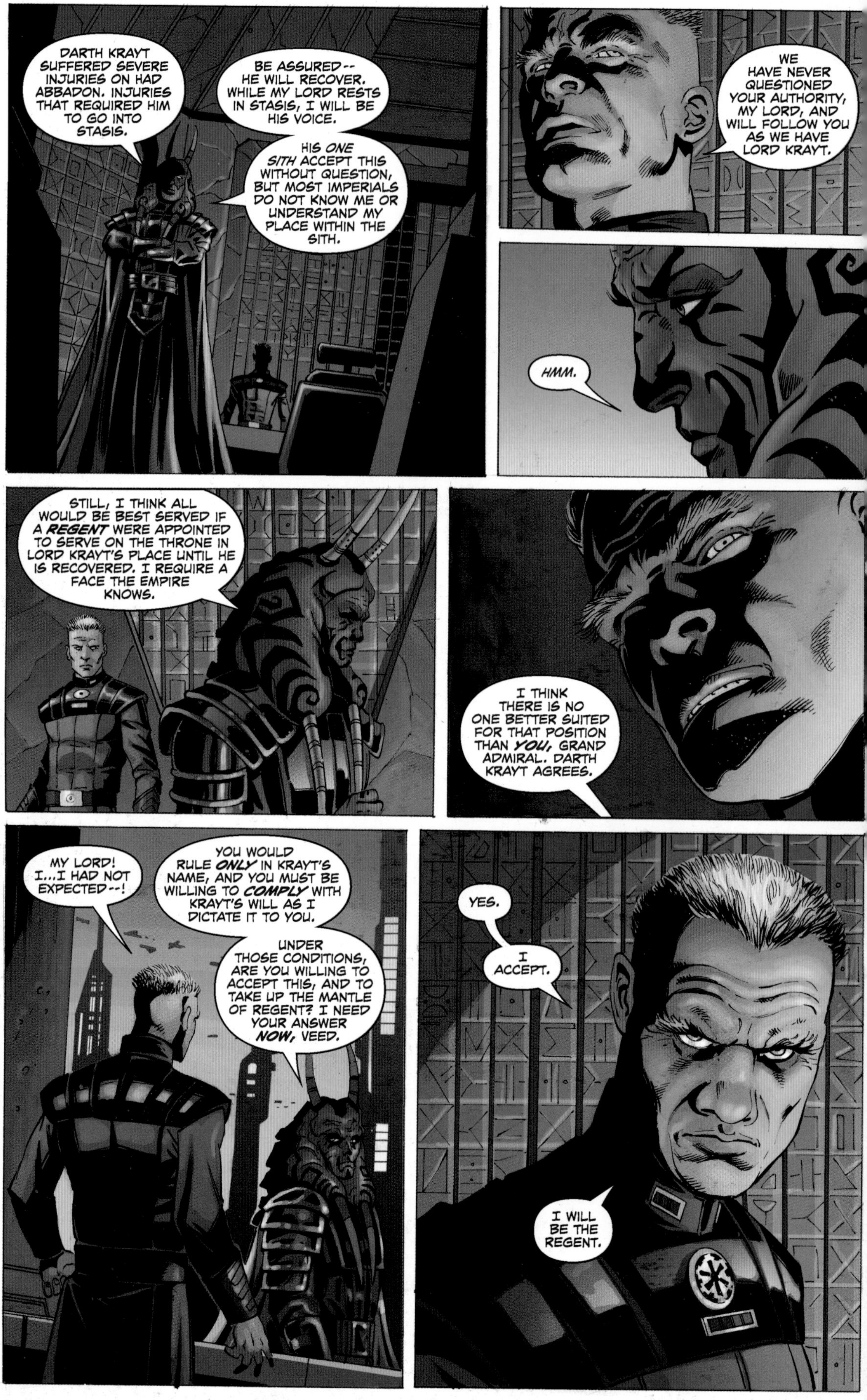
DARTH KRAYT SUFFERED SEVERE INJURIES ON HAD ABBADON. INJURIES THAT REQUIRED HIM TO GO INTO STASIS.
BE ASSURED-- HE WILL RECOVER. WHILE MY LORD RESTS IN STASIS, I WILL BE HIS VOICE.
HIS ONE SITH ACCEPT THIS WITHOUT QUESTION, BUT MOST IMPERIALS DO NOT KNOW ME OR UNDERSTAND MY PLACE WITHIN THE SITH.
WE HAVE NEVER QUESTIONED YOUR AUTHORITY, MY LORD, AND WILL FOLLOW YOU AS WE HAVE LORD KRAYT.
HMM.
STILL, I THINK ALL WOULD BE BEST SERVED IF A REGENT WERE APPOINTED TO SERVE ON THE THRONE IN LORD KRAYT'S PLACE UNTIL HE IS RECOVERED. I REQUIRE A FACE THE EMPIRE KNOWS.
I THINK THERE IS NO ONE BETTER SUITED FOR THAT POSITION THAN YOU, GRAND ADMIRAL. DARTH KRAYT AGREES.
MY LORD! I...I HAD NOT EXPECTED--!
YOU WOULD RULE ONLY IN KRAYT'S NAME, AND YOU MUST BE WILLING TO COMPLY WITH KRAYT'S WILL AS I DICTATE IT TO YOU.
UNDER THOSE CONDITIONS, ARE YOU WILLING TO ACCEPT THIS, AND TO TAKE UP THE MANTLE OF REGENT? I NEED YOUR ANSWER NOW, VEED.
YES.
I ACCEPT.
I WILL BE THE REGENT.

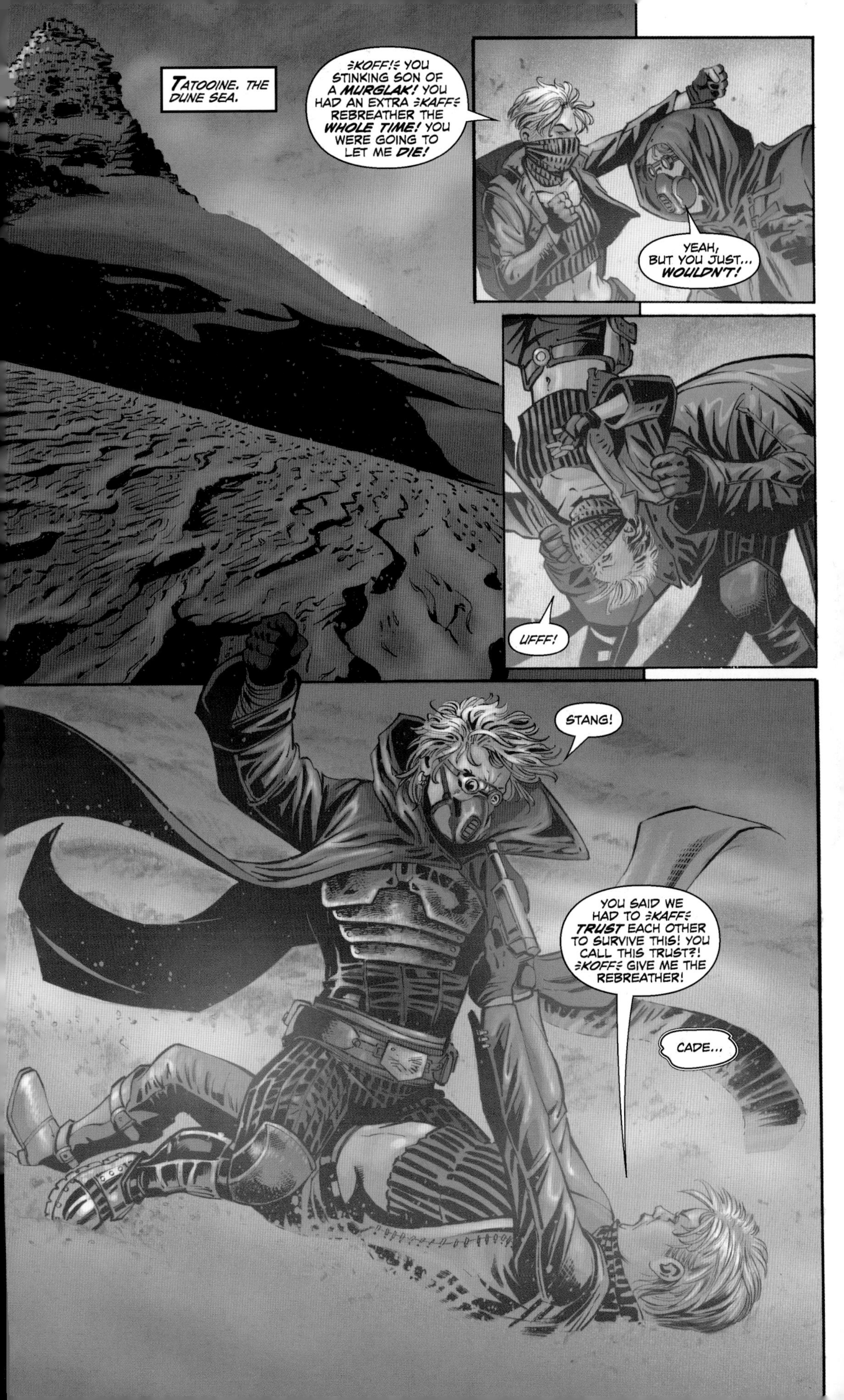
TATOOINE. THE DUNE SEA.
=KOFF!= YOU STINKING SON OF A MURGLAK! YOU HAD AN EXTRA =KAFF= REBREATHER THE WHOLE TIME! YOU WERE GOING TO LET ME DIE!
YEAH, BUT YOU JUST... WOULDN'T!
UFFF!
STANG!
YOU SAID WE HAD TO =KAFF= TRUST EACH OTHER TO SURVIVE THIS! YOU CALL THIS TRUST?! =KOFF= GIVE ME THE REBREATHER!
CADE...

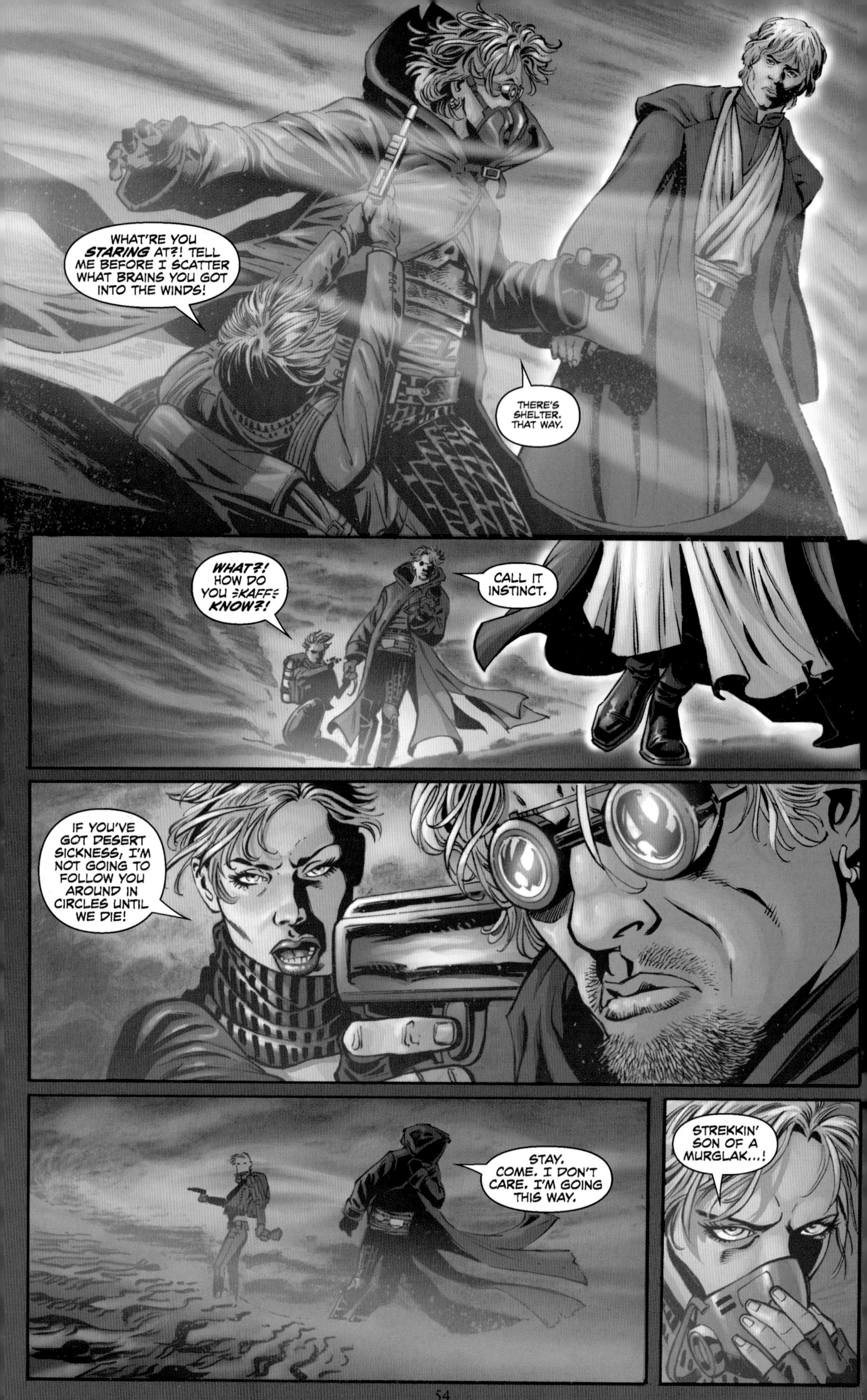
WHAT'RE YOU STARING AT?! TELL ME BEFORE I SCATTER WHAT BRAINS YOU GOT INTO THE WINDS!
THERE'S SHELTER. THAT WAY.
WHAT?! HOW DO YOU =KAFF= KNOW?!
CALL IT INSTINCT.
IF YOU'VE GOT DESERT SICKNESS, I'M NOT GOING TO FOLLOW YOU AROUND IN CIRCLES UNTIL WE DIE!
STAY. COME. I DON'T CARE. I'M GOING THIS WAY.
STREKKIN' SON OF A MURGLAK...!

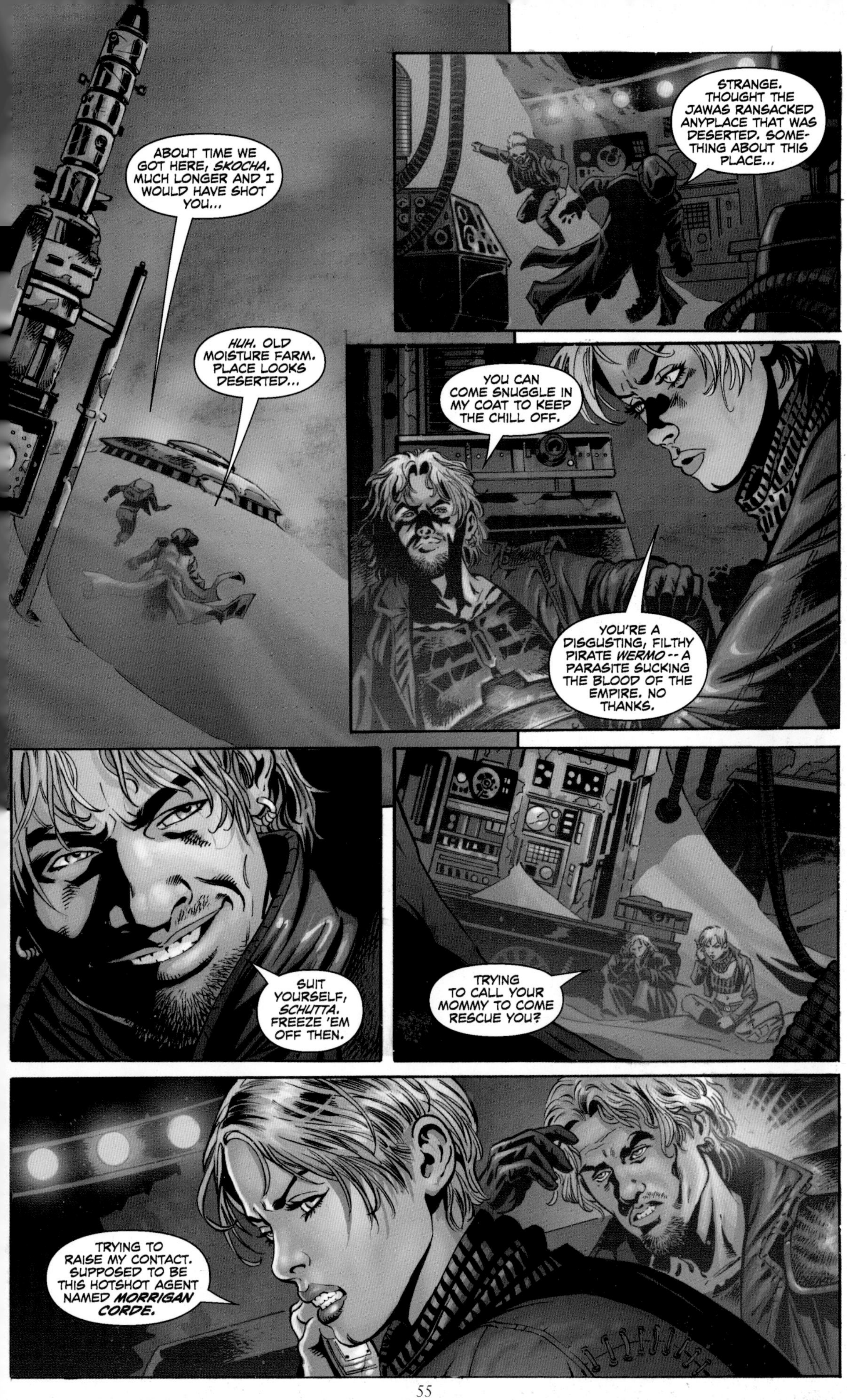
ABOUT TIME WE GOT HERE, *SKOCHA*. MUCH LONGER AND I WOULD HAVE SHOT YOU...
HUH. OLD MOISTURE FARM. PLACE LOOKS DESERTED...
STRANGE. THOUGHT THE JAWAS RANSACKED ANYPLACE THAT WAS DESERTED. SOME-THING ABOUT THIS PLACE...
YOU CAN COME SNUGGLE IN MY COAT TO KEEP THE CHILL OFF.
YOU'RE A DISGUSTING, FILTHY PIRATE *WERMO* -- A PARASITE SUCKING THE BLOOD OF THE EMPIRE. NO THANKS.
SUIT YOURSELF, *SCHUTTA*. FREEZE 'EM OFF THEN.
TRYING TO CALL YOUR MOMMY TO COME RESCUE YOU?
TRYING TO RAISE MY CONTACT. SUPPOSED TO BE THIS HOTSHOT AGENT NAMED ***MORRIGAN CORDE.***

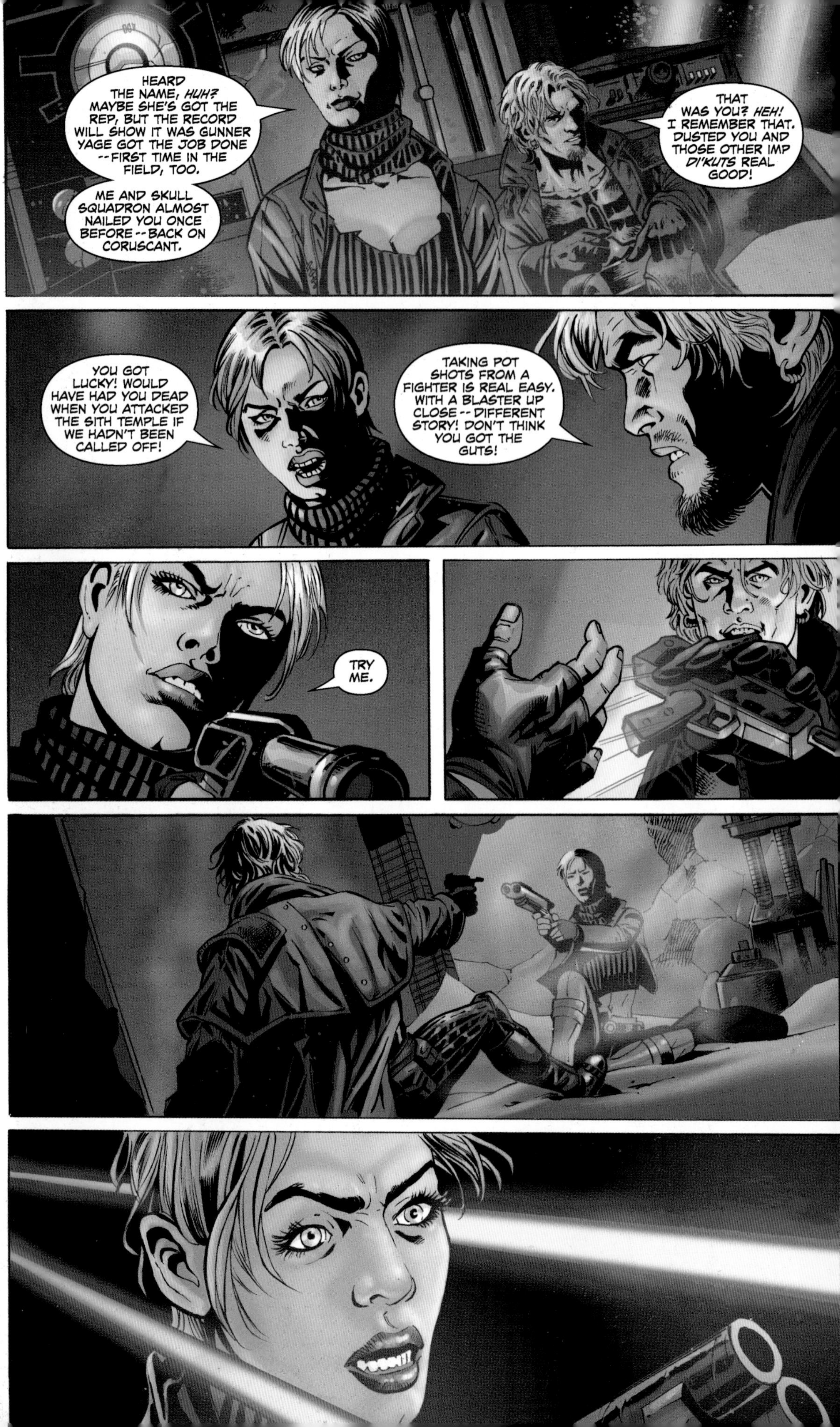
HEARD THE NAME, *HUH?* MAYBE SHE'S GOT THE REP, BUT THE RECORD WILL SHOW IT WAS GUNNER YAGE GOT THE JOB DONE --FIRST TIME IN THE FIELD, TOO.
ME AND SKULL SQUADRON ALMOST NAILED YOU ONCE BEFORE--BACK ON CORUSCANT.
THAT WAS YOU? *HEH!* I REMEMBER THAT. DUSTED YOU AND THOSE OTHER IMP *DI'KUTS* REAL GOOD!
YOU GOT LUCKY! WOULD HAVE HAD YOU DEAD WHEN YOU ATTACKED THE SITH TEMPLE IF WE HADN'T BEEN CALLED OFF!
TAKING POT SHOTS FROM A FIGHTER IS REAL EASY. WITH A BLASTER UP CLOSE--DIFFERENT STORY! DON'T THINK YOU GOT THE GUTS!
TRY ME.

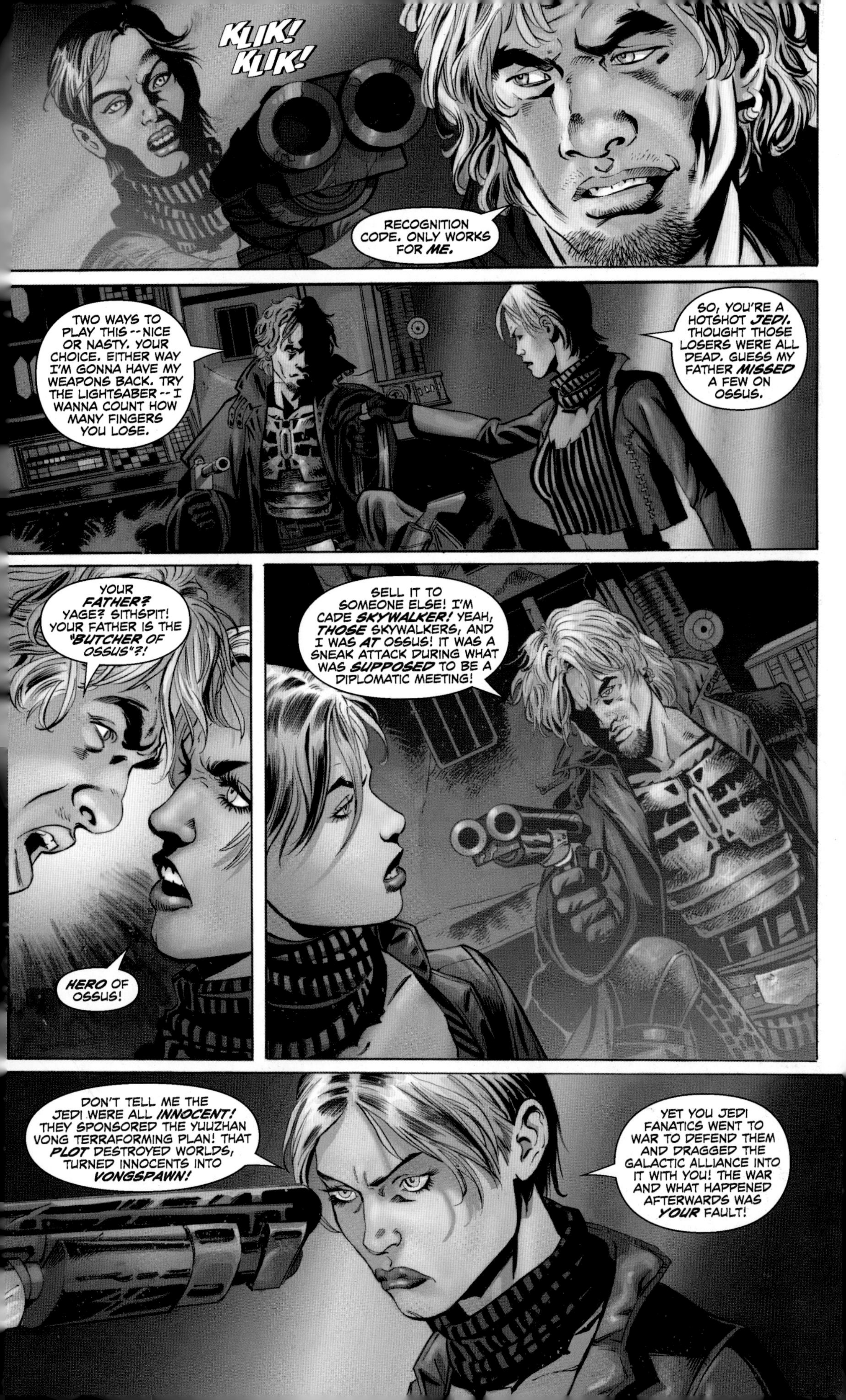
KLIK! KLIK!
RECOGNITION CODE. ONLY WORKS FOR *ME.*
TWO WAYS TO PLAY THIS -- NICE OR NASTY. YOUR CHOICE. EITHER WAY I'M GONNA HAVE MY WEAPONS BACK. TRY THE LIGHTSABER -- I WANNA COUNT HOW MANY FINGERS YOU LOSE.
SO, YOU'RE A HOTSHOT *JEDI.* THOUGHT THOSE LOSERS WERE ALL DEAD. GUESS MY FATHER *MISSED* A FEW ON OSSUS.
YOUR *FATHER?* YAGE? SITHSPIT! YOUR FATHER IS THE *"BUTCHER OF OSSUS"?!*
HERO OF OSSUS!
SELL IT TO SOMEONE ELSE! I'M CADE *SKYWALKER!* YEAH, *THOSE* SKYWALKERS, AND I WAS *AT* OSSUS! IT WAS A SNEAK ATTACK DURING WHAT WAS *SUPPOSED* TO BE A DIPLOMATIC MEETING!
DON'T TELL ME THE JEDI WERE ALL *INNOCENT!* THEY SPONSORED THE YUUZHAN VONG TERRAFORMING PLAN! THAT *PLOT* DESTROYED WORLDS, TURNED INNOCENTS INTO *VONGSPAWN!*
YET YOU JEDI FANATICS WENT TO WAR TO DEFEND THEM AND DRAGGED THE GALACTIC ALLIANCE INTO IT WITH YOU! THE WAR AND WHAT HAPPENED AFTERWARDS WAS *YOUR* FAULT!

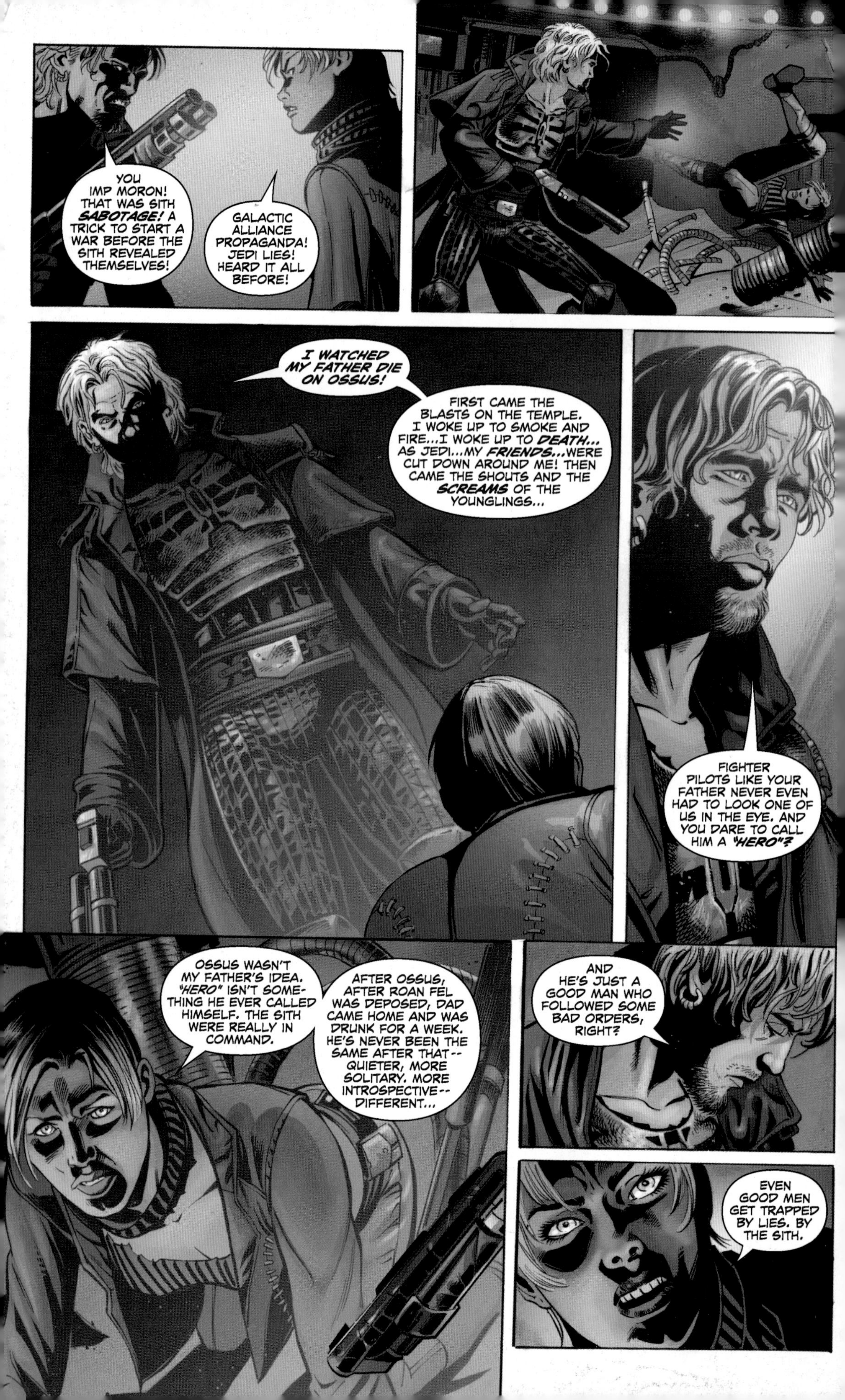
YOU IMP MORON! THAT WAS SITH SABOTAGE! A TRICK TO START A WAR BEFORE THE SITH REVEALED THEMSELVES!
GALACTIC ALLIANCE PROPAGANDA! JEDI LIES! HEARD IT ALL BEFORE!
I WATCHED MY FATHER DIE ON OSSUS!
FIRST CAME THE BLASTS ON THE TEMPLE. I WOKE UP TO SMOKE AND FIRE...I WOKE UP TO DEATH... AS JEDI...MY FRIENDS...WERE CUT DOWN AROUND ME! THEN CAME THE SHOUTS AND THE SCREAMS OF THE YOUNGLINGS...
FIGHTER PILOTS LIKE YOUR FATHER NEVER EVEN HAD TO LOOK ONE OF US IN THE EYE. AND YOU DARE TO CALL HIM A "HERO"?
OSSUS WASN'T MY FATHER'S IDEA. "HERO" ISN'T SOMETHING HE EVER CALLED HIMSELF. THE SITH WERE REALLY IN COMMAND.
AFTER OSSUS, AFTER ROAN FEL WAS DEPOSED, DAD CAME HOME AND WAS DRUNK FOR A WEEK. HE'S NEVER BEEN THE SAME AFTER THAT-- QUIETER, MORE SOLITARY. MORE INTROSPECTIVE-- DIFFERENT...
AND HE'S JUST A GOOD MAN WHO FOLLOWED SOME BAD ORDERS, RIGHT?
EVEN GOOD MEN GET TRAPPED BY LIES. BY THE SITH.

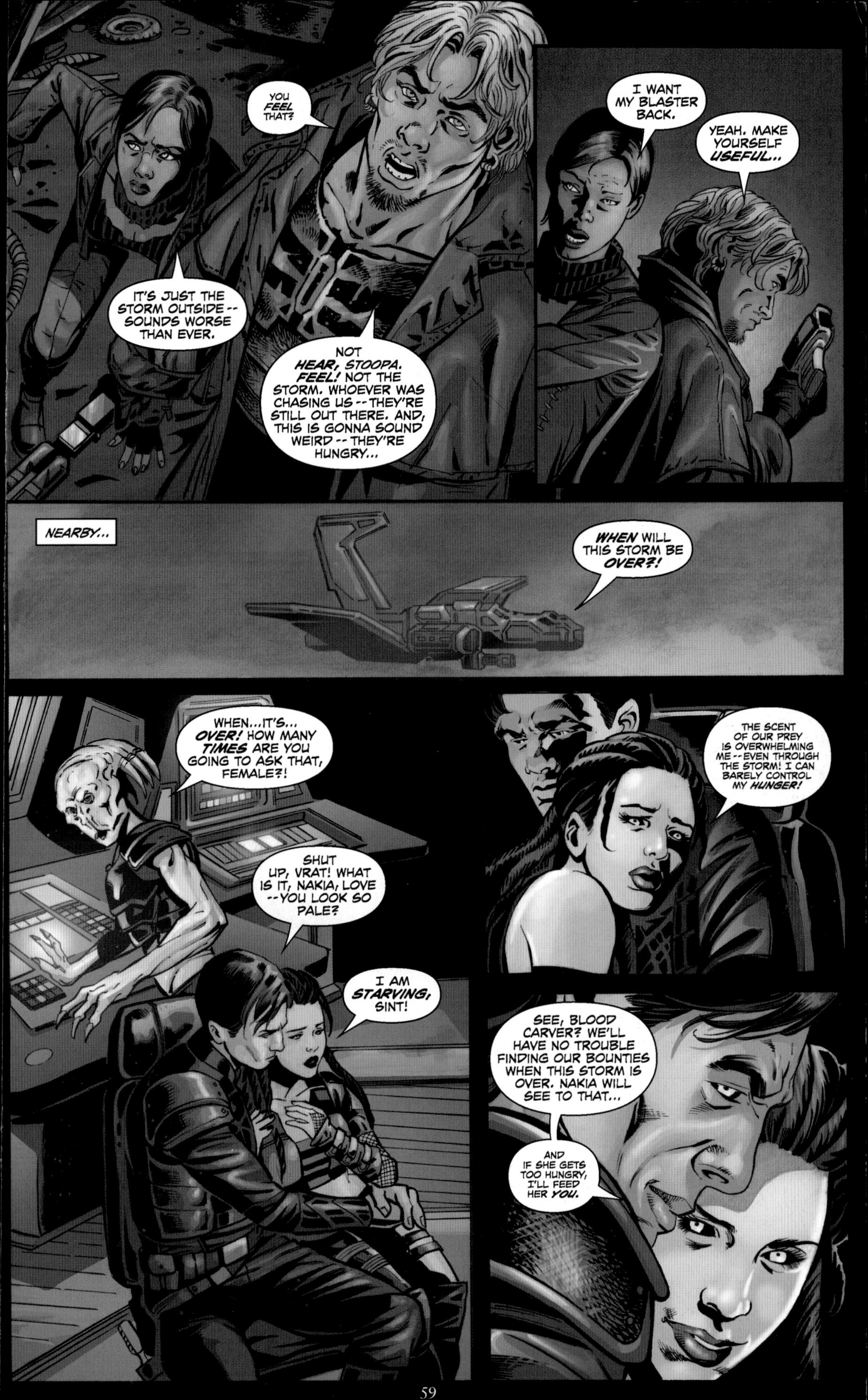
YOU FEEL THAT?
IT'S JUST THE STORM OUTSIDE -- SOUNDS WORSE THAN EVER.
NOT HEAR, STOOPA. FEEL! NOT THE STORM. WHOEVER WAS CHASING US -- THEY'RE STILL OUT THERE. AND, THIS IS GONNA SOUND WEIRD -- THEY'RE HUNGRY...
I WANT MY BLASTER BACK.
YEAH. MAKE YOURSELF USEFUL...
NEARBY...
WHEN WILL THIS STORM BE OVER?!
WHEN...IT'S... OVER! HOW MANY TIMES ARE YOU GOING TO ASK THAT, FEMALE?!
SHUT UP, VRAT! WHAT IS IT, NAKIA, LOVE -- YOU LOOK SO PALE?
I AM STARVING, SINT!
THE SCENT OF OUR PREY IS OVERWHELMING ME -- EVEN THROUGH THE STORM! I CAN BARELY CONTROL MY HUNGER!
SEE, BLOOD CARVER? WE'LL HAVE NO TROUBLE FINDING OUR BOUNTIES WHEN THIS STORM IS OVER. NAKIA WILL SEE TO THAT...
AND IF SHE GETS TOO HUNGRY, I'LL FEED HER YOU.

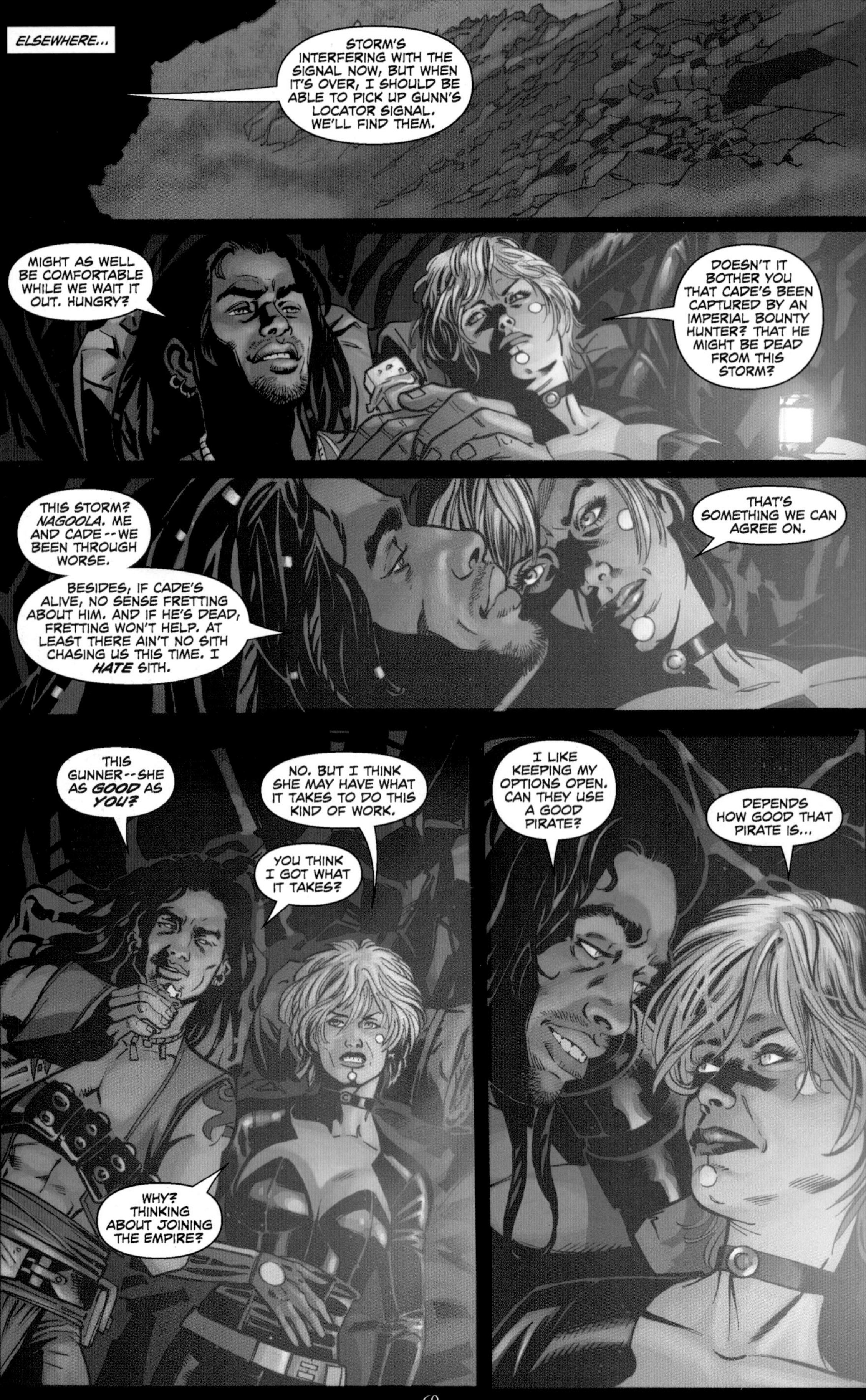
ELSEWHERE...
STORM'S INTERFERING WITH THE SIGNAL NOW, BUT WHEN IT'S OVER, I SHOULD BE ABLE TO PICK UP GUNN'S LOCATOR SIGNAL. WE'LL FIND THEM.
MIGHT AS WELL BE COMFORTABLE WHILE WE WAIT IT OUT. HUNGRY?
DOESN'T IT BOTHER YOU THAT CADE'S BEEN CAPTURED BY AN IMPERIAL BOUNTY HUNTER? THAT HE MIGHT BE DEAD FROM THIS STORM?
THIS STORM? NAGOOLA. ME AND CADE--WE BEEN THROUGH WORSE.
BESIDES, IF CADE'S ALIVE, NO SENSE FRETTING ABOUT HIM. AND IF HE'S DEAD, FRETTING WON'T HELP. AT LEAST THERE AIN'T NO SITH CHASING US THIS TIME. I HATE SITH.
THAT'S SOMETHING WE CAN AGREE ON.
THIS GUNNER--SHE AS GOOD AS YOU?
NO. BUT I THINK SHE MAY HAVE WHAT IT TAKES TO DO THIS KIND OF WORK.
YOU THINK I GOT WHAT IT TAKES?
WHY? THINKING ABOUT JOINING THE EMPIRE?
I LIKE KEEPING MY OPTIONS OPEN. CAN THEY USE A GOOD PIRATE?
DEPENDS HOW GOOD THAT PIRATE IS...

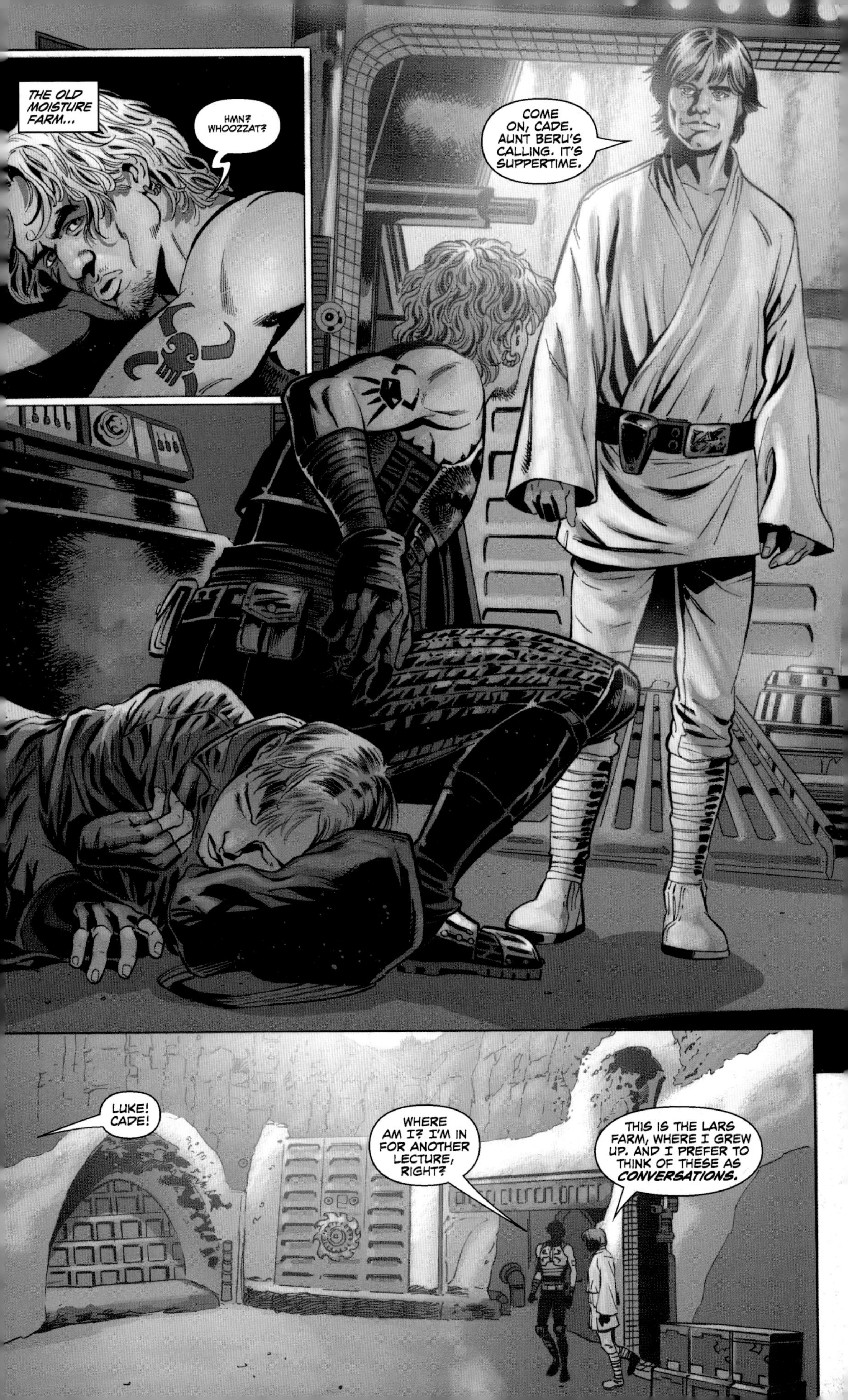
THE OLD MOISTURE FARM...
HMN? WHOOZZAT?
COME ON, CADE. AUNT BERU'S CALLING. IT'S SUPPERTIME.
LUKE! CADE!
WHERE AM I? I'M IN FOR ANOTHER LECTURE, RIGHT?
THIS IS THE LARS FARM, WHERE I GREW UP. AND I PREFER TO THINK OF THESE AS *CONVERSATIONS.*

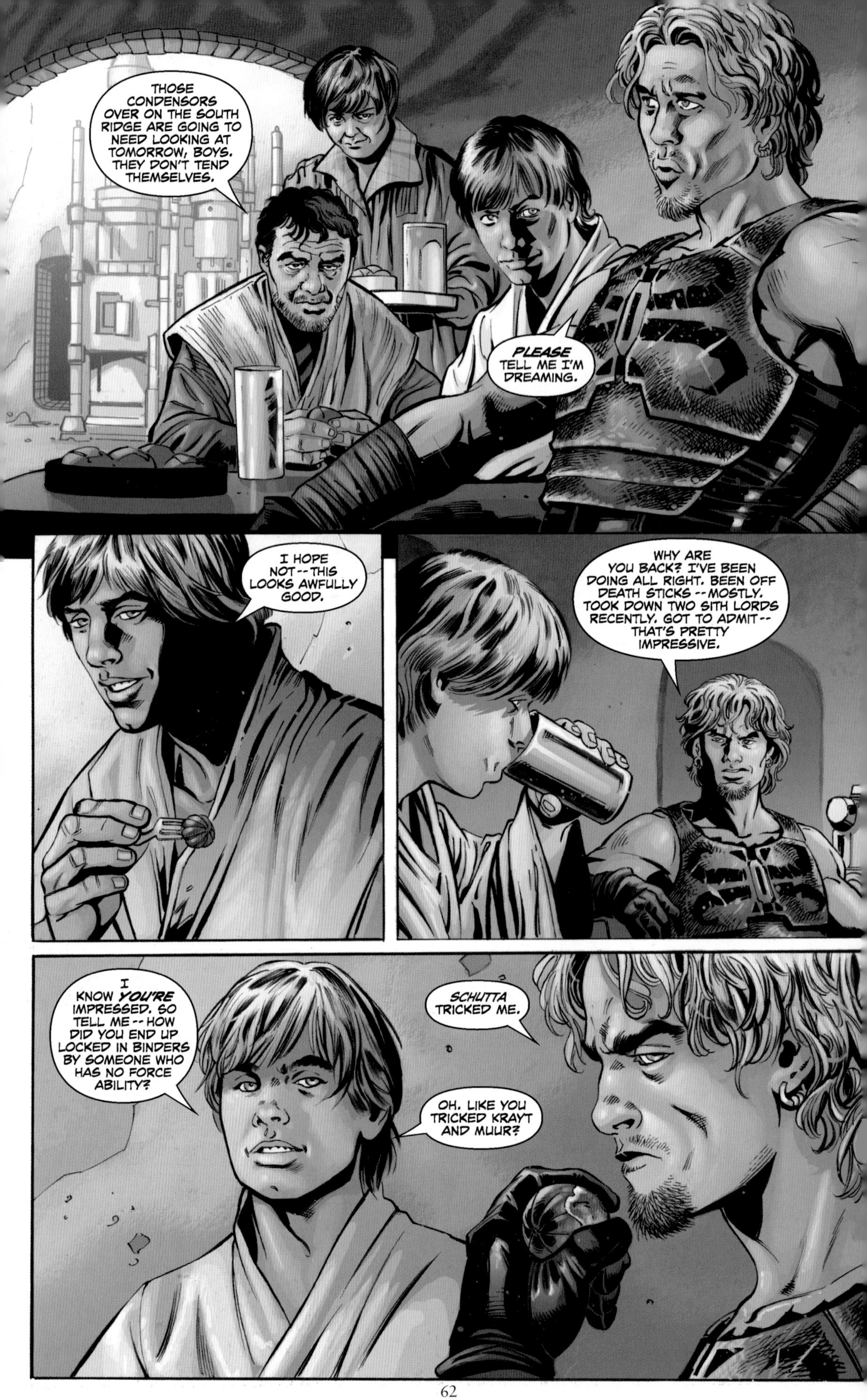
THOSE CONDENSORS OVER ON THE SOUTH RIDGE ARE GOING TO NEED LOOKING AT TOMORROW, BOYS. THEY DON'T TEND THEMSELVES.
PLEASE TELL ME I'M DREAMING.
I HOPE NOT--THIS LOOKS AWFULLY GOOD.
WHY ARE YOU BACK? I'VE BEEN DOING ALL RIGHT. BEEN OFF DEATH STICKS--MOSTLY. TOOK DOWN TWO SITH LORDS RECENTLY. GOT TO ADMIT--THAT'S PRETTY IMPRESSIVE.
I KNOW *YOU'RE* IMPRESSED. SO TELL ME--HOW DID YOU END UP LOCKED IN BINDERS BY SOMEONE WHO HAS NO FORCE ABILITY?
SCHUTTA TRICKED ME.
OH. LIKE YOU TRICKED KRAYT AND MUUR?

HEY! WHERE TH--?

DREAMS CHANGE SUDDENLY. NOT ALL END WELL.

LUKE? WHAT'S GOING...

...ON...?

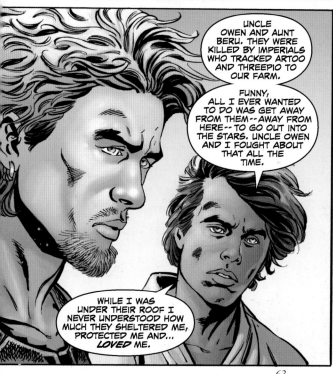

UNCLE OWEN AND AUNT BERU. THEY WERE KILLED BY IMPERIALS WHO TRACKED ARTOO AND THREEPIO TO OUR FARM.

FUNNY, ALL I EVER WANTED TO DO WAS GET AWAY FROM THEM--AWAY FROM HERE--TO GO OUT INTO THE STARS. UNCLE OWEN AND I FOUGHT ABOUT THAT ALL THE TIME.

WHILE I WAS UNDER THEIR ROOF I NEVER UNDERSTOOD HOW MUCH THEY SHELTERED ME, PROTECTED ME AND... *LOVED* ME.

I BURIED THE ONLY PARENTS I EVER KNEW. I COULDN'T GIVE INTO MY GRIEF--OR INTO VENGEANCE. INSTEAD, I FOLLOWED BEN KENOBI--JOINED THE REBELLION...

I GRIEVED FOR THEM LATER...

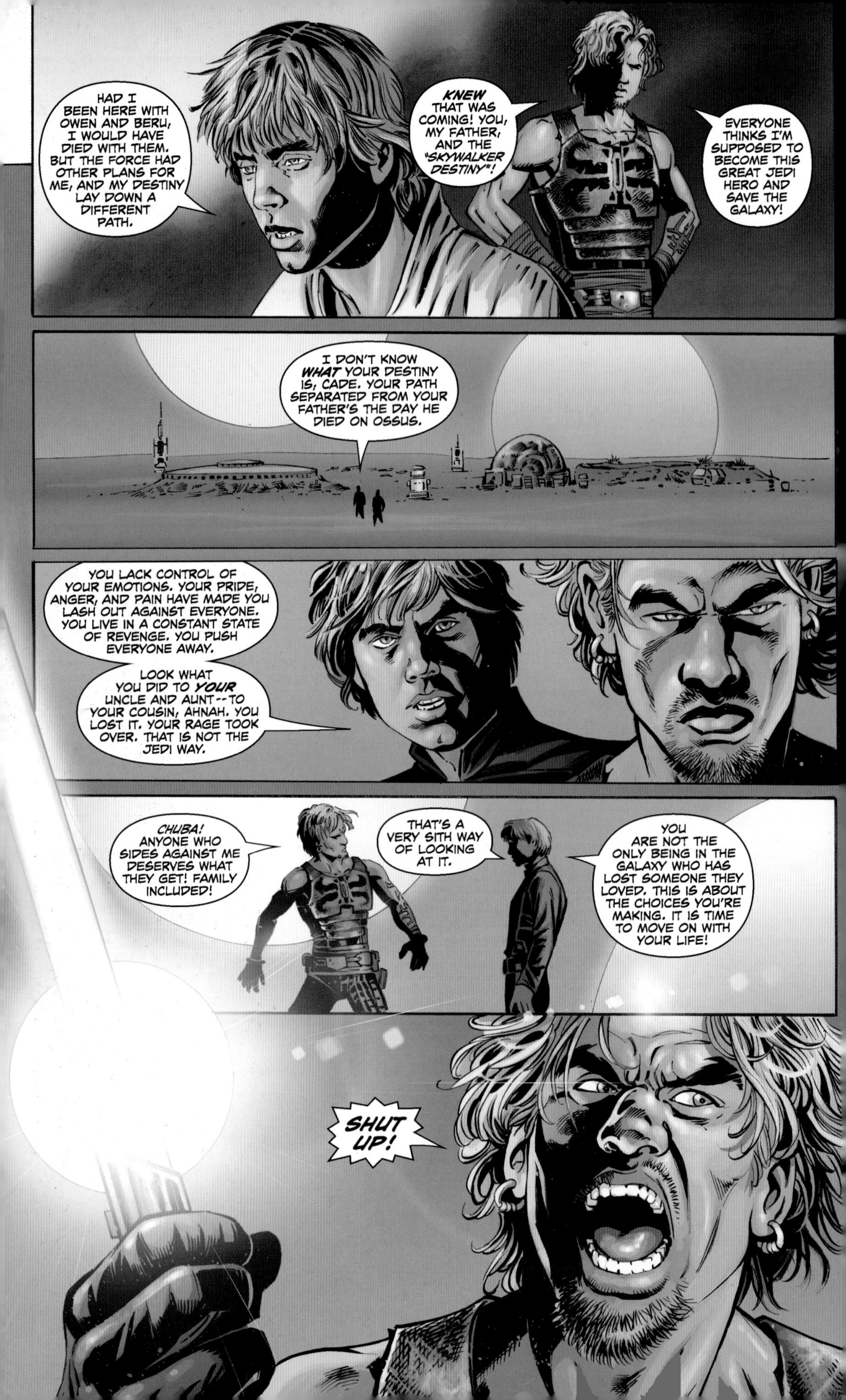
HAD I BEEN HERE WITH OWEN AND BERU, I WOULD HAVE DIED WITH THEM. BUT THE FORCE HAD OTHER PLANS FOR ME, AND MY DESTINY LAY DOWN A DIFFERENT PATH.
KNEW THAT WAS COMING! YOU, MY FATHER, AND THE "SKYWALKER DESTINY"!
EVERYONE THINKS I'M SUPPOSED TO BECOME THIS GREAT JEDI HERO AND SAVE THE GALAXY!
I DON'T KNOW WHAT YOUR DESTINY IS, CADE. YOUR PATH SEPARATED FROM YOUR FATHER'S THE DAY HE DIED ON OSSUS.
YOU LACK CONTROL OF YOUR EMOTIONS. YOUR PRIDE, ANGER, AND PAIN HAVE MADE YOU LASH OUT AGAINST EVERYONE. YOU LIVE IN A CONSTANT STATE OF REVENGE. YOU PUSH EVERYONE AWAY.
LOOK WHAT YOU DID TO YOUR UNCLE AND AUNT--TO YOUR COUSIN, AHNAH. YOU LOST IT. YOUR RAGE TOOK OVER. THAT IS NOT THE JEDI WAY.
CHUBA! ANYONE WHO SIDES AGAINST ME DESERVES WHAT THEY GET! FAMILY INCLUDED!
THAT'S A VERY SITH WAY OF LOOKING AT IT.
YOU ARE NOT THE ONLY BEING IN THE GALAXY WHO HAS LOST SOMEONE THEY LOVED. THIS IS ABOUT THE CHOICES YOU'RE MAKING. IT IS TIME TO MOVE ON WITH YOUR LIFE!
SHUT UP!

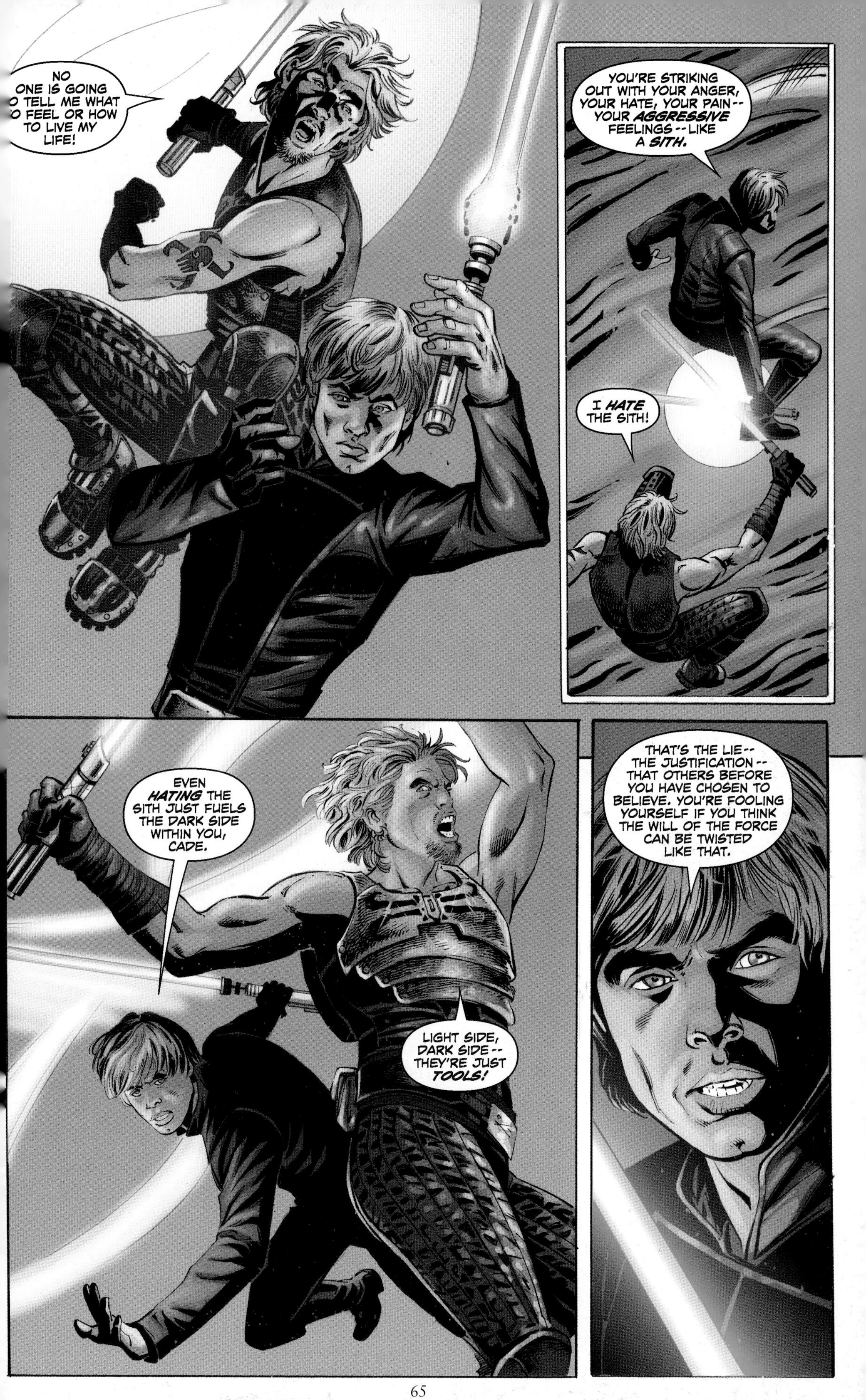
NO ONE IS GOING TO TELL ME WHAT TO FEEL OR HOW TO LIVE MY LIFE!
YOU'RE STRIKING OUT WITH YOUR ANGER, YOUR HATE, YOUR PAIN-- YOUR AGGRESSIVE FEELINGS --LIKE A SITH.
I HATE THE SITH!
EVEN HATING THE SITH JUST FUELS THE DARK SIDE WITHIN YOU, CADE.
LIGHT SIDE, DARK SIDE-- THEY'RE JUST TOOLS!
THAT'S THE LIE-- THE JUSTIFICATION-- THAT OTHERS BEFORE YOU HAVE CHOSEN TO BELIEVE. YOU'RE FOOLING YOURSELF IF YOU THINK THE WILL OF THE FORCE CAN BE TWISTED LIKE THAT.

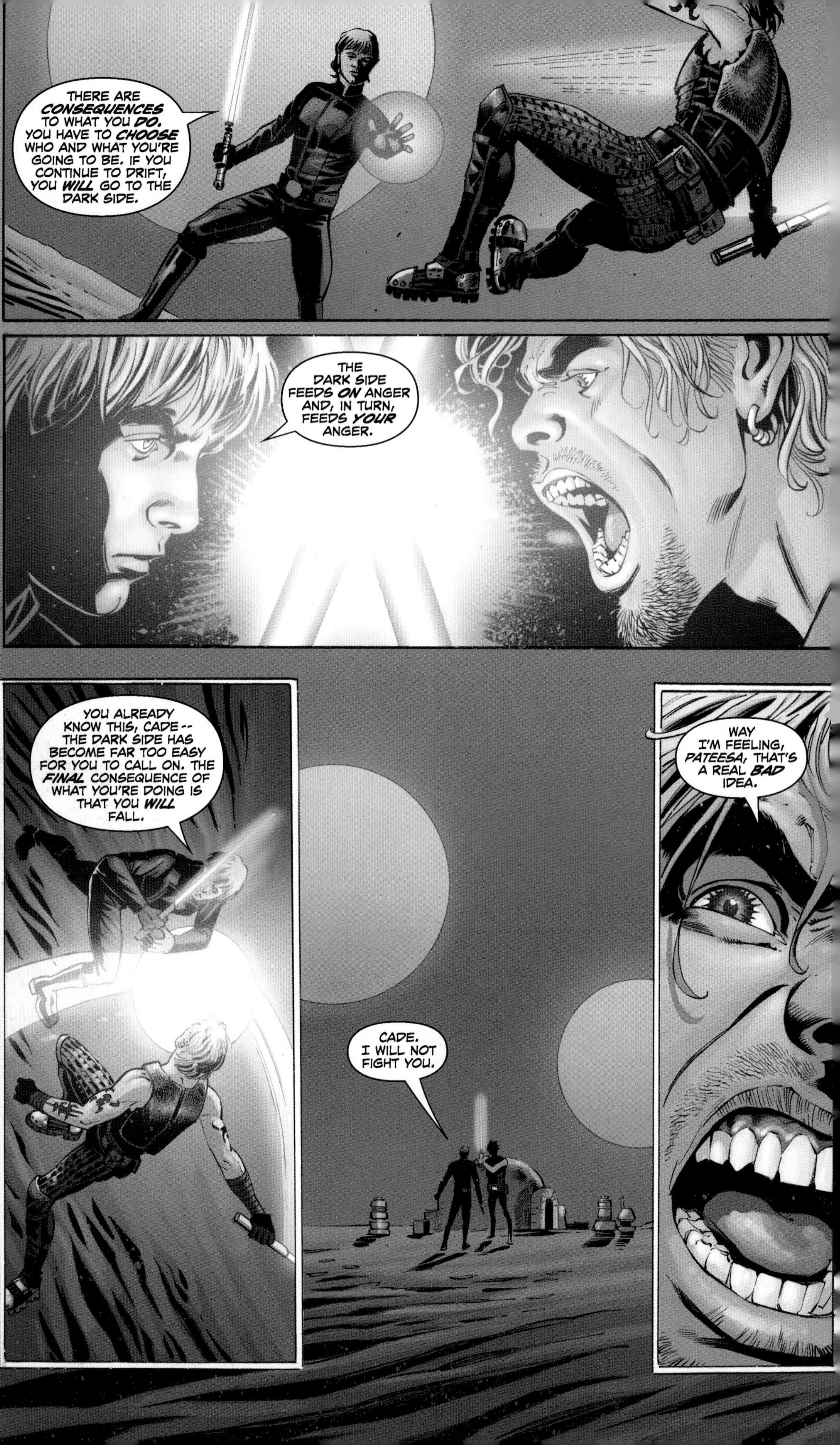
THERE ARE CONSEQUENCES TO WHAT YOU DO. YOU HAVE TO CHOOSE WHO AND WHAT YOU'RE GOING TO BE. IF YOU CONTINUE TO DRIFT, YOU WILL GO TO THE DARK SIDE.
THE DARK SIDE FEEDS ON ANGER AND, IN TURN, FEEDS YOUR ANGER.
YOU ALREADY KNOW THIS, CADE-- THE DARK SIDE HAS BECOME FAR TOO EASY FOR YOU TO CALL ON. THE FINAL CONSEQUENCE OF WHAT YOU'RE DOING IS THAT YOU WILL FALL.
CADE. I WILL NOT FIGHT YOU.
WAY I'M FEELING, PATEESA, THAT'S A REAL BAD IDEA.

THEN STRIKE ME DOWN WITH ALL YOUR ANGER AND YOUR HATE. COMPLETE YOUR JOURNEY TO THE DARK SIDE.

AND THEN GO JOIN THE SITH. YOU'RE ALMOST ONE NOW.

STANG! DOESN'T ANYONE *GET* IT?! I'M *NOT* A SITH *OR* A JEDI! I'M NOT LIKE MY FATHER, OR YOUR FATHER. OR *YOU*. I JUST WANT TO BE LEFT *ALONE!*

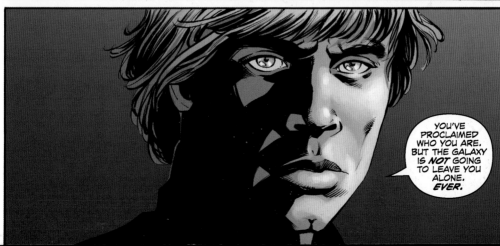

YOU'VE PROCLAIMED WHO YOU ARE. BUT THE GALAXY IS *NOT* GOING TO LEAVE YOU ALONE. *EVER.*

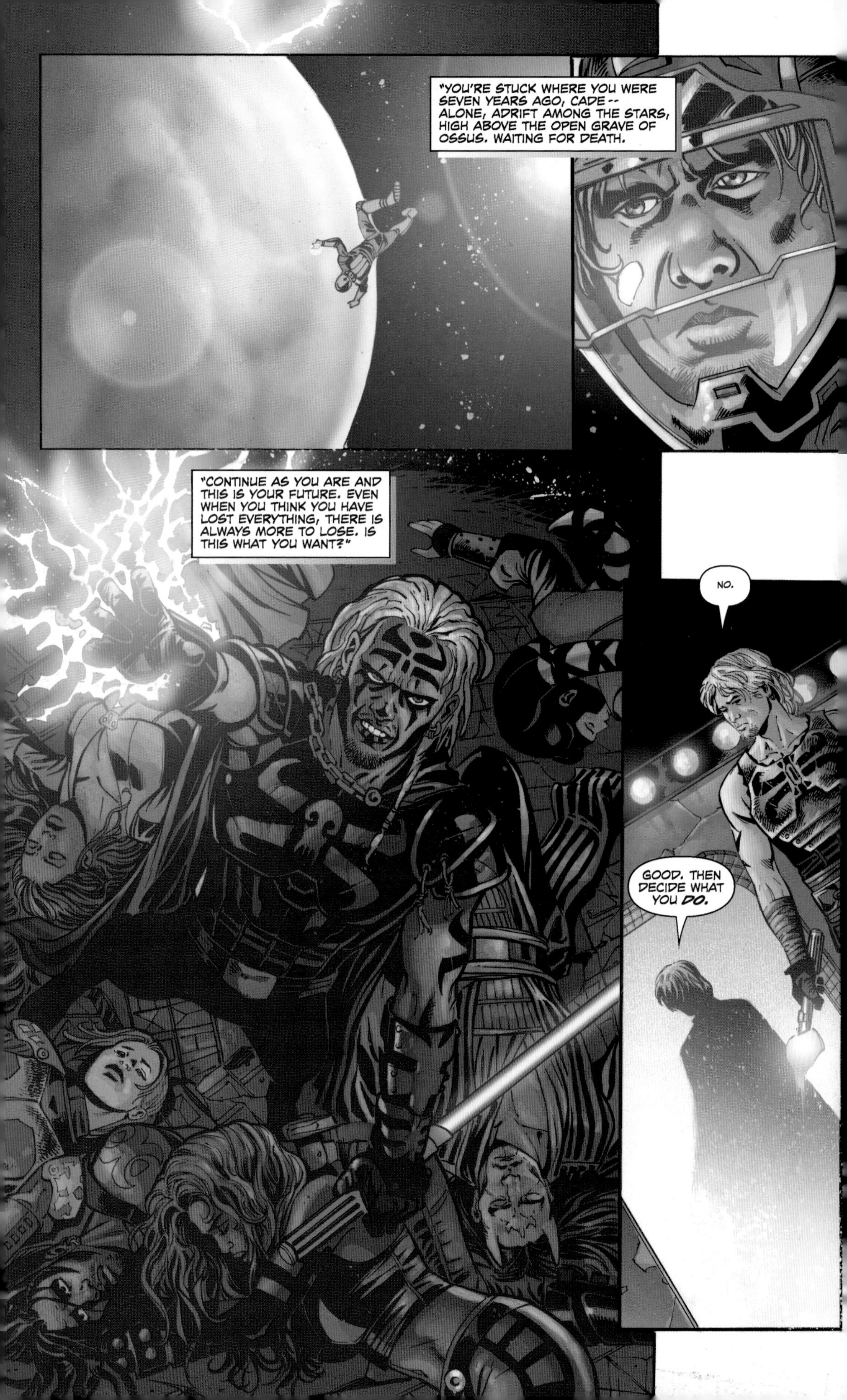
"YOU'RE STUCK WHERE YOU WERE SEVEN YEARS AGO, CADE-- ALONE, ADRIFT AMONG THE STARS, HIGH ABOVE THE OPEN GRAVE OF OSSUS. WAITING FOR DEATH.
"CONTINUE AS YOU ARE AND THIS IS YOUR FUTURE. EVEN WHEN YOU THINK YOU HAVE LOST EVERYTHING, THERE IS ALWAYS MORE TO LOSE. IS THIS WHAT YOU WANT?"
NO.
GOOD. THEN DECIDE WHAT YOU *DO*.

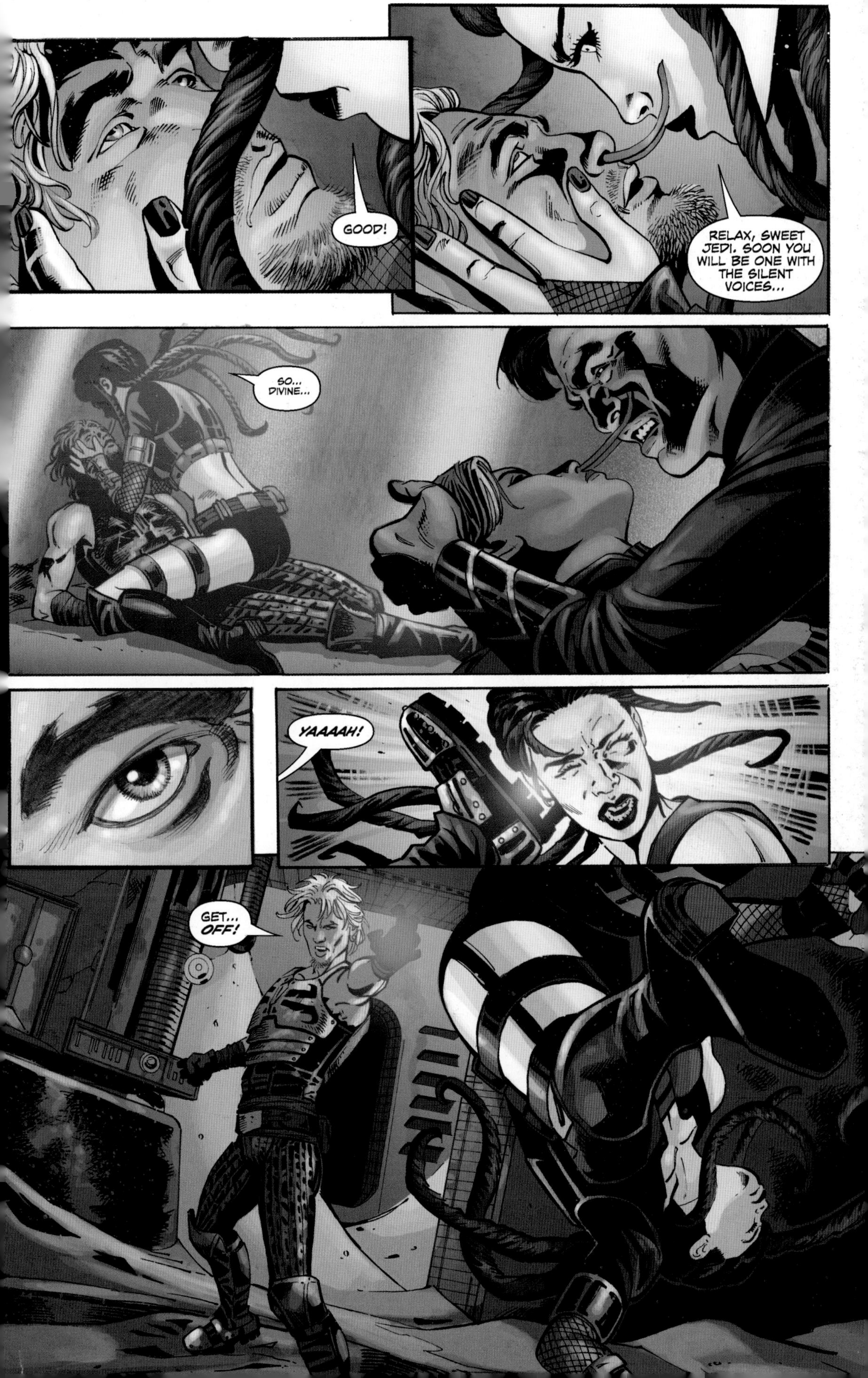
GOOD!
RELAX, SWEET JEDI. SOON YOU WILL BE ONE WITH THE SILENT VOICES...
SO... DIVINE...
YAAAAH!
GET... OFF!

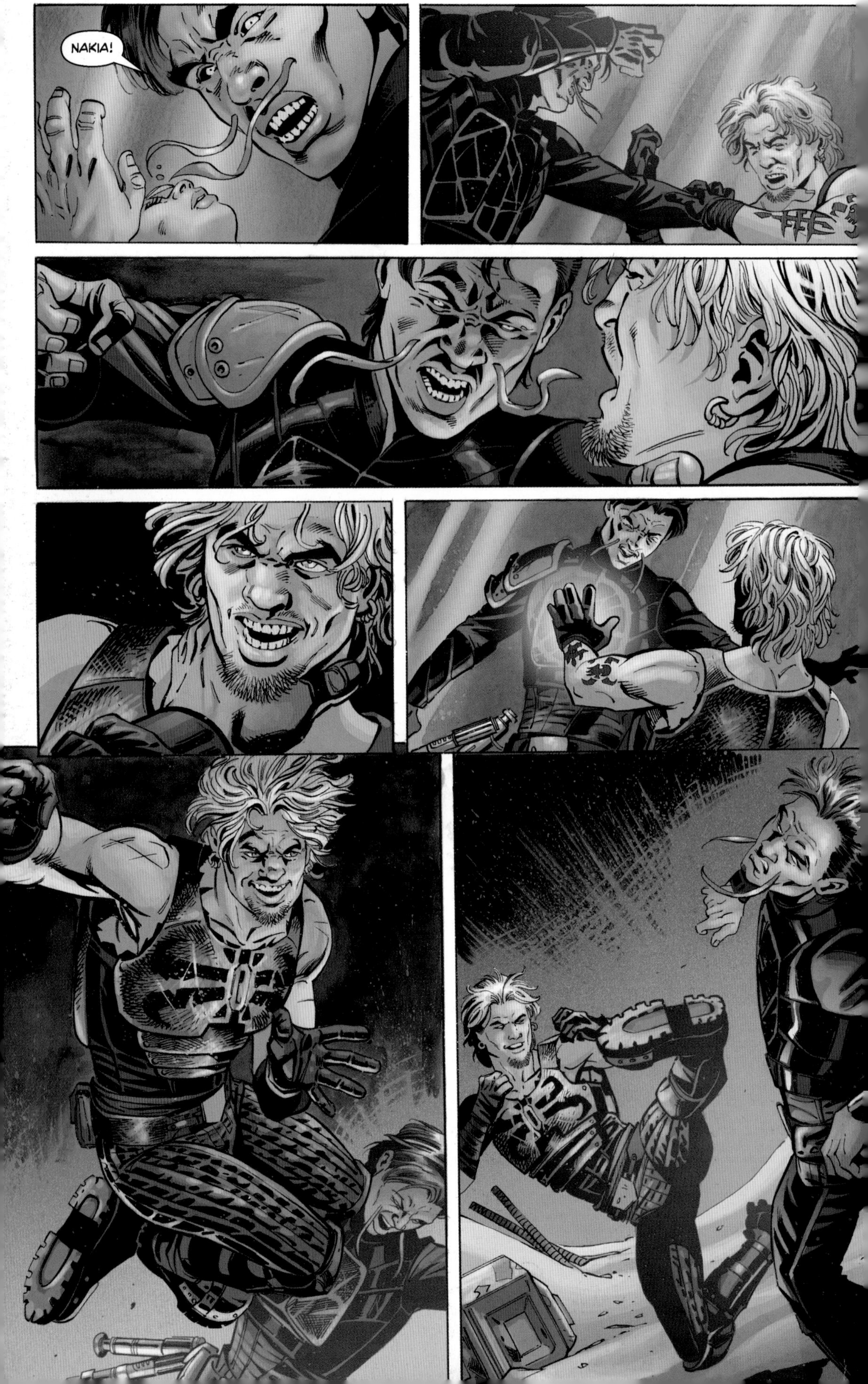
NAKIA!

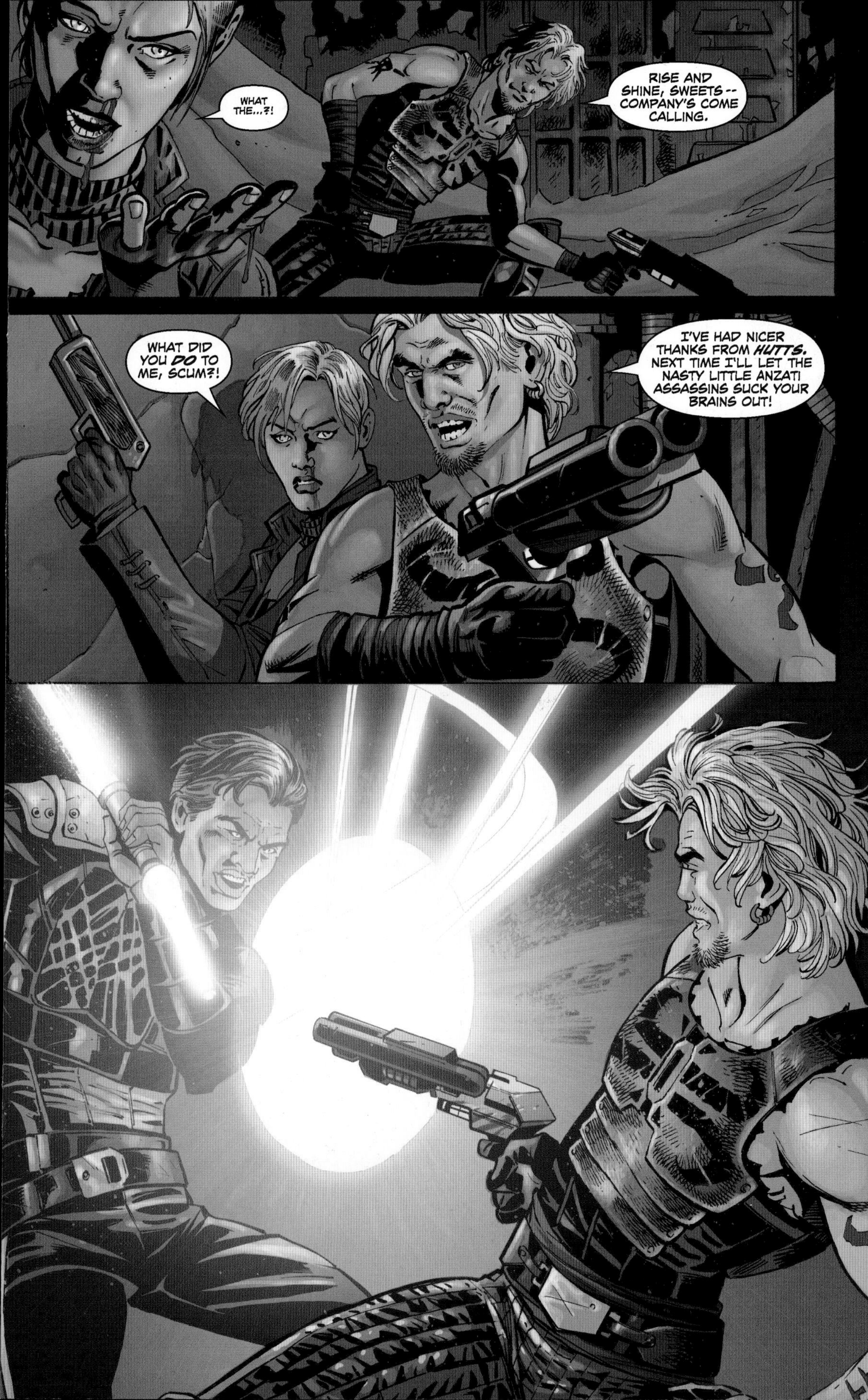
WHAT THE...?!
RISE AND SHINE, SWEETS -- COMPANY'S COME CALLING.
WHAT DID YOU *DO* TO ME, SCUM?!
I'VE HAD NICER THANKS FROM *HUTTS.* NEXT TIME I'LL LET THE NASTY LITTLE ANZATI ASSASSINS SUCK YOUR BRAINS OUT!

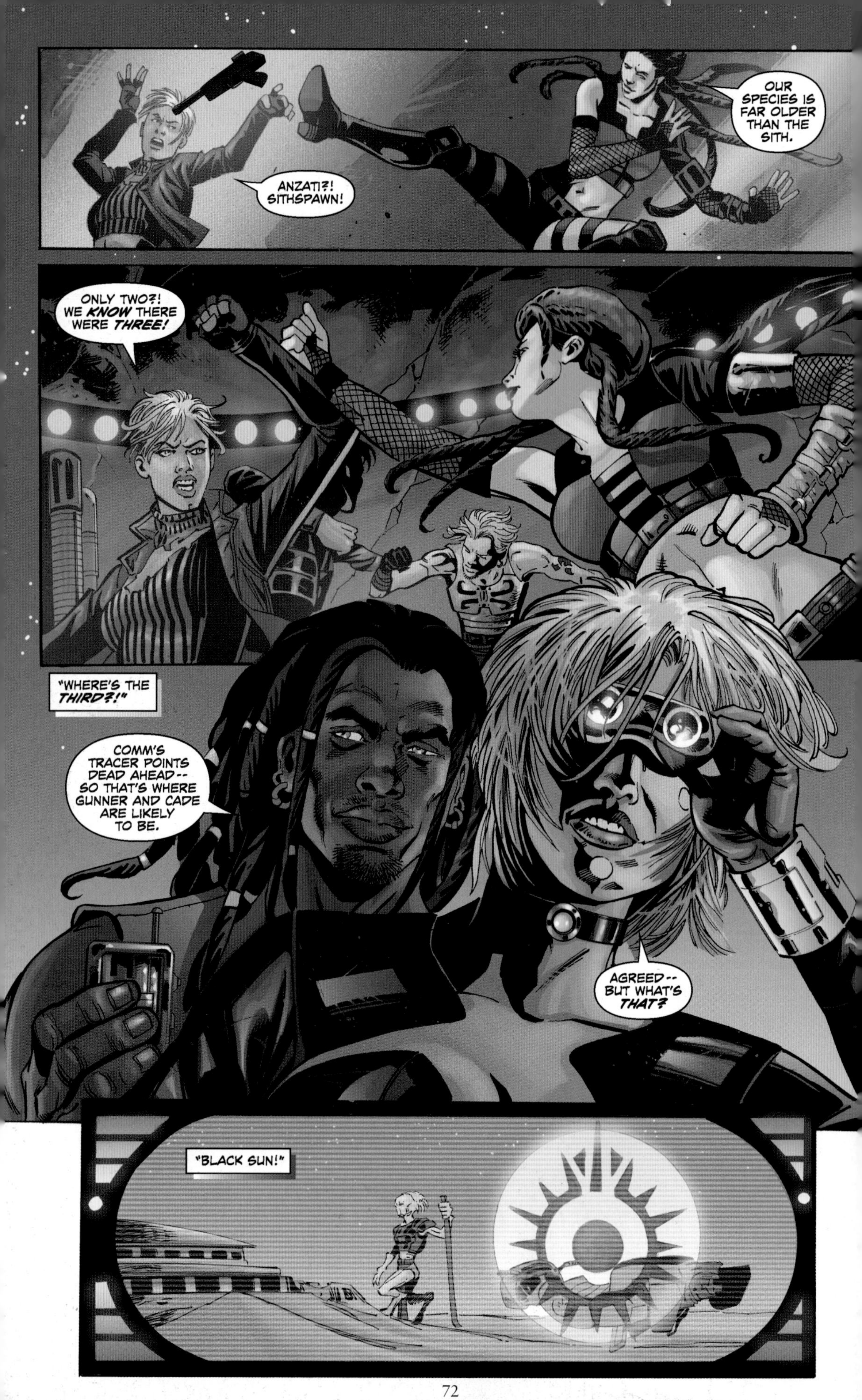
OUR SPECIES IS FAR OLDER THAN THE SITH.
ANZATI?! SITHSPAWN!
ONLY TWO?! WE KNOW THERE WERE THREE!
"WHERE'S THE THIRD?!"
COMM'S TRACER POINTS DEAD AHEAD-- SO THAT'S WHERE GUNNER AND CADE ARE LIKELY TO BE.
AGREED-- BUT WHAT'S THAT?
"BLACK SUN!"

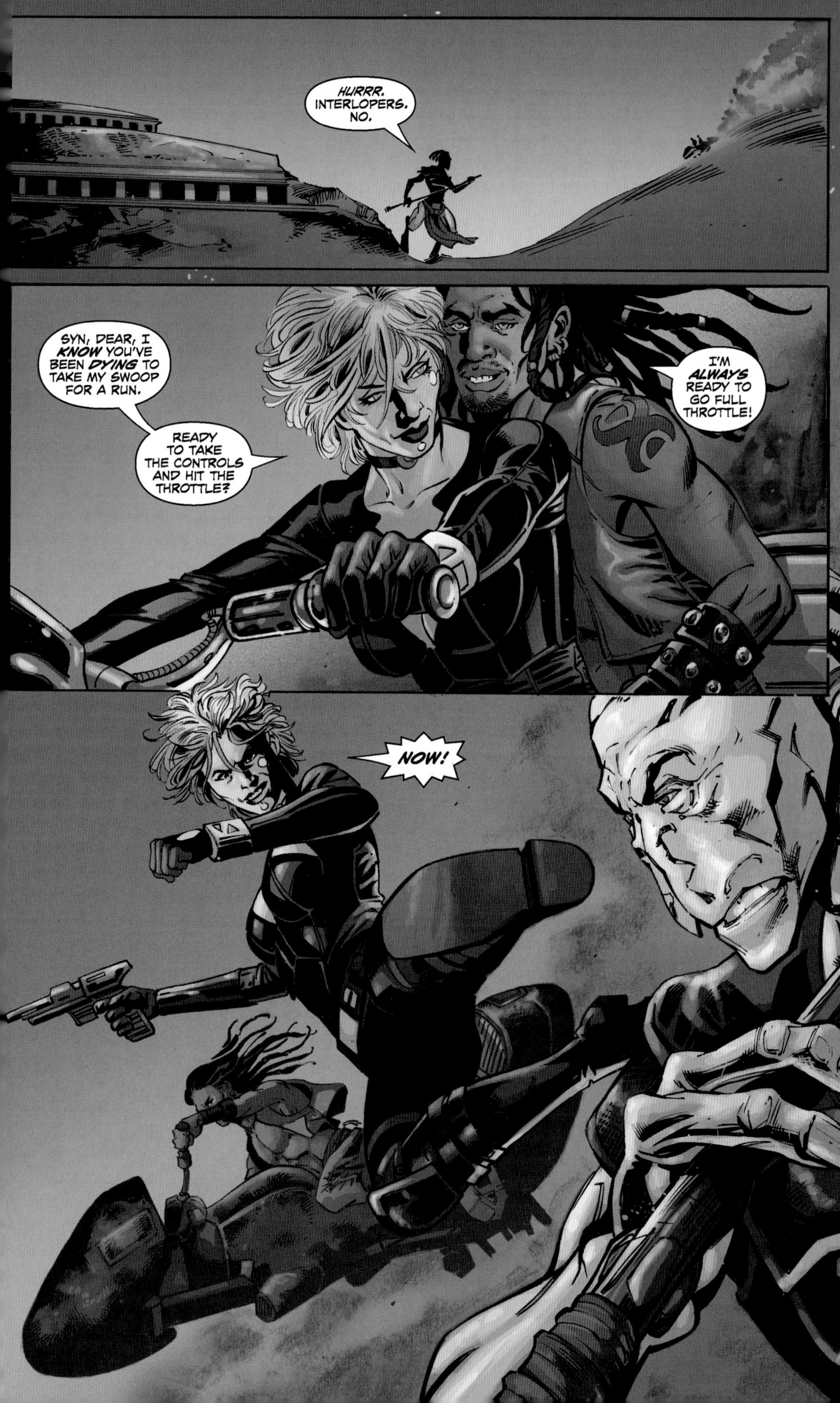
HURRR. INTERLOPERS. NO.
SYN, DEAR, I KNOW YOU'VE BEEN DYING TO TAKE MY SWOOP FOR A RUN.
READY TO TAKE THE CONTROLS AND HIT THE THROTTLE?
I'M ALWAYS READY TO GO FULL THROTTLE!
NOW!

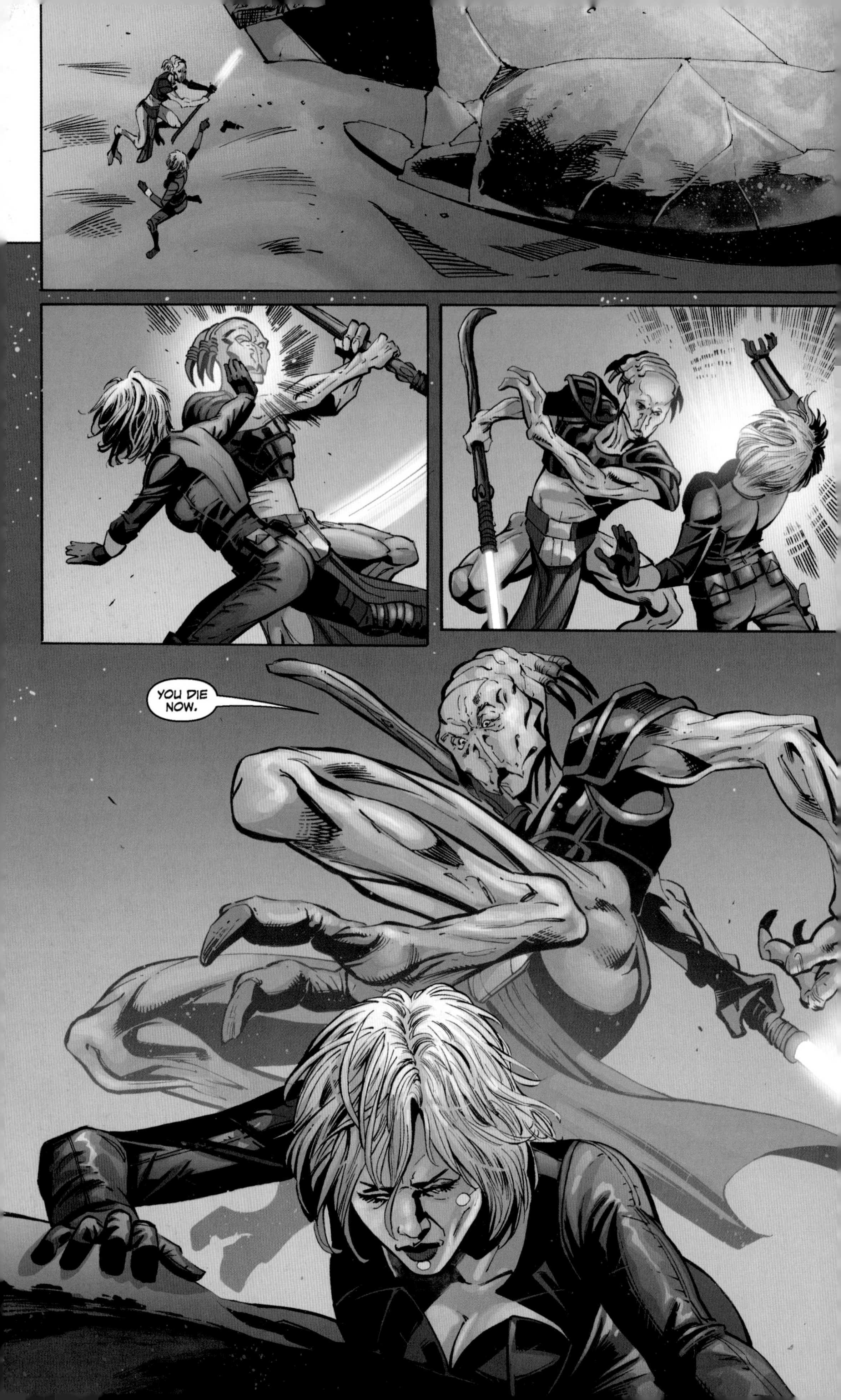
YOU DIE NOW.

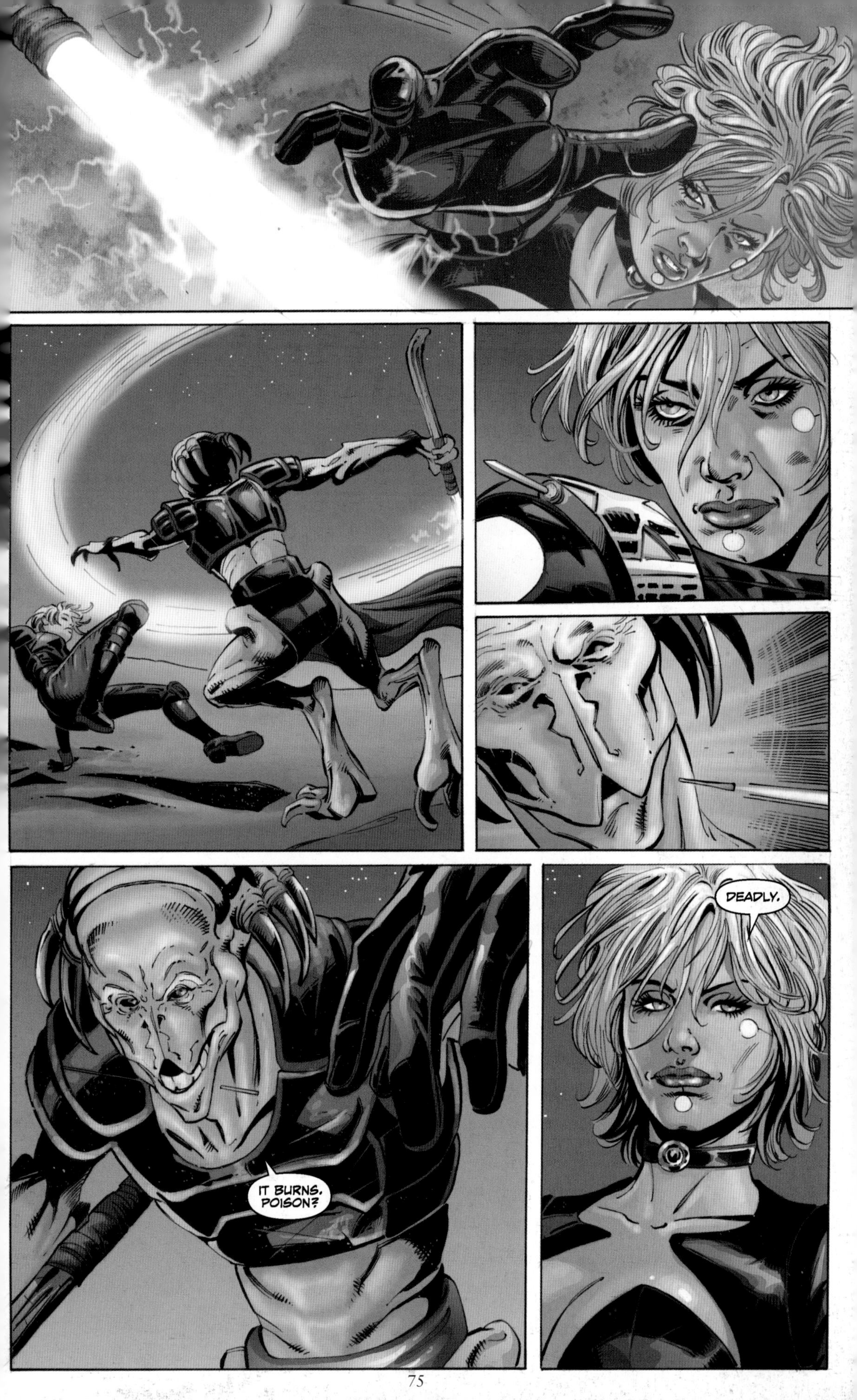
IT BURNS. POISON?
DEADLY.

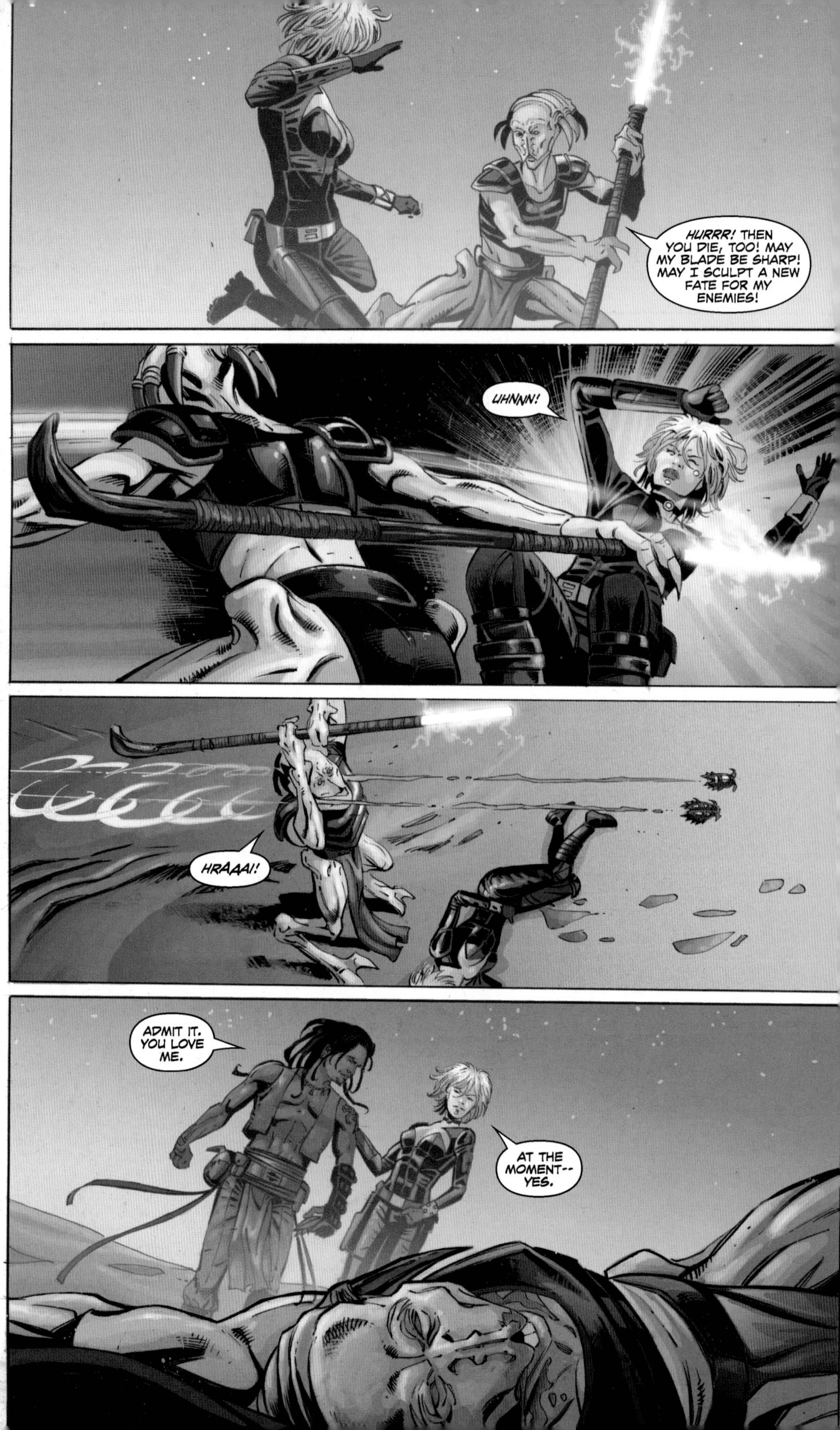
HURRR! THEN YOU DIE, TOO! MAY MY BLADE BE SHARP! MAY I SCULPT A NEW FATE FOR MY ENEMIES!
UHNNN!
HRAAAI!
ADMIT IT. YOU LOVE ME.
AT THE MOMENT-- YES.

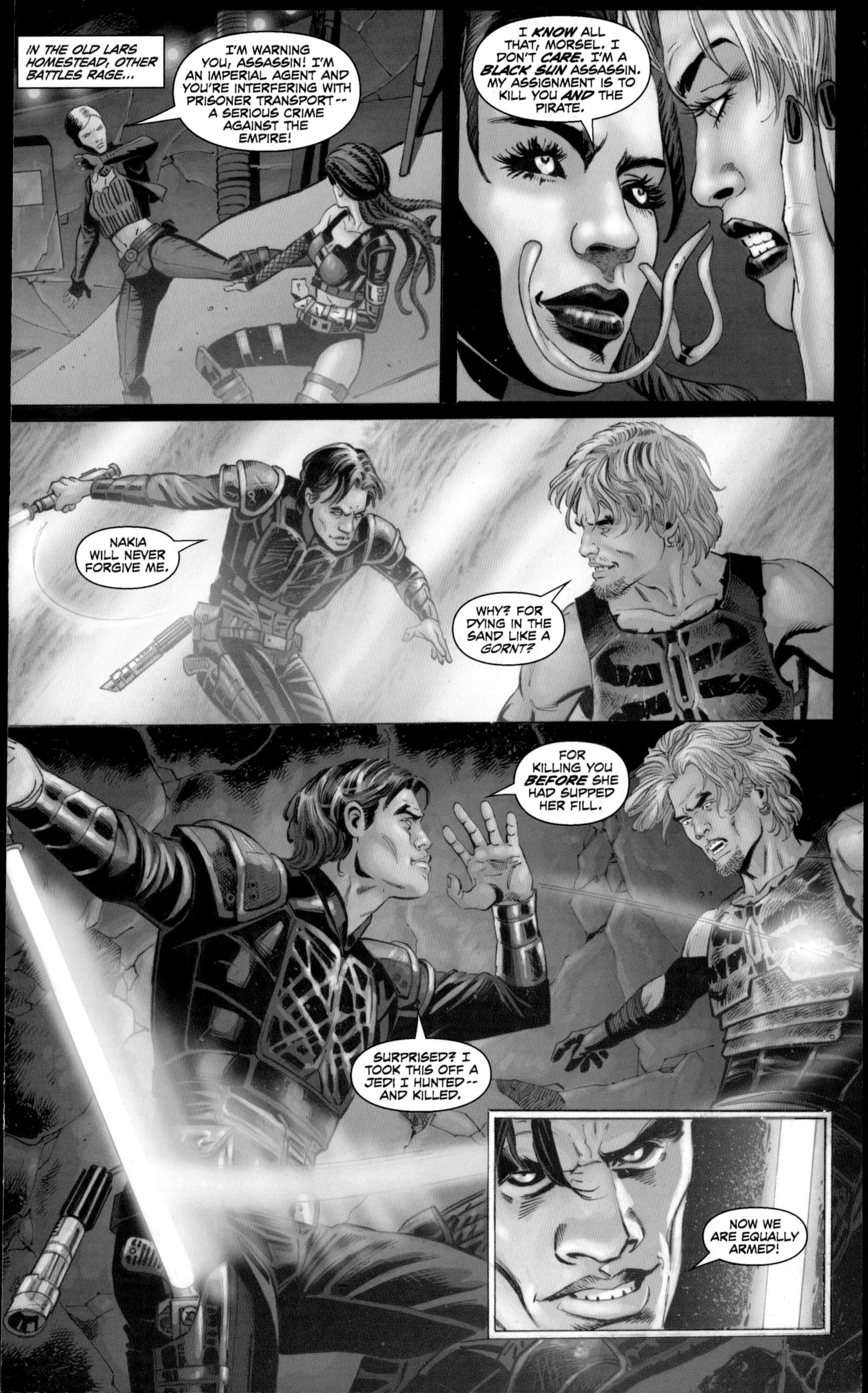

IN THE OLD LARS HOMESTEAD, OTHER BATTLES RAGE...
I'M WARNING YOU, ASSASSIN! I'M AN IMPERIAL AGENT AND YOU'RE INTERFERING WITH PRISONER TRANSPORT-- A SERIOUS CRIME AGAINST THE EMPIRE!
I KNOW ALL THAT, MORSEL. I DON'T CARE. I'M A BLACK SUN ASSASSIN. MY ASSIGNMENT IS TO KILL YOU AND THE PIRATE.
NAKIA WILL NEVER FORGIVE ME.
WHY? FOR DYING IN THE SAND LIKE A GORNT?
FOR KILLING YOU BEFORE SHE HAD SUPPED HER FILL.
SURPRISED? I TOOK THIS OFF A JEDI I HUNTED-- AND KILLED.
NOW WE ARE EQUALLY ARMED!

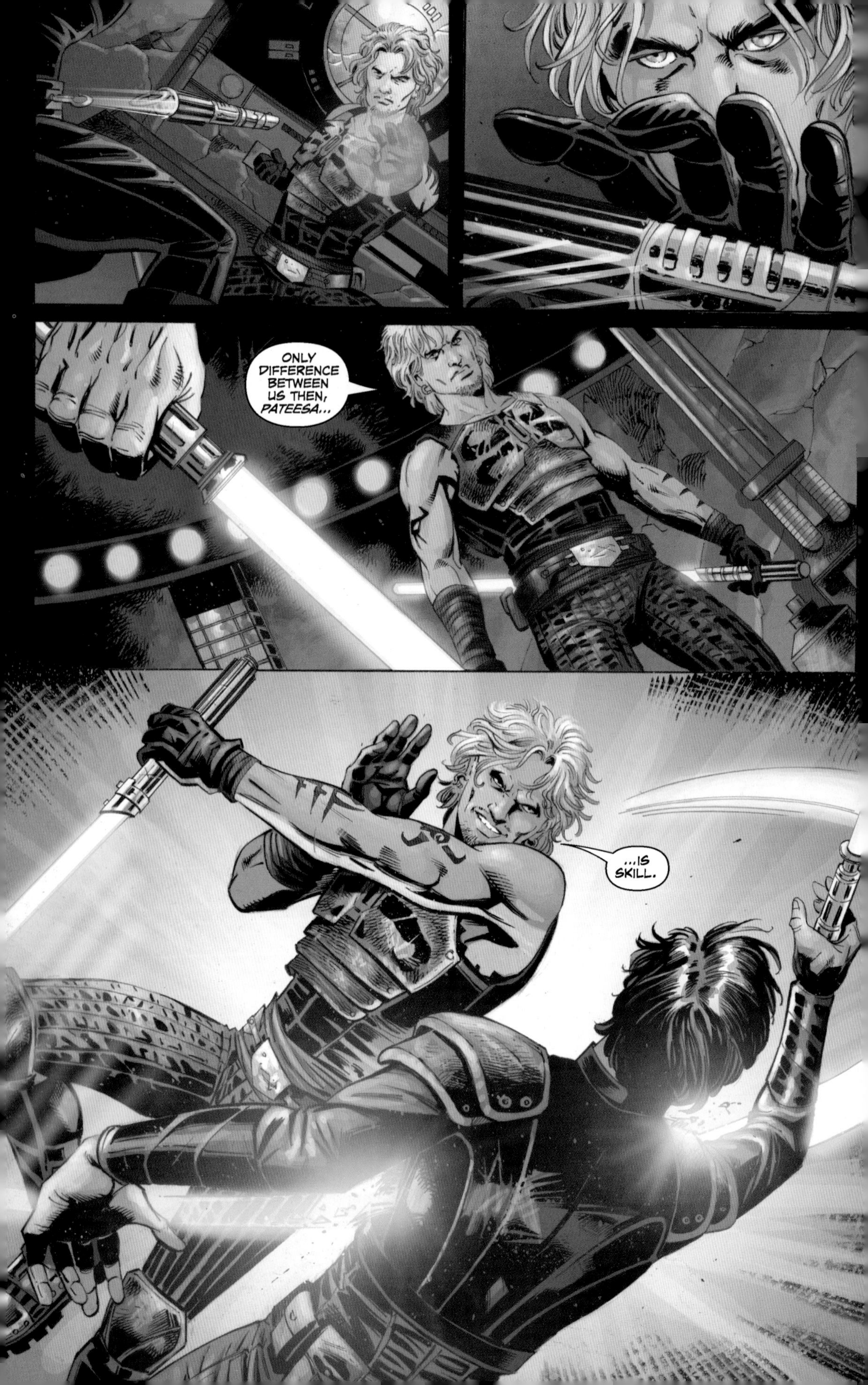
ONLY DIFFERENCE BETWEEN US THEN, PATEESA...
...IS SKILL.

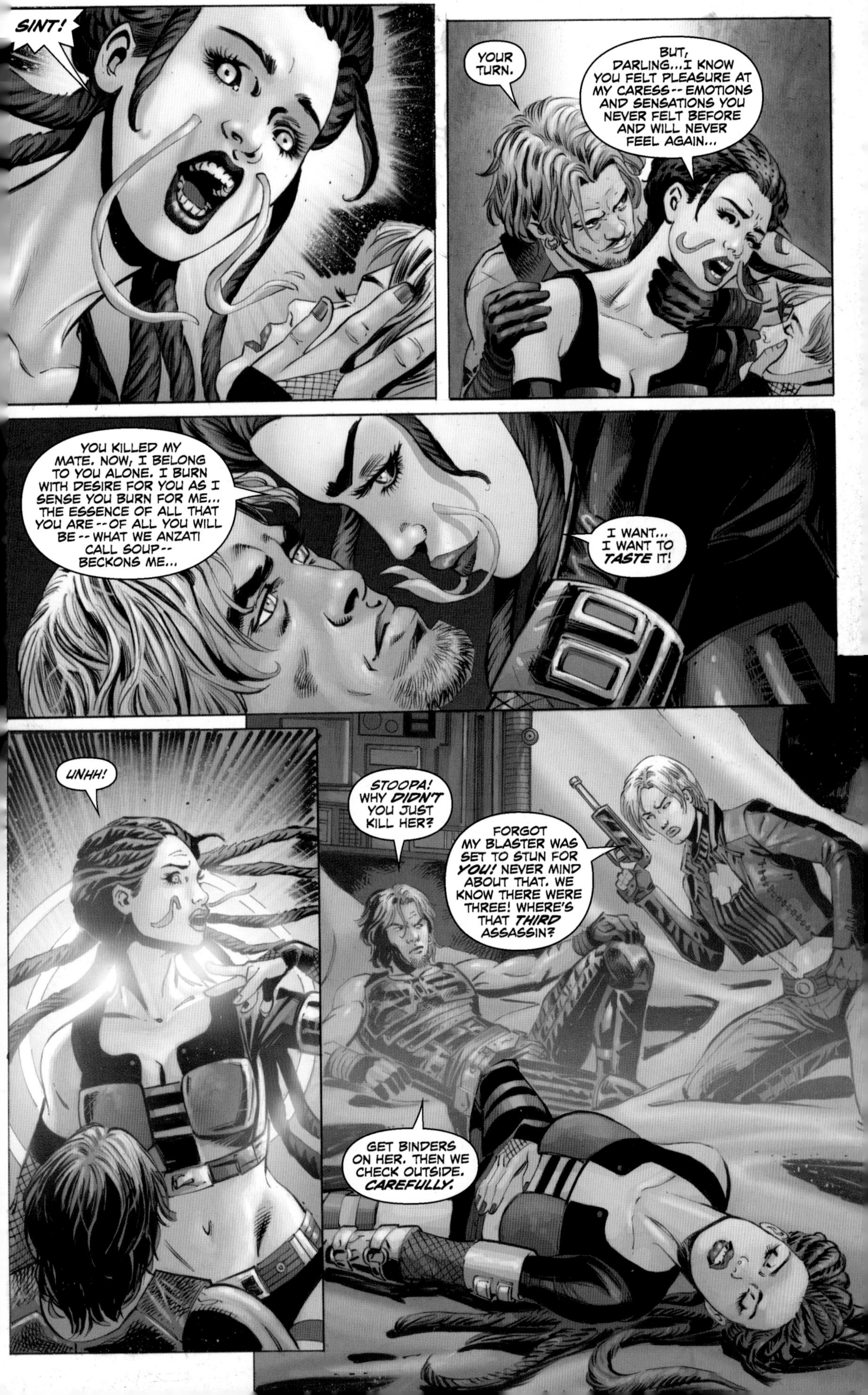
SINT!
YOUR TURN.
BUT, DARLING...I KNOW YOU FELT PLEASURE AT MY CARESS--EMOTIONS AND SENSATIONS YOU NEVER FELT BEFORE AND WILL NEVER FEEL AGAIN...
YOU KILLED MY MATE. NOW, I BELONG TO YOU ALONE. I BURN WITH DESIRE FOR YOU AS I SENSE YOU BURN FOR ME... THE ESSENCE OF ALL THAT YOU ARE--OF ALL YOU WILL BE--WHAT WE ANZATI CALL SOUP--BECKONS ME...
I WANT... I WANT TO TASTE IT!
UNHH!
STOOPA! WHY DIDN'T YOU JUST KILL HER?
FORGOT MY BLASTER WAS SET TO STUN FOR YOU! NEVER MIND ABOUT THAT. WE KNOW THERE WERE THREE! WHERE'S THAT THIRD ASSASSIN?
GET BINDERS ON HER. THEN WE CHECK OUTSIDE. CAREFULLY.

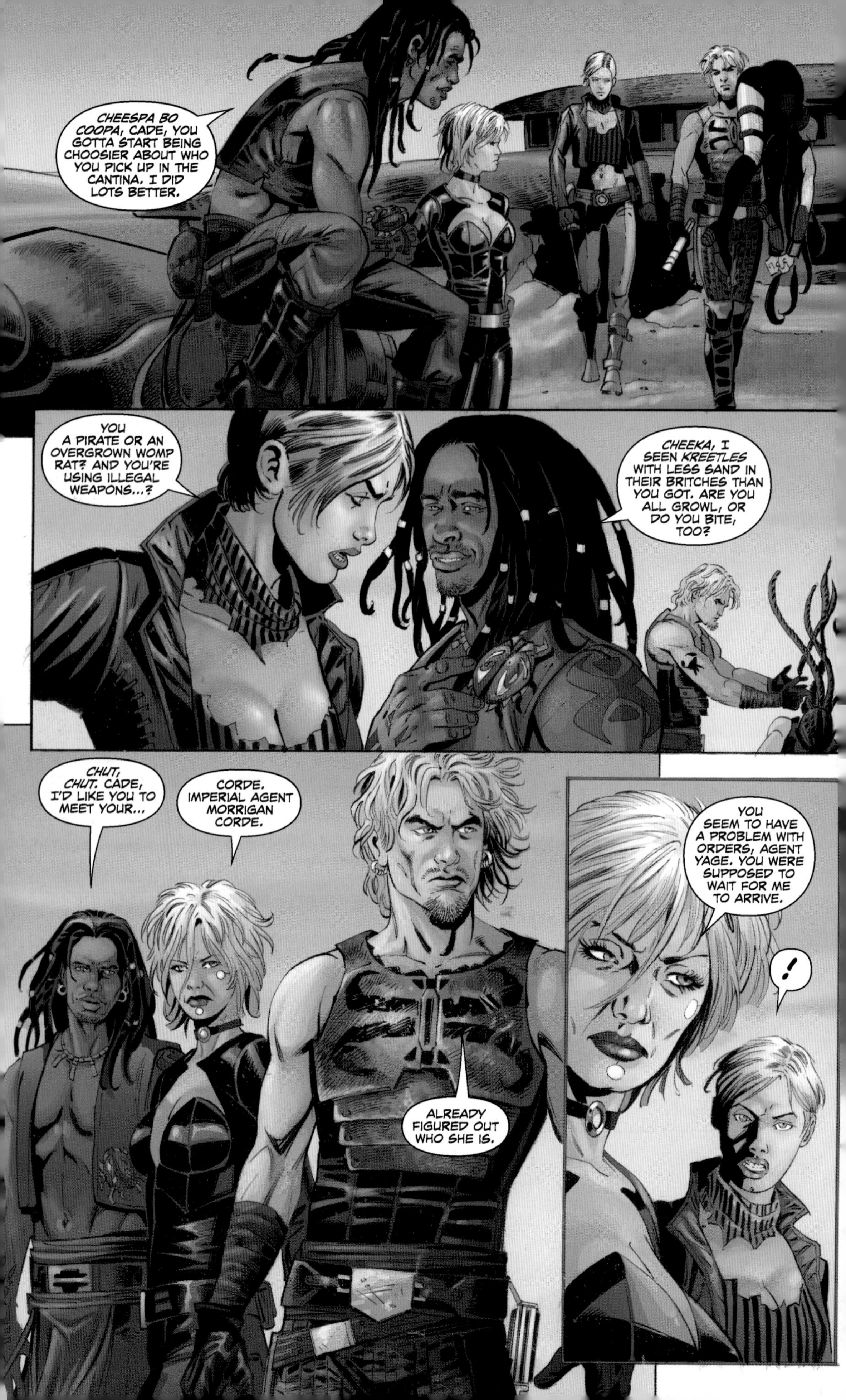
CHEESPA BO COOPA, CADE, YOU GOTTA START BEING CHOOSIER ABOUT WHO YOU PICK UP IN THE CANTINA. I DID LOTS BETTER.
YOU A PIRATE OR AN OVERGROWN WOMP RAT? AND YOU'RE USING ILLEGAL WEAPONS...?
CHEEKA, I SEEN KREETLES WITH LESS SAND IN THEIR BRITCHES THAN YOU GOT. ARE YOU ALL GROWL, OR DO YOU BITE, TOO?
CHUT, CHUT. CADE, I'D LIKE YOU TO MEET YOUR...
CORDE. IMPERIAL AGENT MORRIGAN CORDE.
ALREADY FIGURED OUT WHO SHE IS.
YOU SEEM TO HAVE A PROBLEM WITH ORDERS, AGENT YAGE. YOU WERE SUPPOSED TO WAIT FOR ME TO ARRIVE.
!

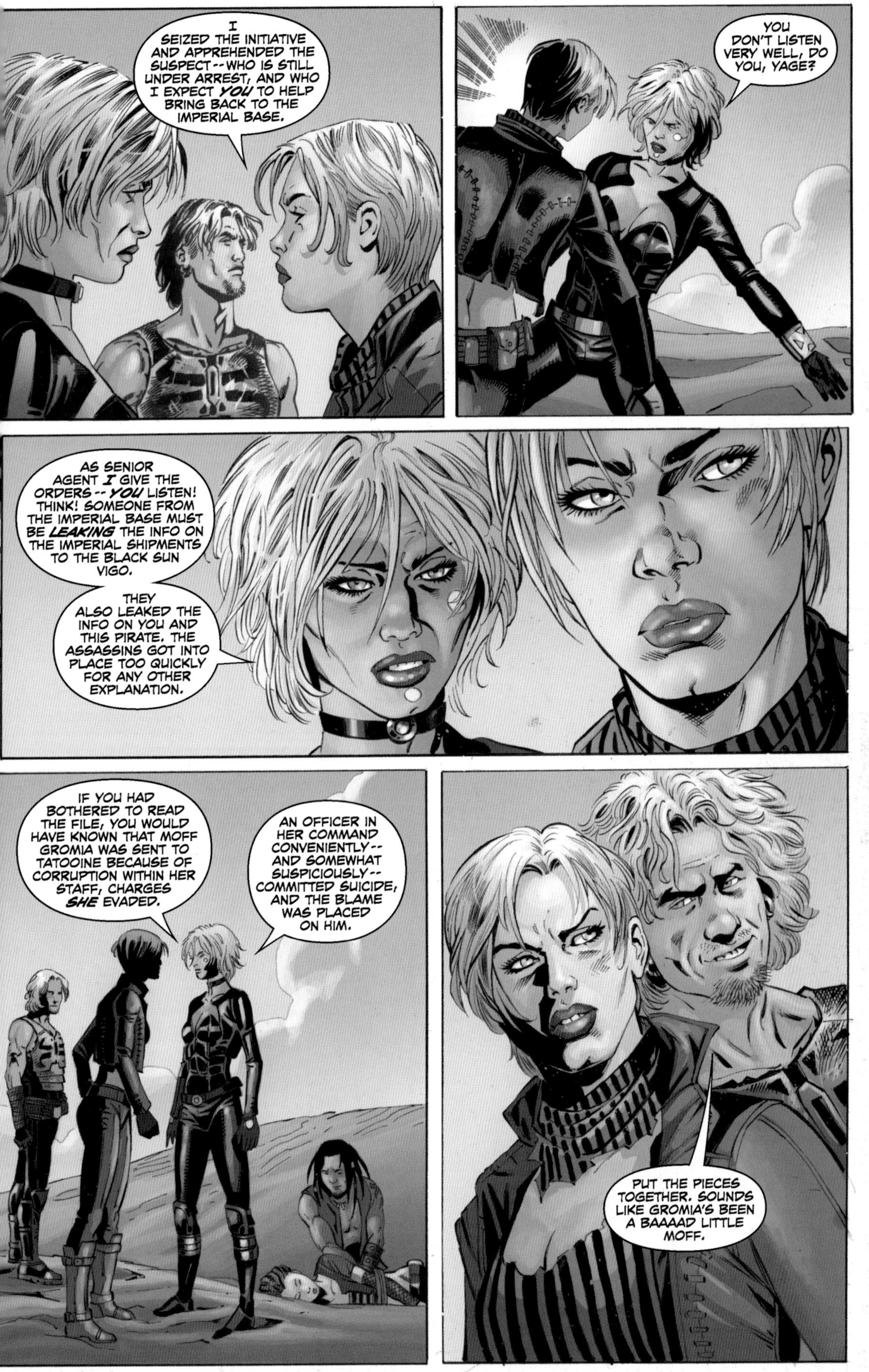
I SEIZED THE INITIATIVE AND APPREHENDED THE SUSPECT--WHO IS STILL UNDER ARREST, AND WHO I EXPECT *YOU* TO HELP BRING BACK TO THE IMPERIAL BASE.
YOU DON'T LISTEN VERY WELL, DO YOU, YAGE?
AS SENIOR AGENT *I* GIVE THE ORDERS--*YOU* LISTEN! THINK! SOMEONE FROM THE IMPERIAL BASE MUST BE *LEAKING* THE INFO ON THE IMPERIAL SHIPMENTS TO THE BLACK SUN VIGO.
THEY ALSO LEAKED THE INFO ON YOU AND THIS PIRATE. THE ASSASSINS GOT INTO PLACE TOO QUICKLY FOR ANY OTHER EXPLANATION.
IF YOU HAD BOTHERED TO READ THE FILE, YOU WOULD HAVE KNOWN THAT MOFF GROMIA WAS SENT TO TATOOINE BECAUSE OF CORRUPTION WITHIN HER STAFF, CHARGES *SHE* EVADED.
AN OFFICER IN HER COMMAND CONVENIENTLY--AND SOMEWHAT SUSPICIOUSLY--COMMITTED SUICIDE, AND THE BLAME WAS PLACED ON HIM.
PUT THE PIECES TOGETHER. SOUNDS LIKE GROMIA'S BEEN A BAAAAD LITTLE MOFF.

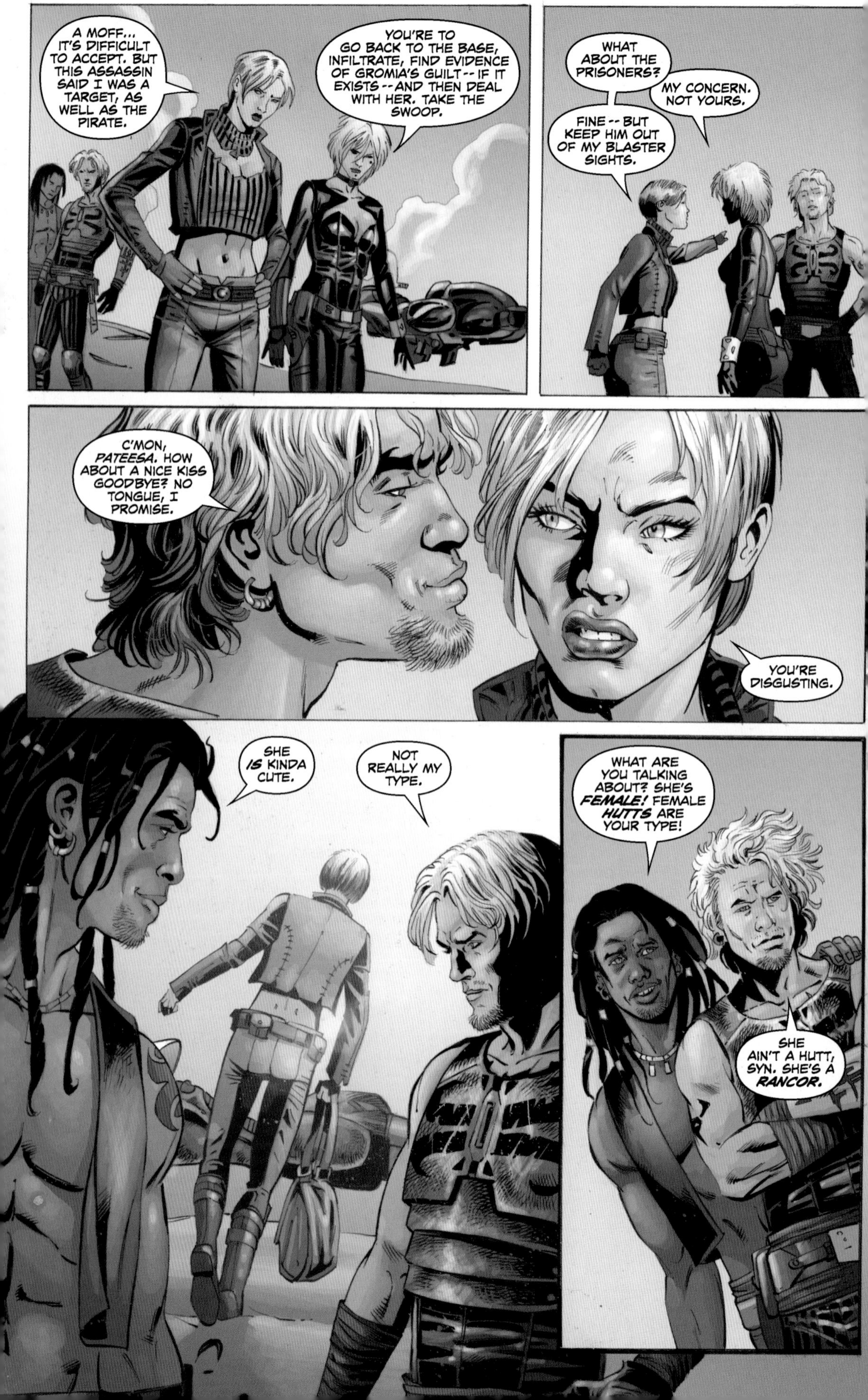
A MOFF... IT'S DIFFICULT TO ACCEPT. BUT THIS ASSASSIN SAID I WAS A TARGET, AS WELL AS THE PIRATE.
YOU'RE TO GO BACK TO THE BASE, INFILTRATE, FIND EVIDENCE OF GROMIA'S GUILT -- IF IT EXISTS -- AND THEN DEAL WITH HER. TAKE THE SWOOP.
WHAT ABOUT THE PRISONERS?
MY CONCERN. NOT YOURS.
FINE -- BUT KEEP HIM OUT OF MY BLASTER SIGHTS.
C'MON, *PATEESA*. HOW ABOUT A NICE KISS GOODBYE? NO TONGUE, I PROMISE.
YOU'RE DISGUSTING.
SHE *IS* KINDA CUTE.
NOT REALLY MY TYPE.
WHAT ARE YOU TALKING ABOUT? SHE'S ***FEMALE!*** FEMALE ***HUTTS*** ARE YOUR TYPE!
SHE AIN'T A HUTT, SYN. SHE'S A ***RANCOR.***

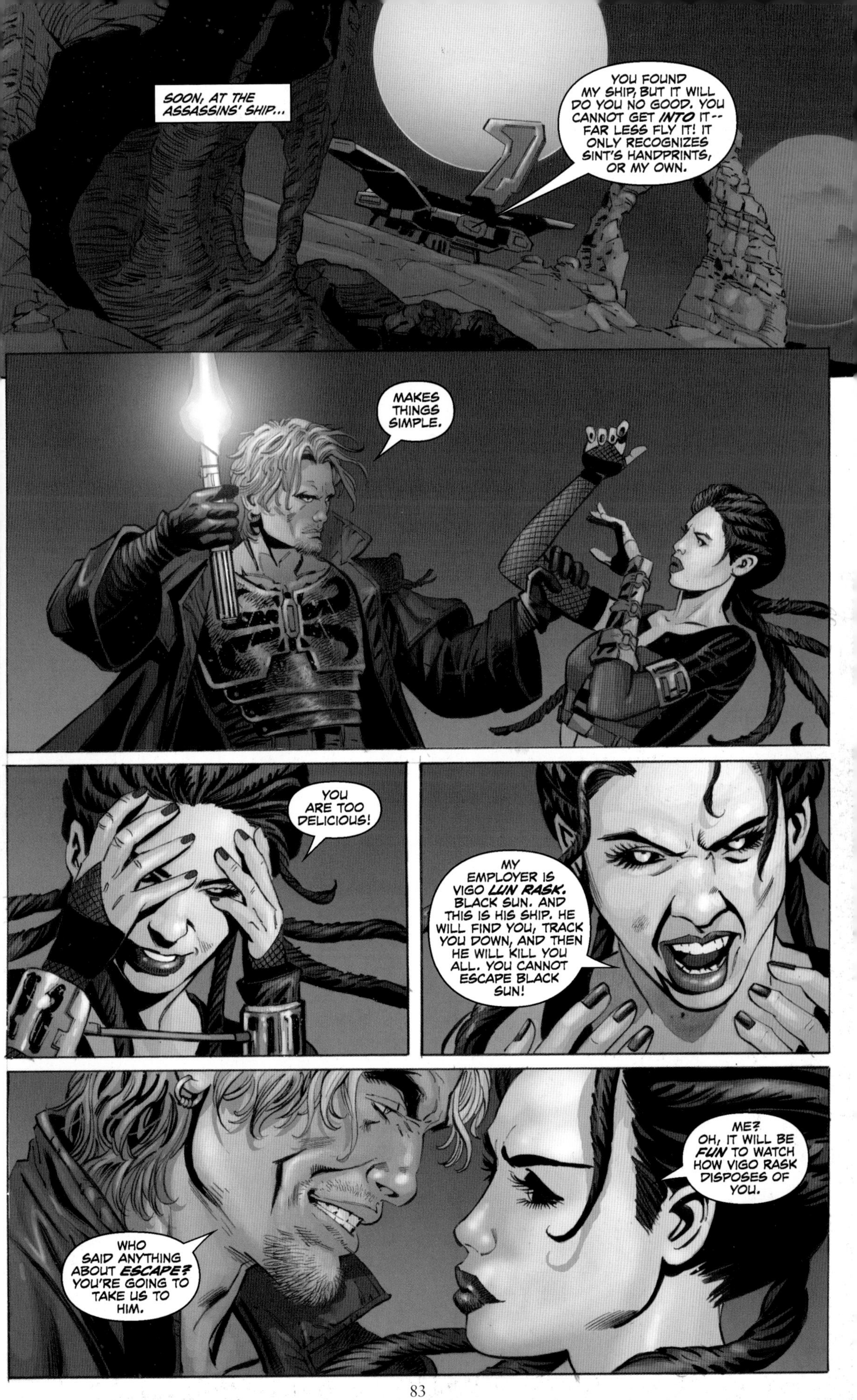
SOON, AT THE ASSASSINS' SHIP...
YOU FOUND MY SHIP, BUT IT WILL DO YOU NO GOOD. YOU CANNOT GET INTO IT-- FAR LESS FLY IT! IT ONLY RECOGNIZES SINT'S HANDPRINTS, OR MY OWN.
MAKES THINGS SIMPLE.
YOU ARE TOO DELICIOUS!
MY EMPLOYER IS VIGO LUN RASK. BLACK SUN. AND THIS IS HIS SHIP. HE WILL FIND YOU, TRACK YOU DOWN, AND THEN HE WILL KILL YOU ALL. YOU CANNOT ESCAPE BLACK SUN!
ME? OH, IT WILL BE FUN TO WATCH HOW VIGO RASK DISPOSES OF YOU.
WHO SAID ANYTHING ABOUT ESCAPE? YOU'RE GOING TO TAKE US TO HIM.

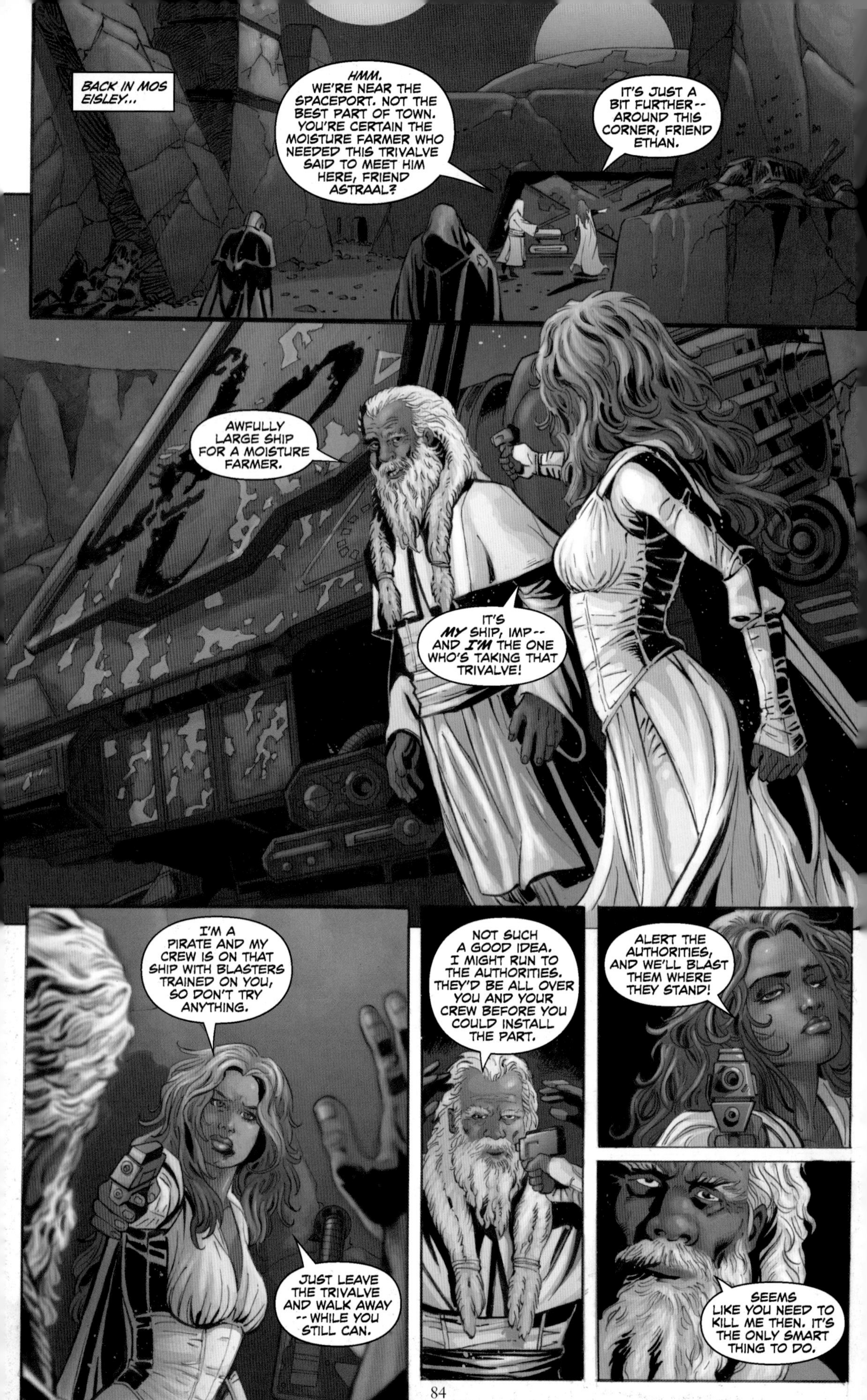

BACK IN MOS EISLEY...
HMM. WE'RE NEAR THE SPACEPORT. NOT THE BEST PART OF TOWN. YOU'RE CERTAIN THE MOISTURE FARMER WHO NEEDED THIS TRIVALVE SAID TO MEET HIM HERE, FRIEND ASTRAAL?
IT'S JUST A BIT FURTHER-- AROUND THIS CORNER, FRIEND ETHAN.
AWFULLY LARGE SHIP FOR A MOISTURE FARMER.
IT'S MY SHIP, IMP-- AND I'M THE ONE WHO'S TAKING THAT TRIVALVE!
I'M A PIRATE AND MY CREW IS ON THAT SHIP WITH BLASTERS TRAINED ON YOU, SO DON'T TRY ANYTHING.
JUST LEAVE THE TRIVALVE AND WALK AWAY --WHILE YOU STILL CAN.
NOT SUCH A GOOD IDEA. I MIGHT RUN TO THE AUTHORITIES. THEY'D BE ALL OVER YOU AND YOUR CREW BEFORE YOU COULD INSTALL THE PART.
ALERT THE AUTHORITIES, AND WE'LL BLAST THEM WHERE THEY STAND!
SEEMS LIKE YOU NEED TO KILL ME THEN. IT'S THE ONLY SMART THING TO DO.

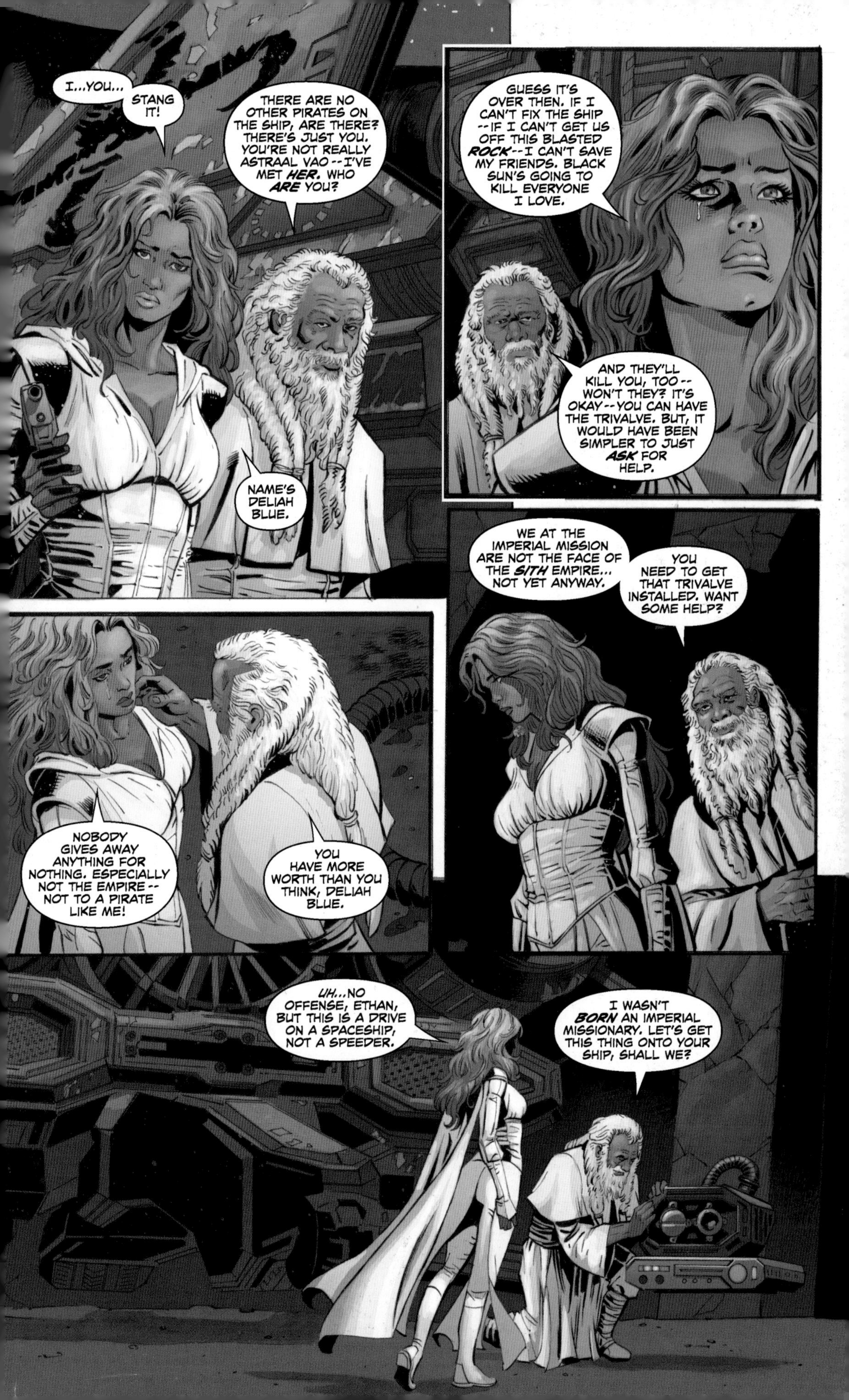
I...YOU...
STANG IT!
THERE ARE NO OTHER PIRATES ON THE SHIP, ARE THERE? THERE'S JUST YOU. YOU'RE NOT REALLY ASTRAAL VAO--I'VE MET HER. WHO ARE YOU?
NAME'S DELIAH BLUE.
GUESS IT'S OVER THEN. IF I CAN'T FIX THE SHIP--IF I CAN'T GET US OFF THIS BLASTED ROCK--I CAN'T SAVE MY FRIENDS. BLACK SUN'S GOING TO KILL EVERYONE I LOVE.
AND THEY'LL KILL YOU, TOO--WON'T THEY? IT'S OKAY--YOU CAN HAVE THE TRIVALVE. BUT, IT WOULD HAVE BEEN SIMPLER TO JUST ASK FOR HELP.
NOBODY GIVES AWAY ANYTHING FOR NOTHING. ESPECIALLY NOT THE EMPIRE--NOT TO A PIRATE LIKE ME!
YOU HAVE MORE WORTH THAN YOU THINK, DELIAH BLUE.
WE AT THE IMPERIAL MISSION ARE NOT THE FACE OF THE SITH EMPIRE... NOT YET ANYWAY.
YOU NEED TO GET THAT TRIVALVE INSTALLED. WANT SOME HELP?
UH...NO OFFENSE, ETHAN, BUT THIS IS A DRIVE ON A SPACESHIP, NOT A SPEEDER.
I WASN'T BORN AN IMPERIAL MISSIONARY. LET'S GET THIS THING ONTO YOUR SHIP, SHALL WE?

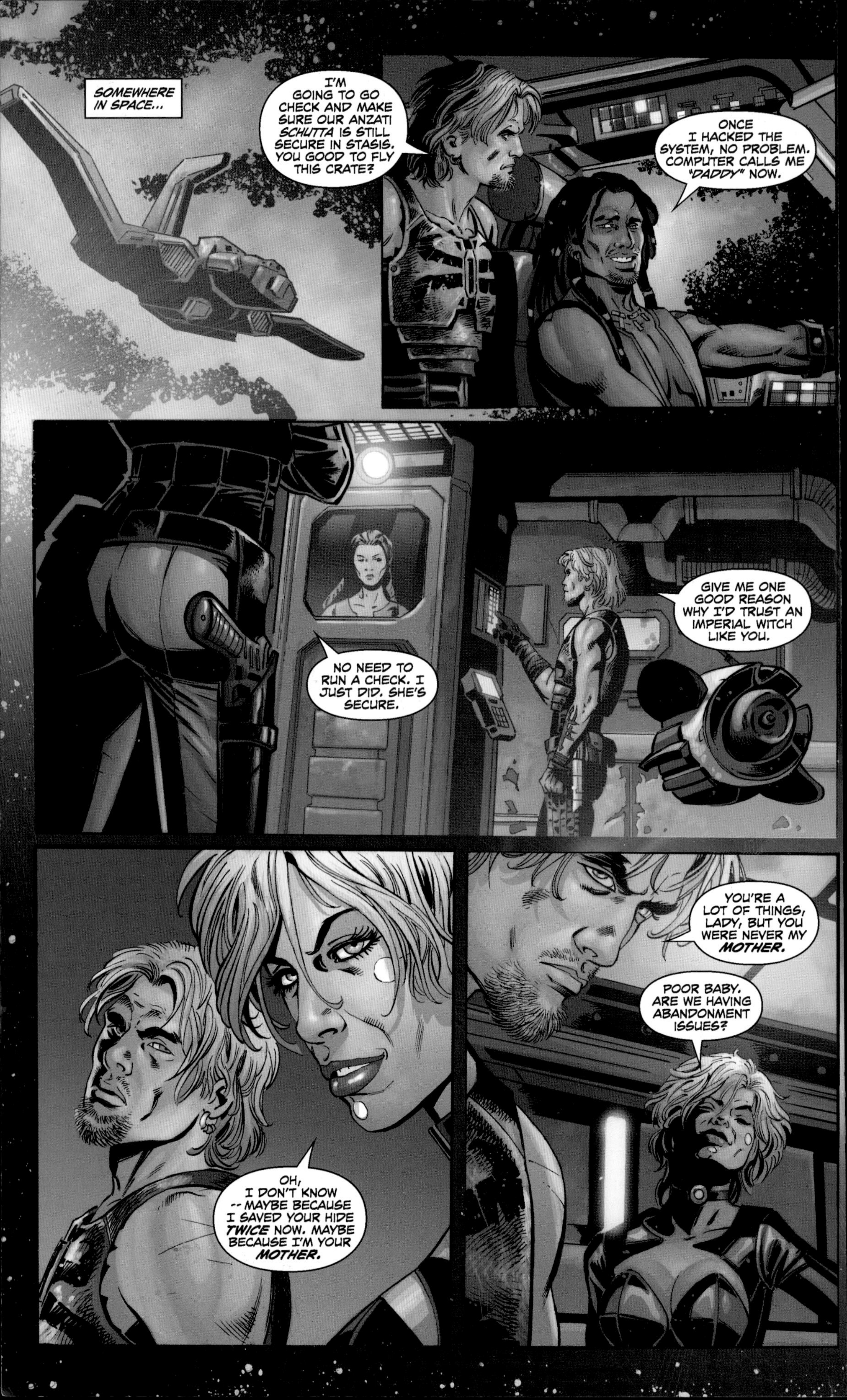
SOMEWHERE IN SPACE...
I'M GOING TO GO CHECK AND MAKE SURE OUR ANZATI SCHUTTA IS STILL SECURE IN STASIS. YOU GOOD TO FLY THIS CRATE?
ONCE I HACKED THE SYSTEM, NO PROBLEM. COMPUTER CALLS ME "DADDY" NOW.
NO NEED TO RUN A CHECK. I JUST DID. SHE'S SECURE.
GIVE ME ONE GOOD REASON WHY I'D TRUST AN IMPERIAL WITCH LIKE YOU.
OH, I DON'T KNOW -- MAYBE BECAUSE I SAVED YOUR HIDE TWICE NOW. MAYBE BECAUSE I'M YOUR MOTHER.
YOU'RE A LOT OF THINGS, LADY, BUT YOU WERE NEVER MY MOTHER.
POOR BABY. ARE WE HAVING ABANDONMENT ISSUES?

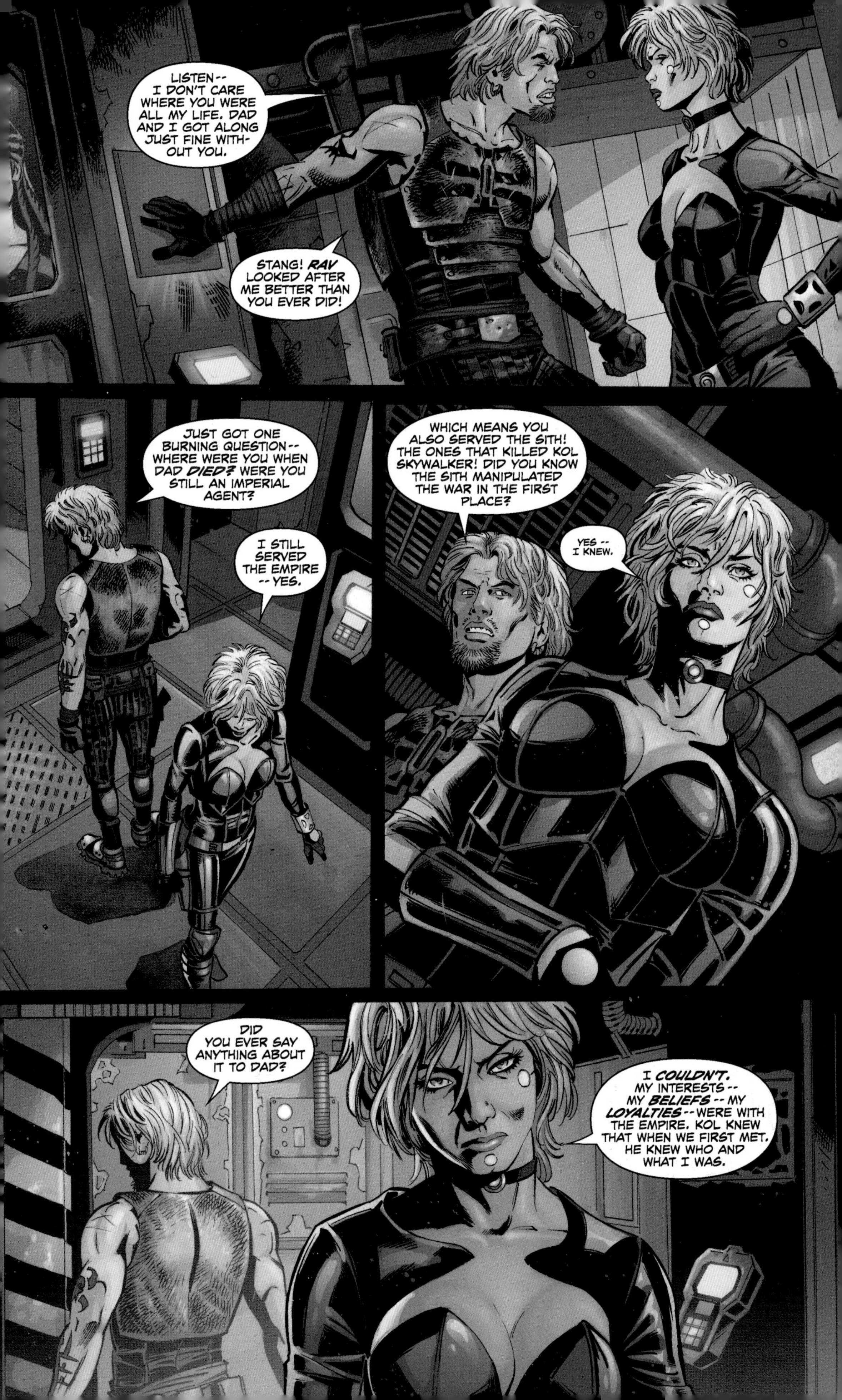
LISTEN-- I DON'T CARE WHERE YOU WERE ALL MY LIFE. DAD AND I GOT ALONG JUST FINE WITH-OUT YOU.
STANG! RAV LOOKED AFTER ME BETTER THAN YOU EVER DID!
JUST GOT ONE BURNING QUESTION-- WHERE WERE YOU WHEN DAD DIED? WERE YOU STILL AN IMPERIAL AGENT?
I STILL SERVED THE EMPIRE --YES.
WHICH MEANS YOU ALSO SERVED THE SITH! THE ONES THAT KILLED KOL SKYWALKER! DID YOU KNOW THE SITH MANIPULATED THE WAR IN THE FIRST PLACE?
YES -- I KNEW.
DID YOU EVER SAY ANYTHING ABOUT IT TO DAD?
I COULDN'T. MY INTERESTS-- MY BELIEFS-- MY LOYALTIES--WERE WITH THE EMPIRE. KOL KNEW THAT WHEN WE FIRST MET. HE KNEW WHO AND WHAT I WAS.

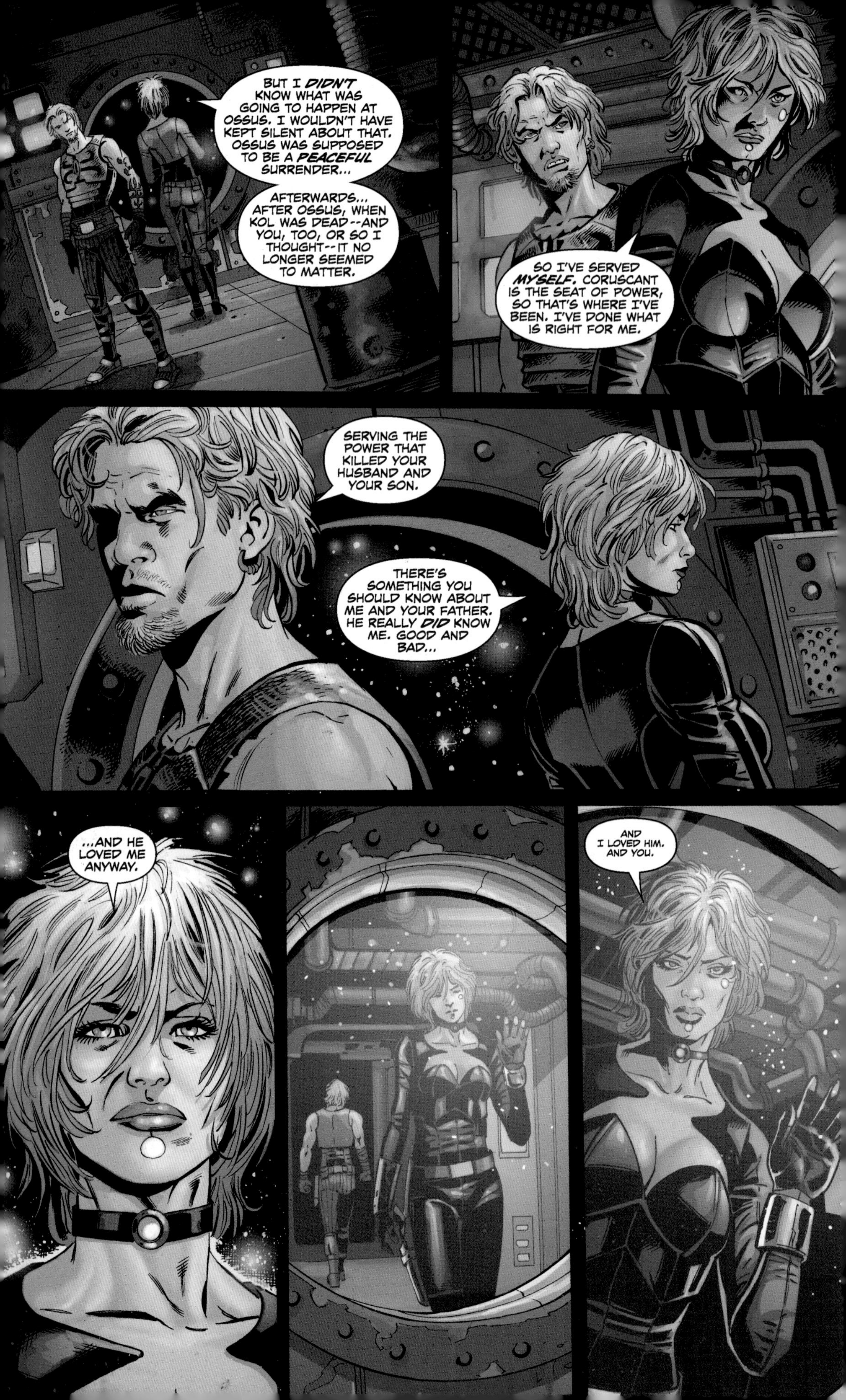
BUT I DIDN'T KNOW WHAT WAS GOING TO HAPPEN AT OSSUS. I WOULDN'T HAVE KEPT SILENT ABOUT THAT. OSSUS WAS SUPPOSED TO BE A PEACEFUL SURRENDER...
AFTERWARDS... AFTER OSSUS, WHEN KOL WAS DEAD--AND YOU, TOO, OR SO I THOUGHT--IT NO LONGER SEEMED TO MATTER.
SO I'VE SERVED MYSELF. CORUSCANT IS THE SEAT OF POWER, SO THAT'S WHERE I'VE BEEN. I'VE DONE WHAT IS RIGHT FOR ME.
SERVING THE POWER THAT KILLED YOUR HUSBAND AND YOUR SON.
THERE'S SOMETHING YOU SHOULD KNOW ABOUT ME AND YOUR FATHER. HE REALLY DID KNOW ME. GOOD AND BAD...
...AND HE LOVED ME ANYWAY.
AND I LOVED HIM. AND YOU.

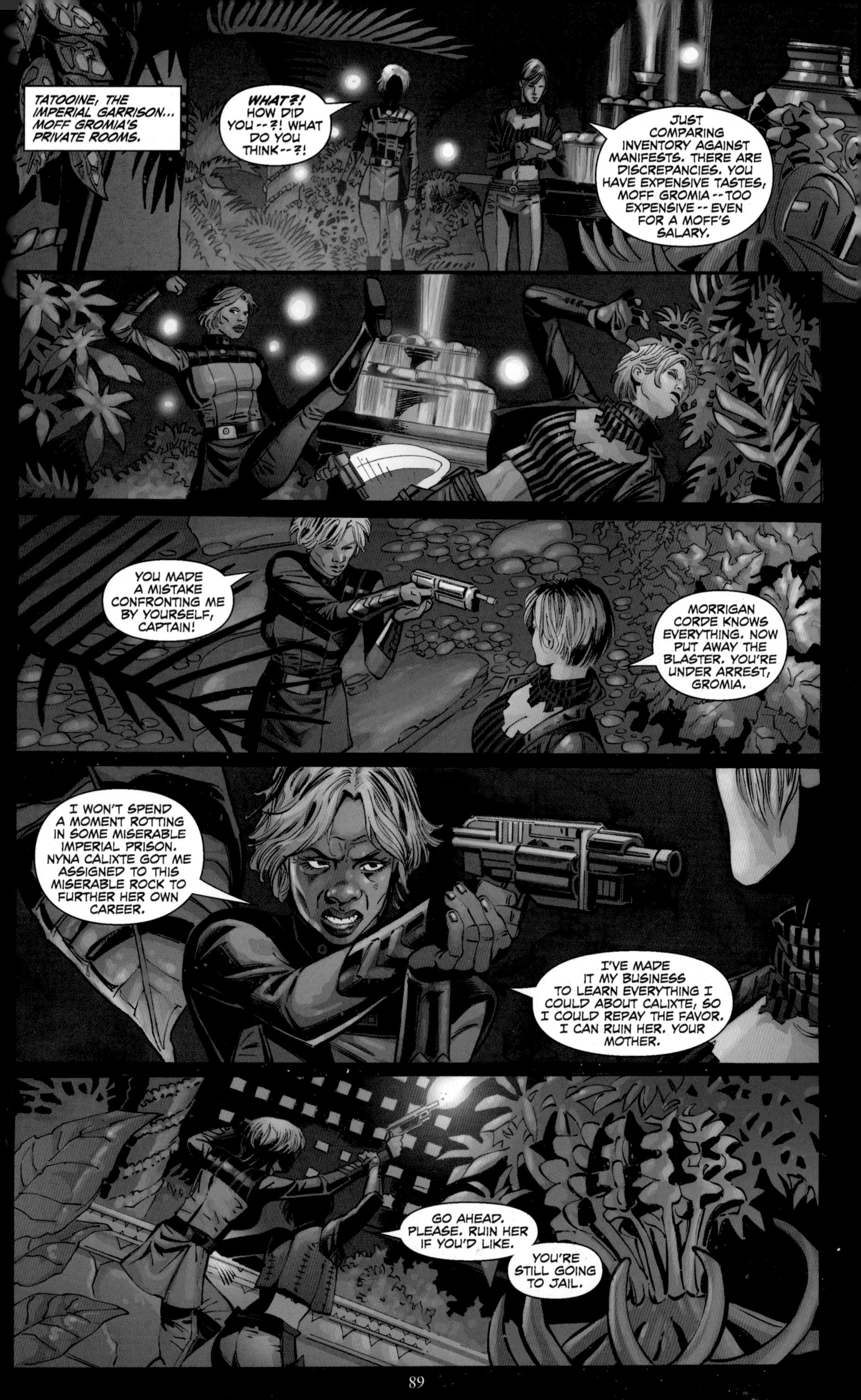
TATOOINE, THE IMPERIAL GARRISON... MOFF GROMIA'S PRIVATE ROOMS.
WHAT?! HOW DID YOU--?! WHAT DO YOU THINK--?!
JUST COMPARING INVENTORY AGAINST MANIFESTS. THERE ARE DISCREPANCIES. YOU HAVE EXPENSIVE TASTES, MOFF GROMIA--TOO EXPENSIVE--EVEN FOR A MOFF'S SALARY.
YOU MADE A MISTAKE CONFRONTING ME BY YOURSELF, CAPTAIN!
MORRIGAN CORDE KNOWS EVERYTHING. NOW PUT AWAY THE BLASTER. YOU'RE UNDER ARREST, GROMIA.
I WON'T SPEND A MOMENT ROTTING IN SOME MISERABLE IMPERIAL PRISON. NYNA CALIXTE GOT ME ASSIGNED TO THIS MISERABLE ROCK TO FURTHER HER OWN CAREER.
I'VE MADE IT MY BUSINESS TO LEARN EVERYTHING I COULD ABOUT CALIXTE, SO I COULD REPAY THE FAVOR. I CAN RUIN HER. YOUR MOTHER.
GO AHEAD. PLEASE. RUIN HER IF YOU'D LIKE.
YOU'RE STILL GOING TO JAIL.

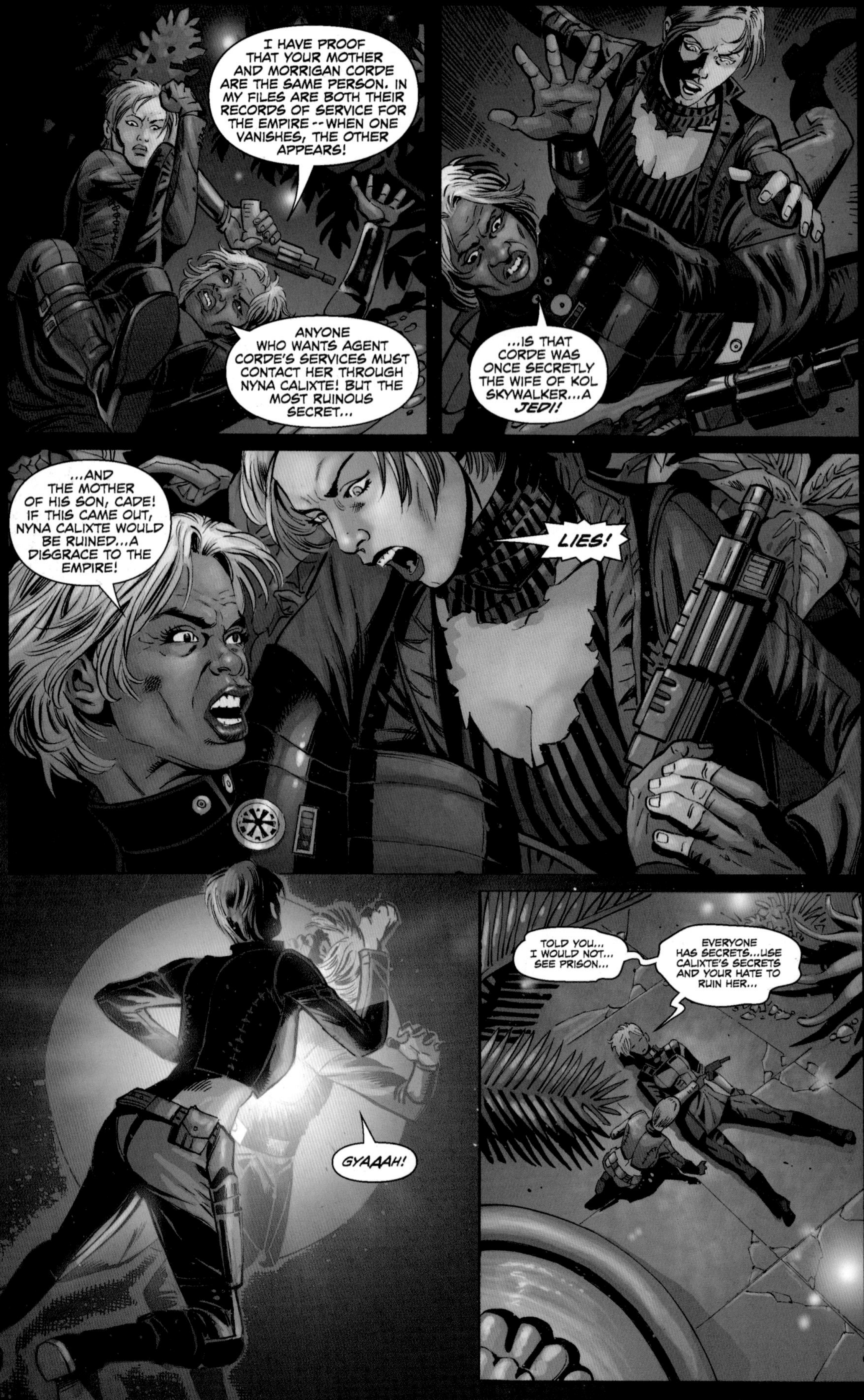

I HAVE PROOF THAT YOUR MOTHER AND MORRIGAN CORDE ARE THE SAME PERSON. IN MY FILES ARE BOTH THEIR RECORDS OF SERVICE FOR THE EMPIRE -- WHEN ONE VANISHES, THE OTHER APPEARS!
ANYONE WHO WANTS AGENT CORDE'S SERVICES MUST CONTACT HER THROUGH NYNA CALIXTE! BUT THE MOST RUINOUS SECRET...
...IS THAT CORDE WAS ONCE SECRETLY THE WIFE OF KOL SKYWALKER...A JEDI!
...AND THE MOTHER OF HIS SON, CADE! IF THIS CAME OUT, NYNA CALIXTE WOULD BE RUINED...A DISGRACE TO THE EMPIRE!
LIES!
GYAAAH!
TOLD YOU... I WOULD NOT... SEE PRISON...
EVERYONE HAS SECRETS...USE CALIXTE'S SECRETS AND YOUR HATE TO RUIN HER...

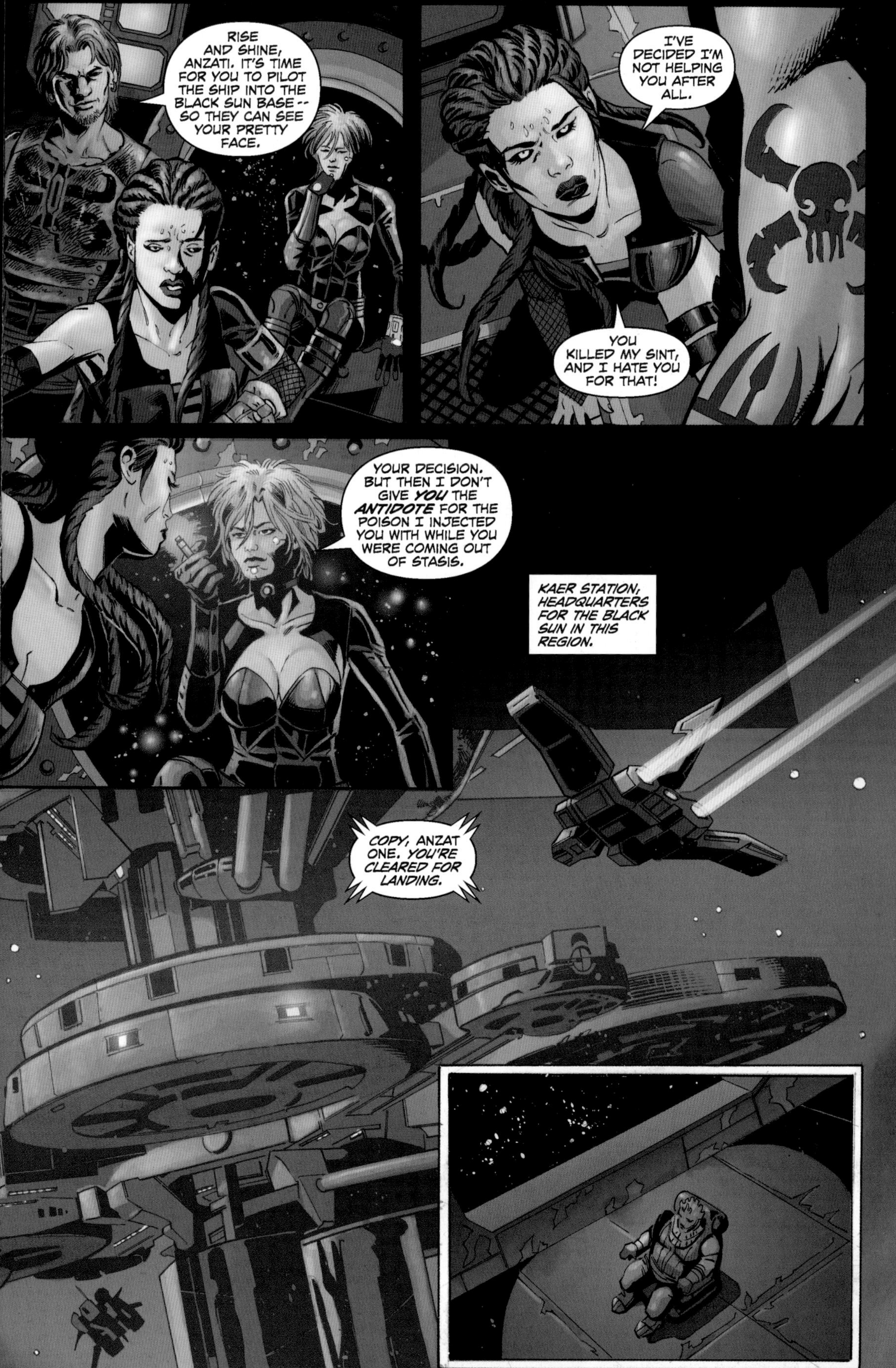
RISE AND SHINE, ANZATI. IT'S TIME FOR YOU TO PILOT THE SHIP INTO THE BLACK SUN BASE -- SO THEY CAN SEE YOUR PRETTY FACE.
I'VE DECIDED I'M NOT HELPING YOU AFTER ALL.
YOU KILLED MY SINT, AND I HATE YOU FOR THAT!
YOUR DECISION. BUT THEN I DON'T GIVE YOU THE ANTIDOTE FOR THE POISON I INJECTED YOU WITH WHILE YOU WERE COMING OUT OF STASIS.
KAER STATION, HEADQUARTERS FOR THE BLACK SUN IN THIS REGION.
COPY, ANZAT ONE. YOU'RE CLEARED FOR LANDING.

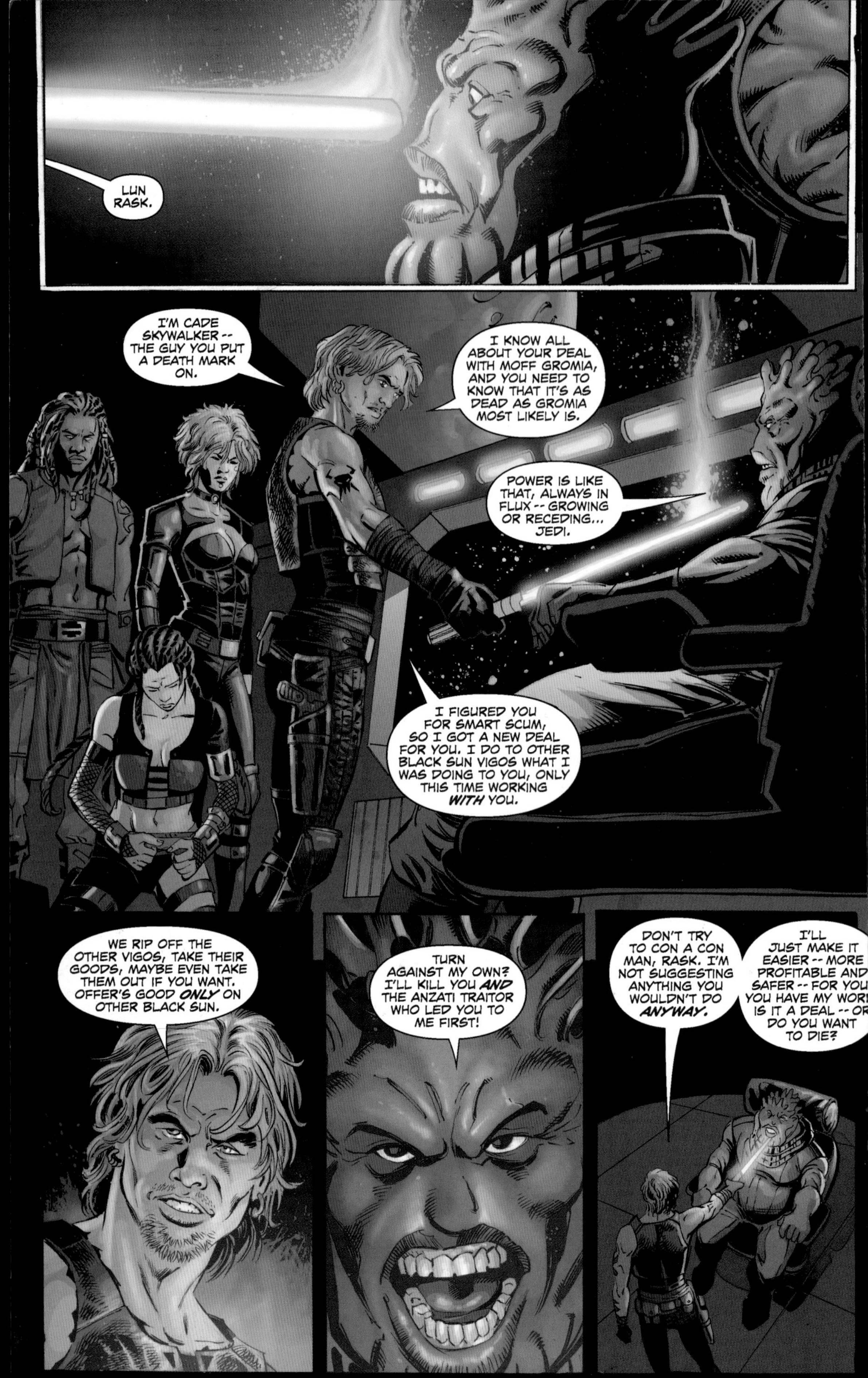
LUN RASK.
I'M CADE SKYWALKER -- THE GUY YOU PUT A DEATH MARK ON.
I KNOW ALL ABOUT YOUR DEAL WITH MOFF GROMIA, AND YOU NEED TO KNOW THAT IT'S AS DEAD AS GROMIA MOST LIKELY IS.
POWER IS LIKE THAT, ALWAYS IN FLUX -- GROWING OR RECEDING... JEDI.
I FIGURED YOU FOR SMART SCUM, SO I GOT A NEW DEAL FOR YOU. I DO TO OTHER BLACK SUN VIGOS WHAT I WAS DOING TO YOU, ONLY THIS TIME WORKING *WITH* YOU.
WE RIP OFF THE OTHER VIGOS, TAKE THEIR GOODS, MAYBE EVEN TAKE THEM OUT IF YOU WANT. OFFER'S GOOD *ONLY* ON OTHER BLACK SUN.
TURN AGAINST MY OWN? I'LL KILL YOU *AND* THE ANZATI TRAITOR WHO LED YOU TO ME FIRST!
DON'T TRY TO CON A CON MAN, RASK. I'M NOT SUGGESTING ANYTHING YOU WOULDN'T DO *ANYWAY*.
I'LL JUST MAKE IT EASIER -- MORE PROFITABLE AND SAFER -- FOR YOU YOU HAVE MY WOR IS IT A DEAL -- OR DO YOU WANT TO DIE?

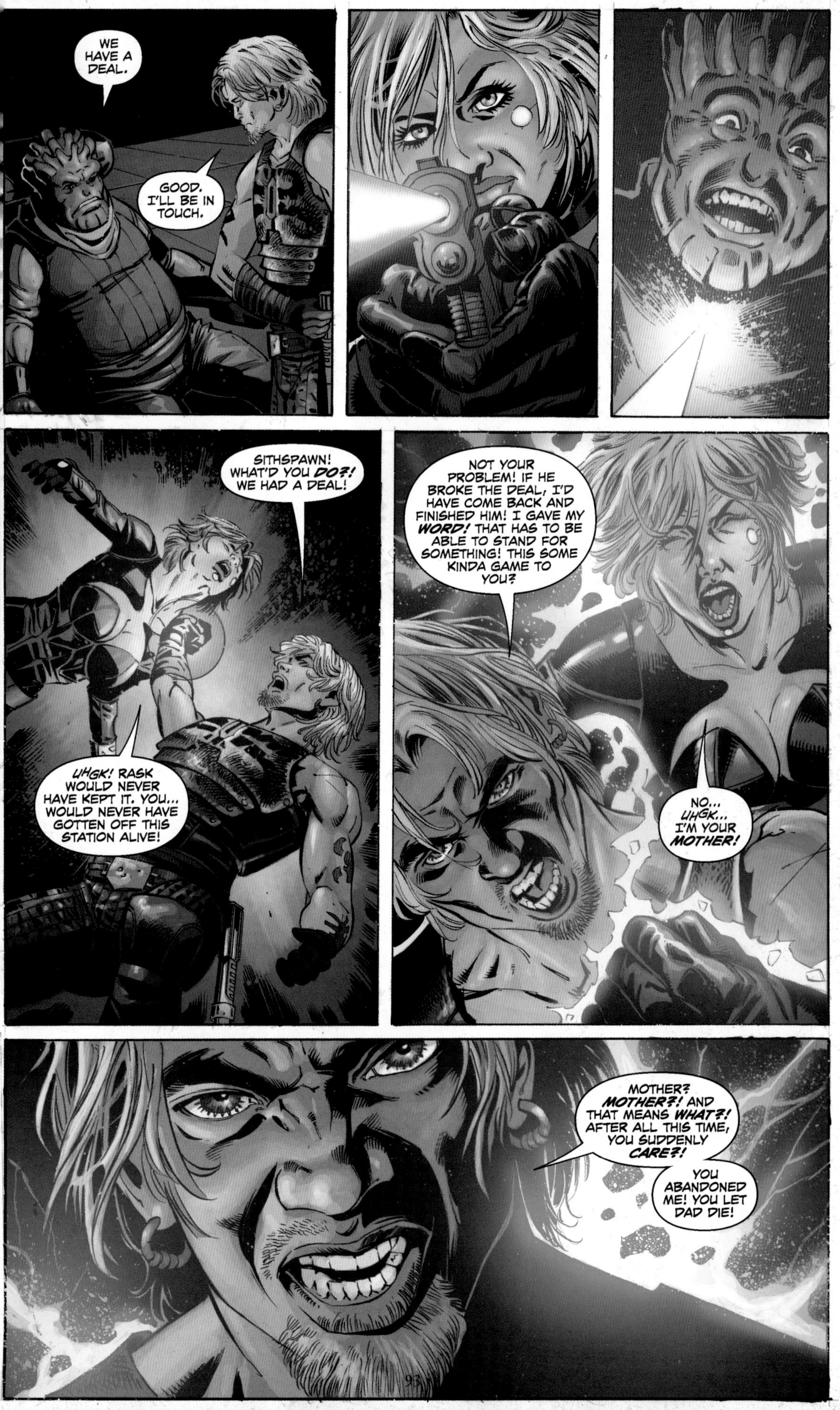
WE HAVE A DEAL.
GOOD. I'LL BE IN TOUCH.
SITHSPAWN! WHAT'D YOU DO?! WE HAD A DEAL!
UHGK! RASK WOULD NEVER HAVE KEPT IT. YOU... WOULD NEVER HAVE GOTTEN OFF THIS STATION ALIVE!
NOT YOUR PROBLEM! IF HE BROKE THE DEAL, I'D HAVE COME BACK AND FINISHED HIM! I GAVE MY WORD! THAT HAS TO BE ABLE TO STAND FOR SOMETHING! THIS SOME KINDA GAME TO YOU?
NO... UHGK... I'M YOUR MOTHER!
MOTHER? MOTHER?! AND THAT MEANS WHAT?! AFTER ALL THIS TIME, YOU SUDDENLY CARE?!
YOU ABANDONED ME! YOU LET DAD DIE!

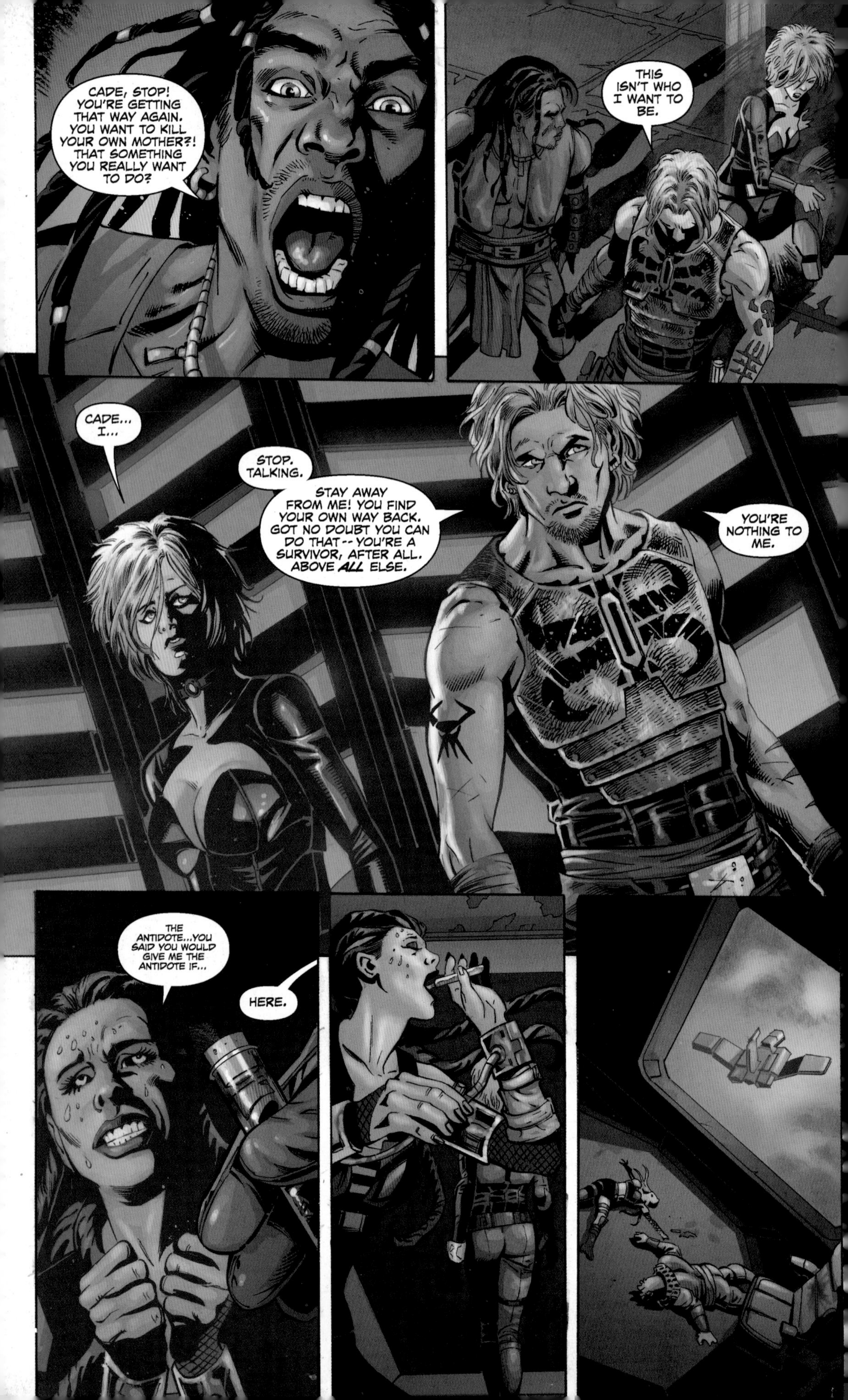
CADE, STOP! YOU'RE GETTING THAT WAY AGAIN. YOU WANT TO KILL YOUR OWN MOTHER?! THAT SOMETHING YOU REALLY WANT TO DO?
THIS ISN'T WHO I WANT TO BE.
CADE... I...
STOP. TALKING.
STAY AWAY FROM ME! YOU FIND YOUR OWN WAY BACK. GOT NO DOUBT YOU CAN DO THAT--YOU'RE A SURVIVOR, AFTER ALL. ABOVE ALL ELSE.
YOU'RE NOTHING TO ME.
THE ANTIDOTE...YOU SAID YOU WOULD GIVE ME THE ANTIDOTE IF...
HERE.

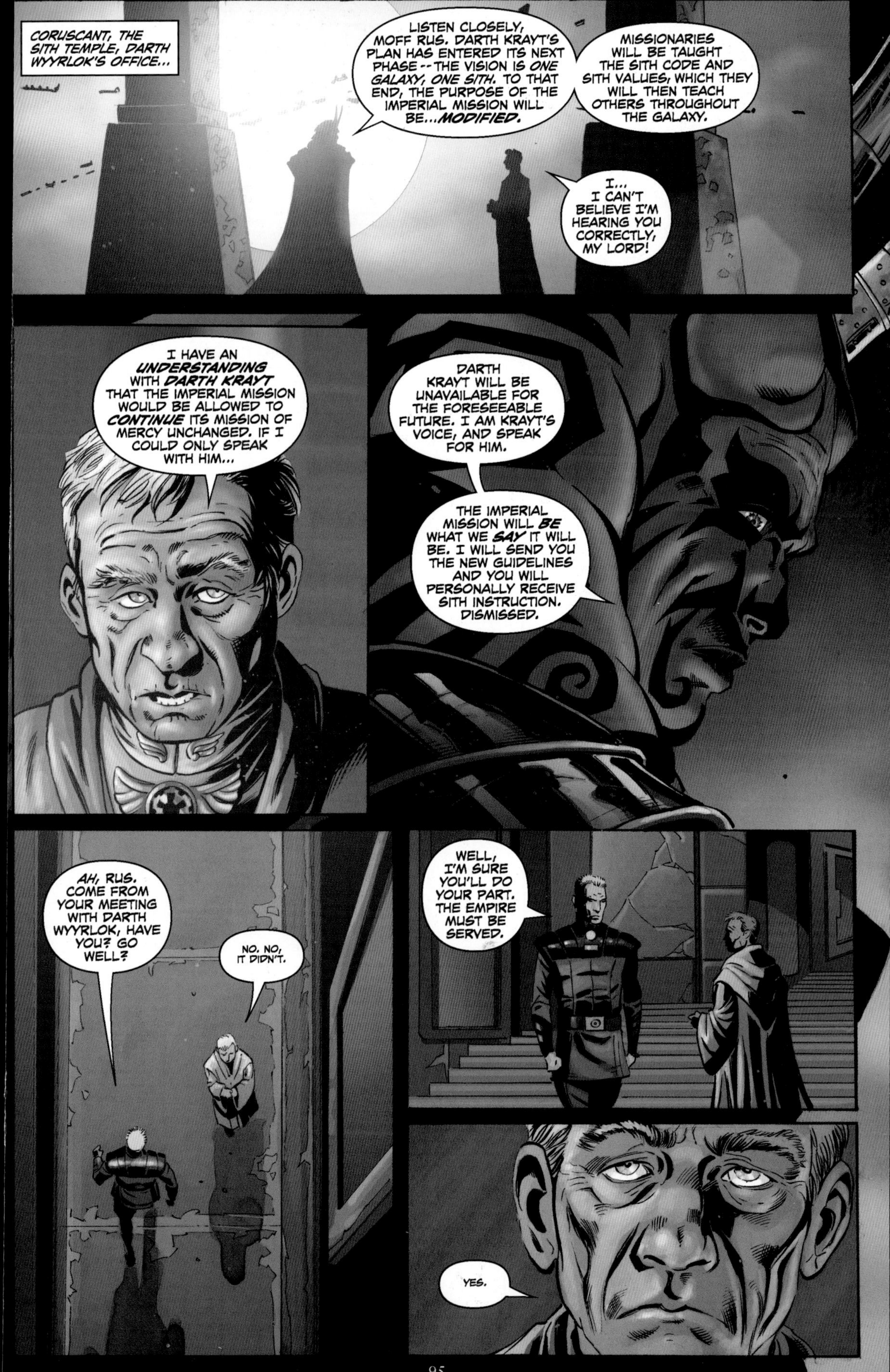
CORUSCANT, THE SITH TEMPLE, DARTH WYYRLOK'S OFFICE...
LISTEN CLOSELY, MOFF RUS. DARTH KRAYT'S PLAN HAS ENTERED ITS NEXT PHASE--THE VISION IS ONE GALAXY, ONE SITH. TO THAT END, THE PURPOSE OF THE IMPERIAL MISSION WILL BE...MODIFIED.
MISSIONARIES WILL BE TAUGHT THE SITH CODE AND SITH VALUES, WHICH THEY WILL THEN TEACH OTHERS THROUGHOUT THE GALAXY.
I... I CAN'T BELIEVE I'M HEARING YOU CORRECTLY, MY LORD!
I HAVE AN UNDERSTANDING WITH DARTH KRAYT THAT THE IMPERIAL MISSION WOULD BE ALLOWED TO CONTINUE ITS MISSION OF MERCY UNCHANGED. IF I COULD ONLY SPEAK WITH HIM...
DARTH KRAYT WILL BE UNAVAILABLE FOR THE FORESEEABLE FUTURE. I AM KRAYT'S VOICE, AND SPEAK FOR HIM.
THE IMPERIAL MISSION WILL BE WHAT WE SAY IT WILL BE. I WILL SEND YOU THE NEW GUIDELINES AND YOU WILL PERSONALLY RECEIVE SITH INSTRUCTION. DISMISSED.
AH, RUS. COME FROM YOUR MEETING WITH DARTH WYYRLOK, HAVE YOU? GO WELL?
NO. NO, IT DIDN'T.
WELL, I'M SURE YOU'LL DO YOUR PART. THE EMPIRE MUST BE SERVED.
YES.

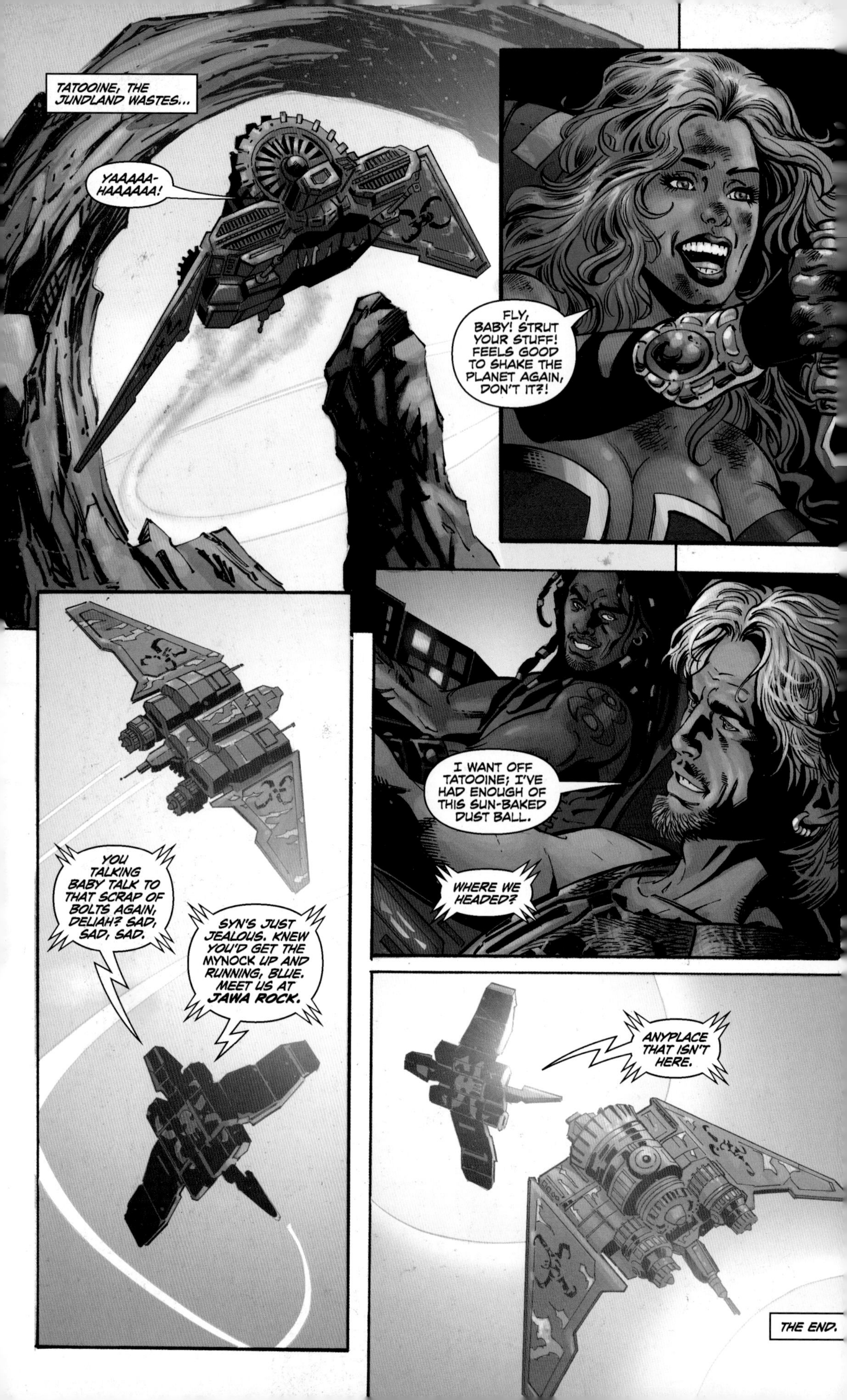
TATOOINE, THE JUNDLAND WASTES...
YAAAAA-HAAAAAA!
FLY, BABY! STRUT YOUR STUFF! FEELS GOOD TO SHAKE THE PLANET AGAIN, DON'T IT?!
YOU TALKING BABY TALK TO THAT SCRAP OF BOLTS AGAIN, DELIAH? SAD, SAD, SAD.
SYN'S JUST JEALOUS. KNEW YOU'D GET THE MYNOCK UP AND RUNNING, BLUE. MEET US AT JAWA ROCK.
I WANT OFF TATOOINE; I'VE HAD ENOUGH OF THIS SUN-BAKED DUST BALL.
WHERE WE HEADED?
ANYPLACE THAT ISN'T HERE.
THE END.

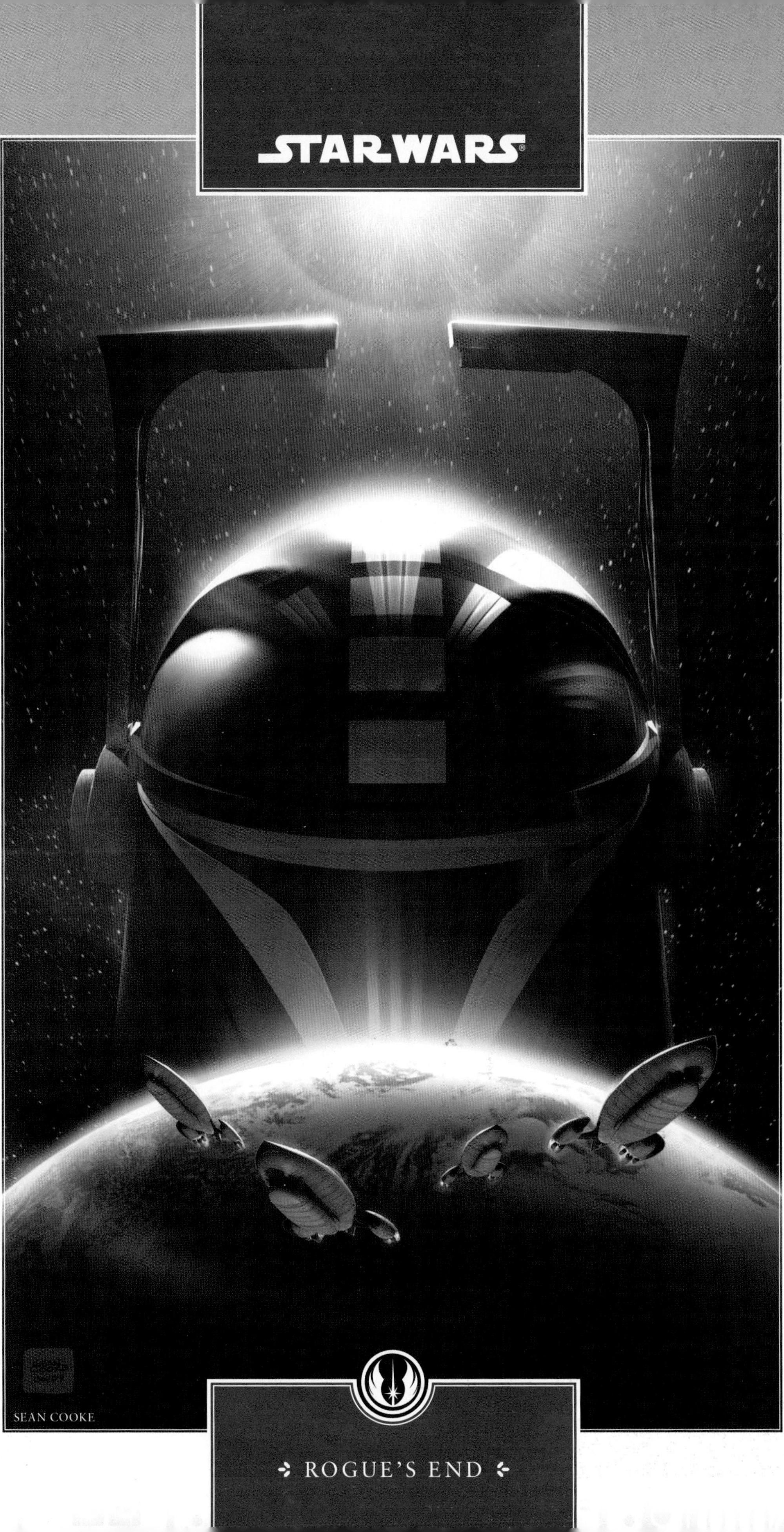
STAR WARS
SEAN COOKE
ROGUE'S END

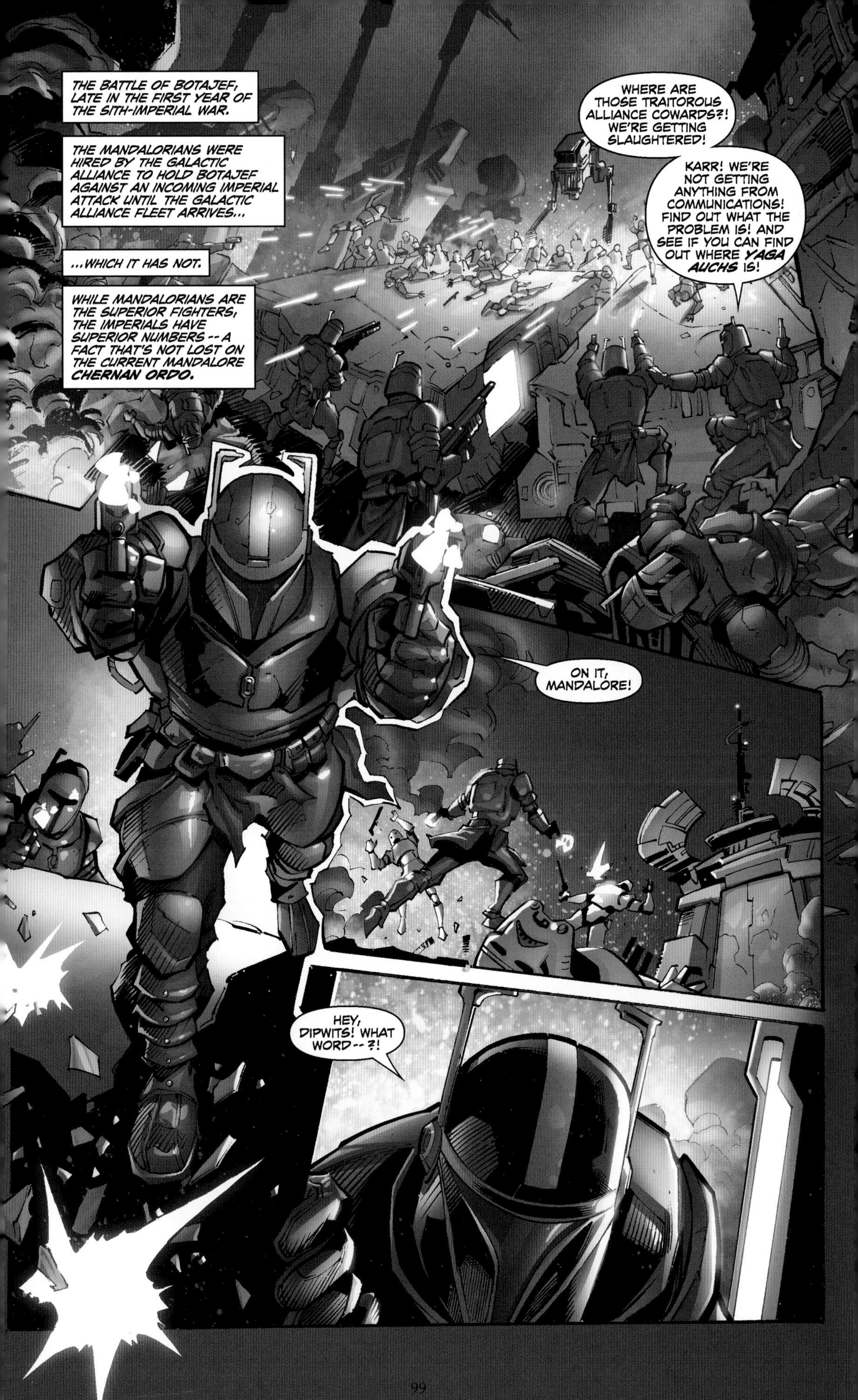
THE BATTLE OF BOTAJEF, LATE IN THE FIRST YEAR OF THE SITH-IMPERIAL WAR.
THE MANDALORIANS WERE HIRED BY THE GALACTIC ALLIANCE TO HOLD BOTAJEF AGAINST AN INCOMING IMPERIAL ATTACK UNTIL THE GALACTIC ALLIANCE FLEET ARRIVES...
...WHICH IT HAS NOT.
WHILE MANDALORIANS ARE THE SUPERIOR FIGHTERS, THE IMPERIALS HAVE SUPERIOR NUMBERS -- A FACT THAT'S NOT LOST ON THE CURRENT MANDALORE CHERNAN ORDO.
WHERE ARE THOSE TRAITOROUS ALLIANCE COWARDS?! WE'RE GETTING SLAUGHTERED!
KARR! WE'RE NOT GETTING ANYTHING FROM COMMUNICATIONS! FIND OUT WHAT THE PROBLEM IS! AND SEE IF YOU CAN FIND OUT WHERE YAGA AUCHS IS!
ON IT, MANDALORE!
HEY, DIPWITS! WHAT WORD--?!

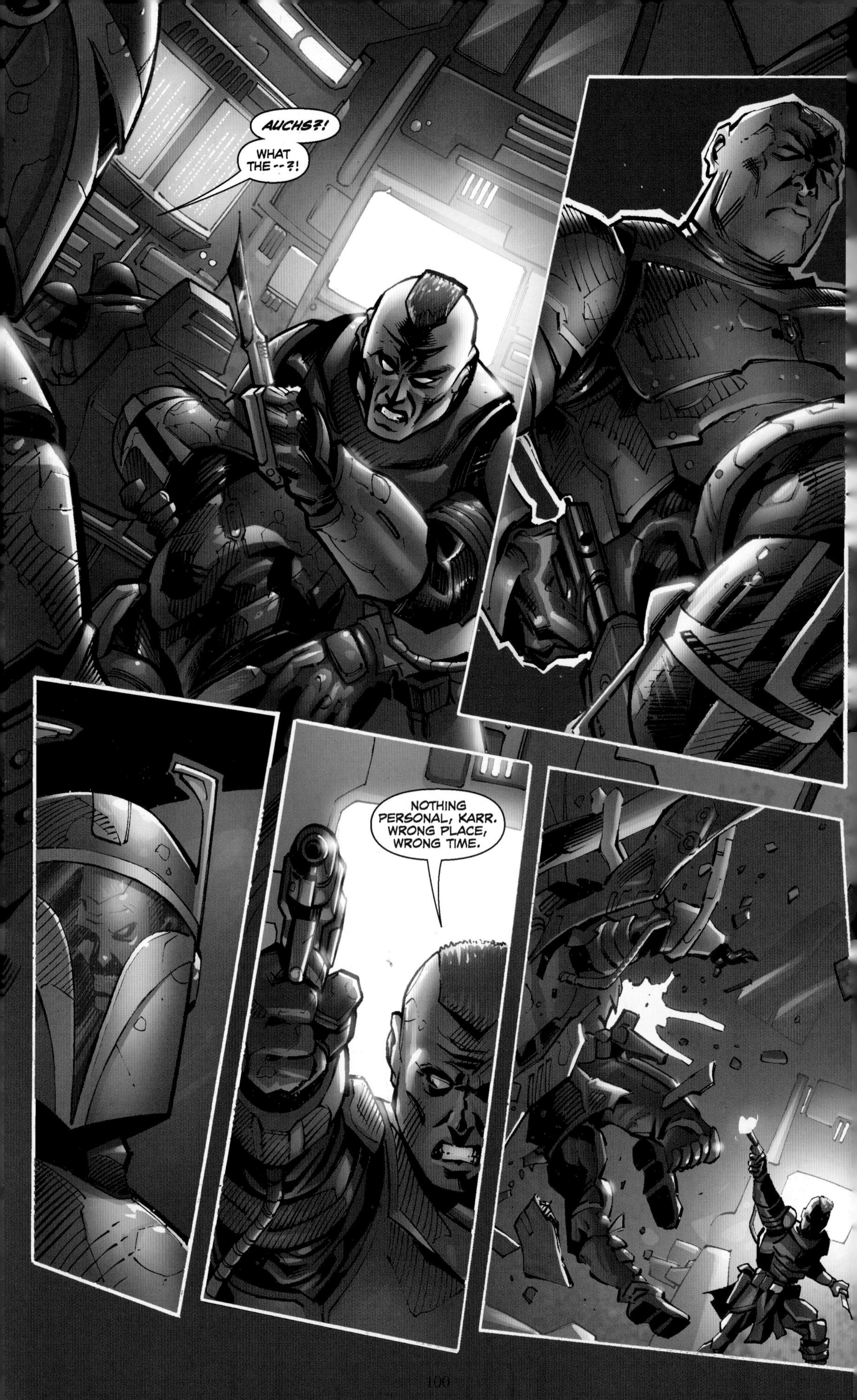
AUCHS?!
WHAT THE--?!
NOTHING PERSONAL, KARR. WRONG PLACE, WRONG TIME.

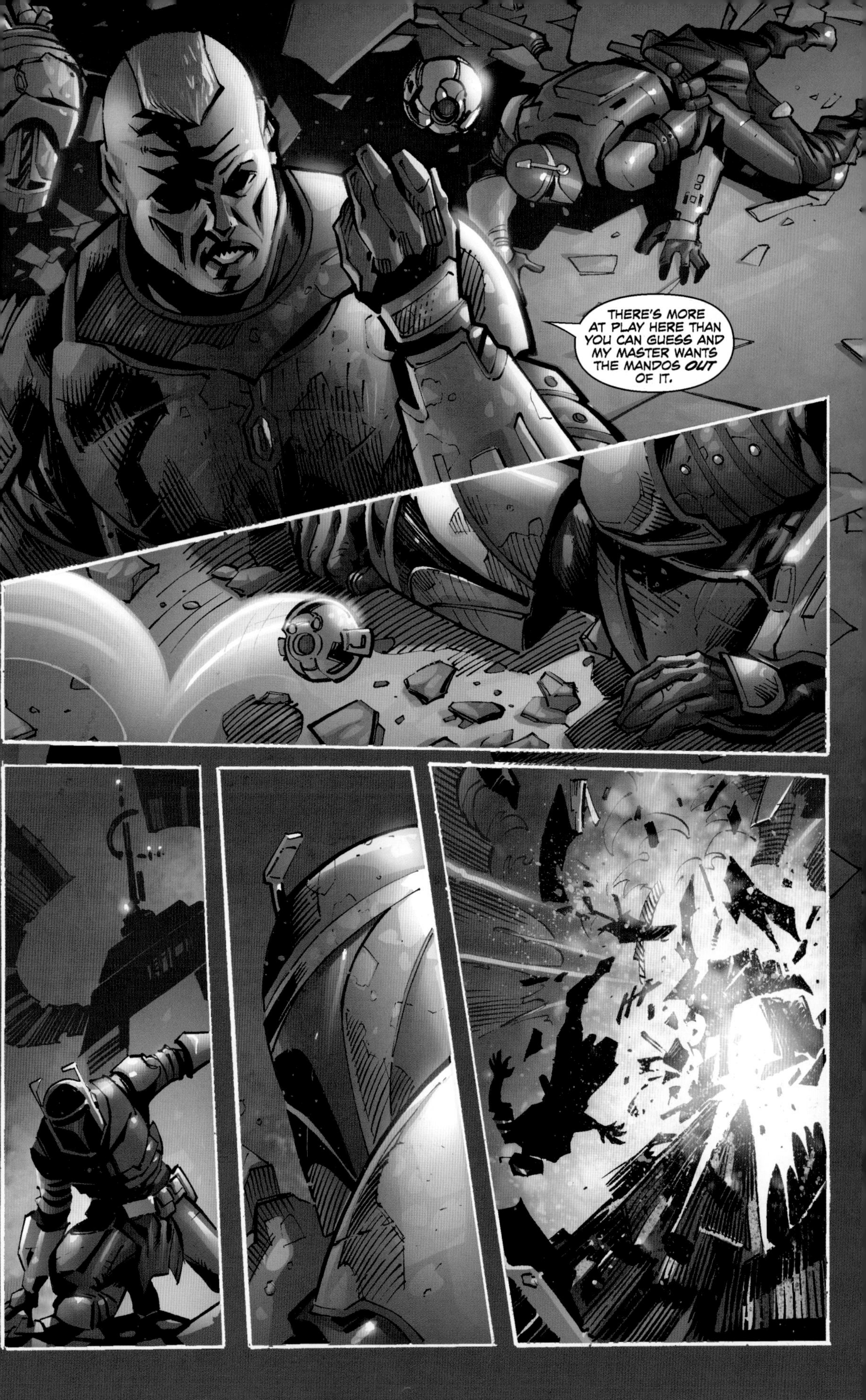
THERE'S MORE AT PLAY HERE THAN YOU CAN GUESS AND MY MASTER WANTS THE MANDOS *OUT* OF IT.

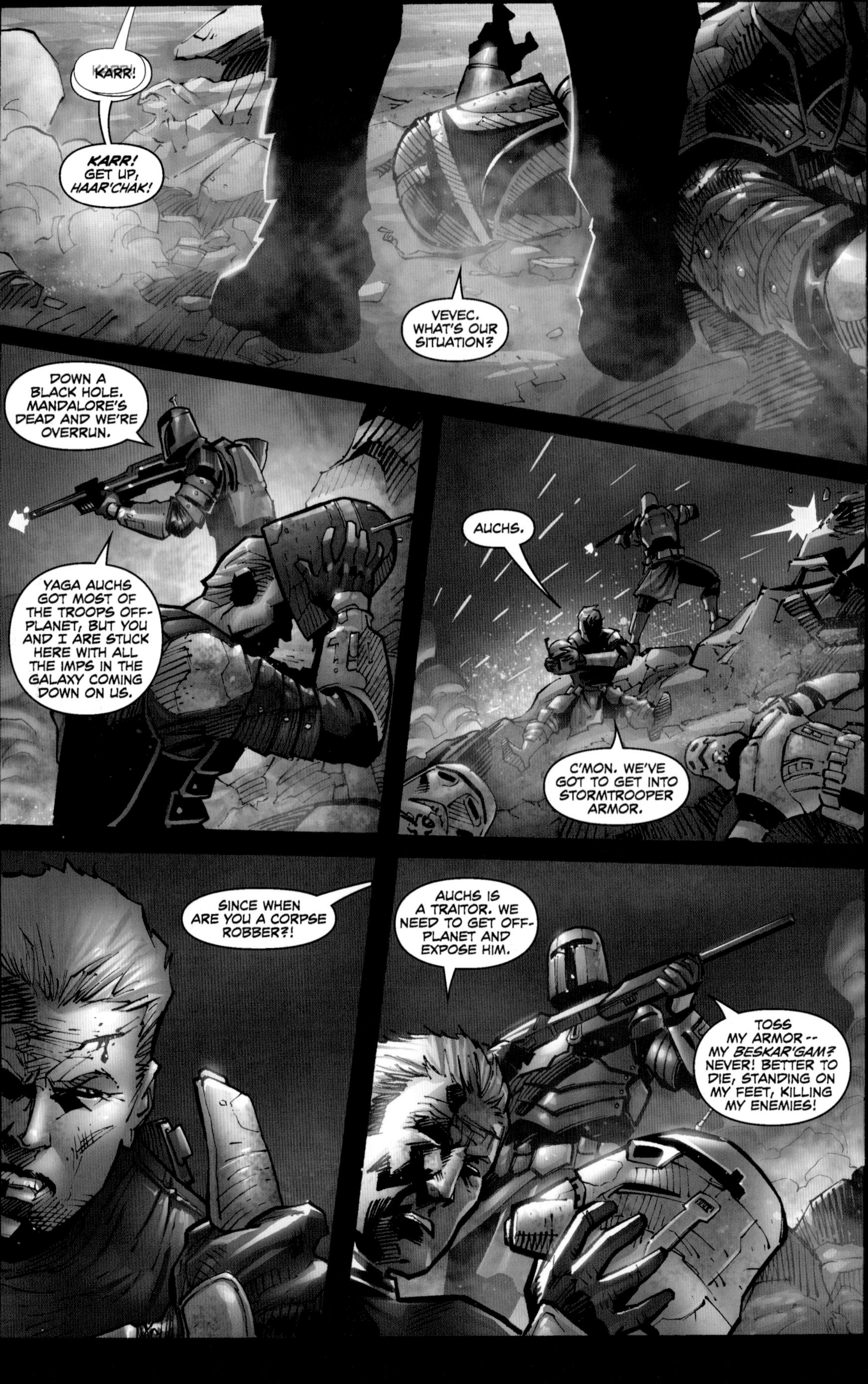
KARR!
KARR! GET UP, HAAR'CHAK!
VEVEC. WHAT'S OUR SITUATION?
DOWN A BLACK HOLE. MANDALORE'S DEAD AND WE'RE OVERRUN.
YAGA AUCHS GOT MOST OF THE TROOPS OFF-PLANET, BUT YOU AND I ARE STUCK HERE WITH ALL THE IMPS IN THE GALAXY COMING DOWN ON US.
AUCHS.
C'MON. WE'VE GOT TO GET INTO STORMTROOPER ARMOR.
SINCE WHEN ARE YOU A CORPSE ROBBER?!
AUCHS IS A TRAITOR. WE NEED TO GET OFF-PLANET AND EXPOSE HIM.
TOSS MY ARMOR -- MY BESKAR'GAM? NEVER! BETTER TO DIE, STANDING ON MY FEET, KILLING MY ENEMIES!

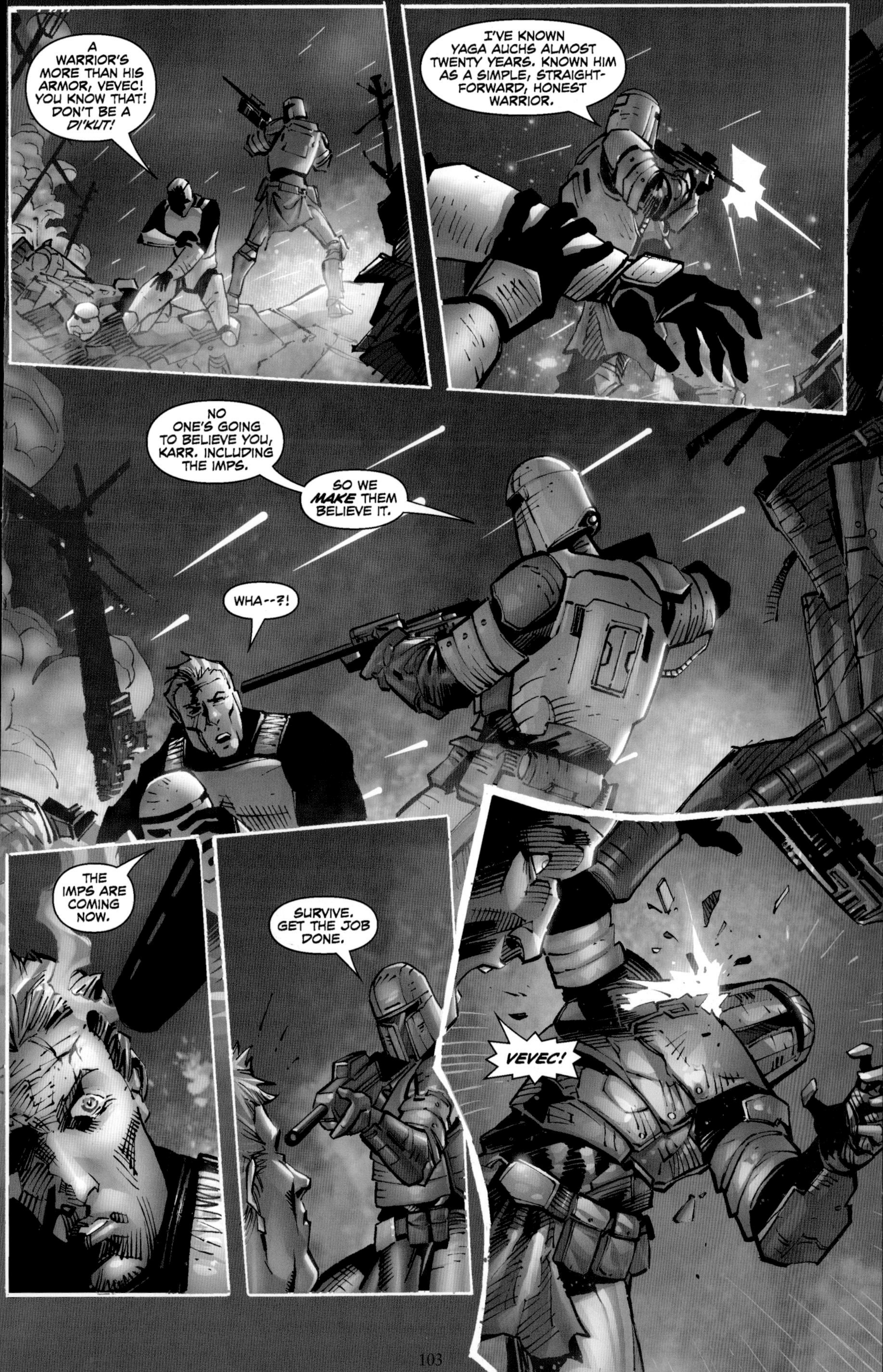
A WARRIOR'S MORE THAN HIS ARMOR, VEVEC! YOU KNOW THAT! DON'T BE A *DI'KUT!*
I'VE KNOWN YAGA AUCHS ALMOST TWENTY YEARS. KNOWN HIM AS A SIMPLE, STRAIGHT-FORWARD, HONEST WARRIOR.
NO ONE'S GOING TO BELIEVE YOU, KARR. INCLUDING THE IMPS.
SO WE *MAKE* THEM BELIEVE IT.
WHA--?!
THE IMPS ARE COMING NOW.
SURVIVE. GET THE JOB DONE.
VEVEC!

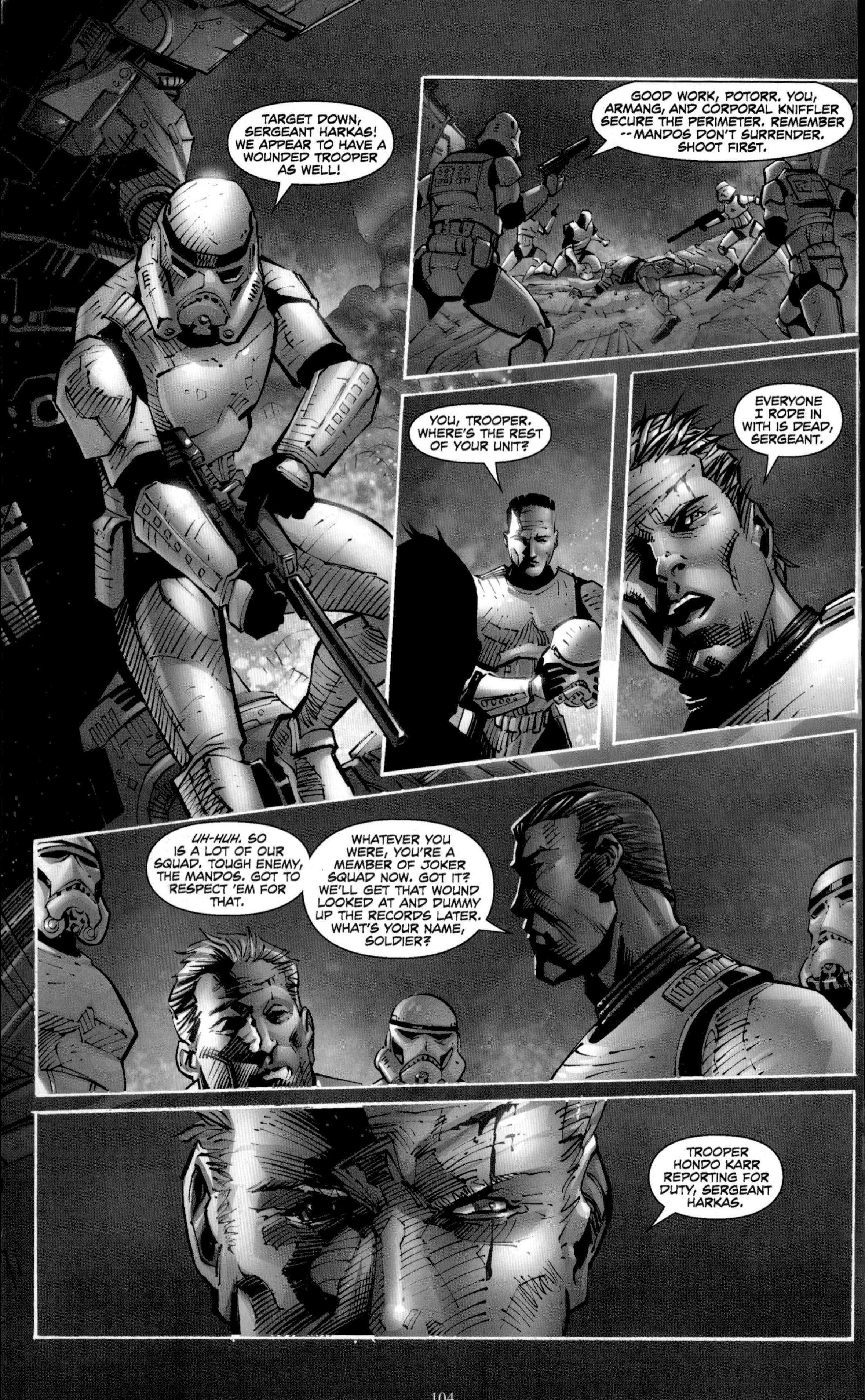
TARGET DOWN, SERGEANT HARKAS! WE APPEAR TO HAVE A WOUNDED TROOPER AS WELL!
GOOD WORK, POTORR. YOU, ARMANG, AND CORPORAL KNIFFLER SECURE THE PERIMETER. REMEMBER --MANDOS DON'T SURRENDER. SHOOT FIRST.
YOU, TROOPER. WHERE'S THE REST OF YOUR UNIT?
EVERYONE I RODE IN WITH IS DEAD, SERGEANT.
UH-HUH. SO IS A LOT OF OUR SQUAD. TOUGH ENEMY, THE MANDOS. GOT TO RESPECT 'EM FOR THAT.
WHATEVER YOU WERE, YOU'RE A MEMBER OF JOKER SQUAD NOW. GOT IT? WE'LL GET THAT WOUND LOOKED AT AND DUMMY UP THE RECORDS LATER. WHAT'S YOUR NAME, SOLDIER?
TROOPER HONDO KARR REPORTING FOR DUTY, SERGEANT HARKAS.

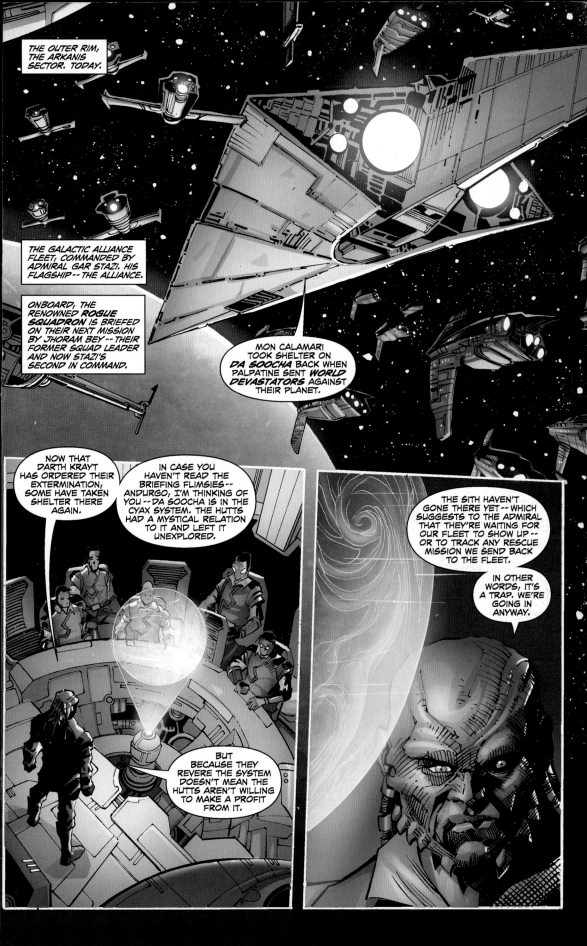

THE OUTER RIM, THE ARKANIS SECTOR. TODAY.

THE GALACTIC ALLIANCE FLEET, COMMANDED BY ADMIRAL GAR STAZI. HIS FLAGSHIP--THE ALLIANCE.

ONBOARD, THE RENOWNED *ROGUE SQUADRON* IS BRIEFED ON THEIR NEXT MISSION BY JHORAM BEY--THEIR FORMER SQUAD LEADER AND NOW STAZI'S SECOND IN COMMAND.

MON CALAMARI TOOK SHELTER ON *DA SOOCHA* BACK WHEN PALPATINE SENT *WORLD DEVASTATORS* AGAINST THEIR PLANET.

NOW THAT DARTH KRAYT HAS ORDERED THEIR EXTERMINATION, SOME HAVE TAKEN SHELTER THERE AGAIN.

IN CASE YOU HAVEN'T READ THE BRIEFING FLIMSIES-- AND DURGO, I'M THINKING OF YOU--DA SOOCHA IS IN THE CYAX SYSTEM. THE HUTTS HAD A MYSTICAL RELATION TO IT AND LEFT IT UNEXPLORED.

THE SITH HAVEN'T GONE THERE YET -- WHICH SUGGESTS TO THE ADMIRAL THAT THEY'RE WAITING FOR OUR FLEET TO SHOW UP -- OR TO TRACK ANY RESCUE MISSION WE SEND BACK TO THE FLEET.

IN OTHER WORDS, IT'S A TRAP. WE'RE GOING IN ANYWAY.

BUT BECAUSE THEY REVERE THE SYSTEM DOESN'T MEAN THE HUTTS AREN'T WILLING TO MAKE A PROFIT FROM IT.

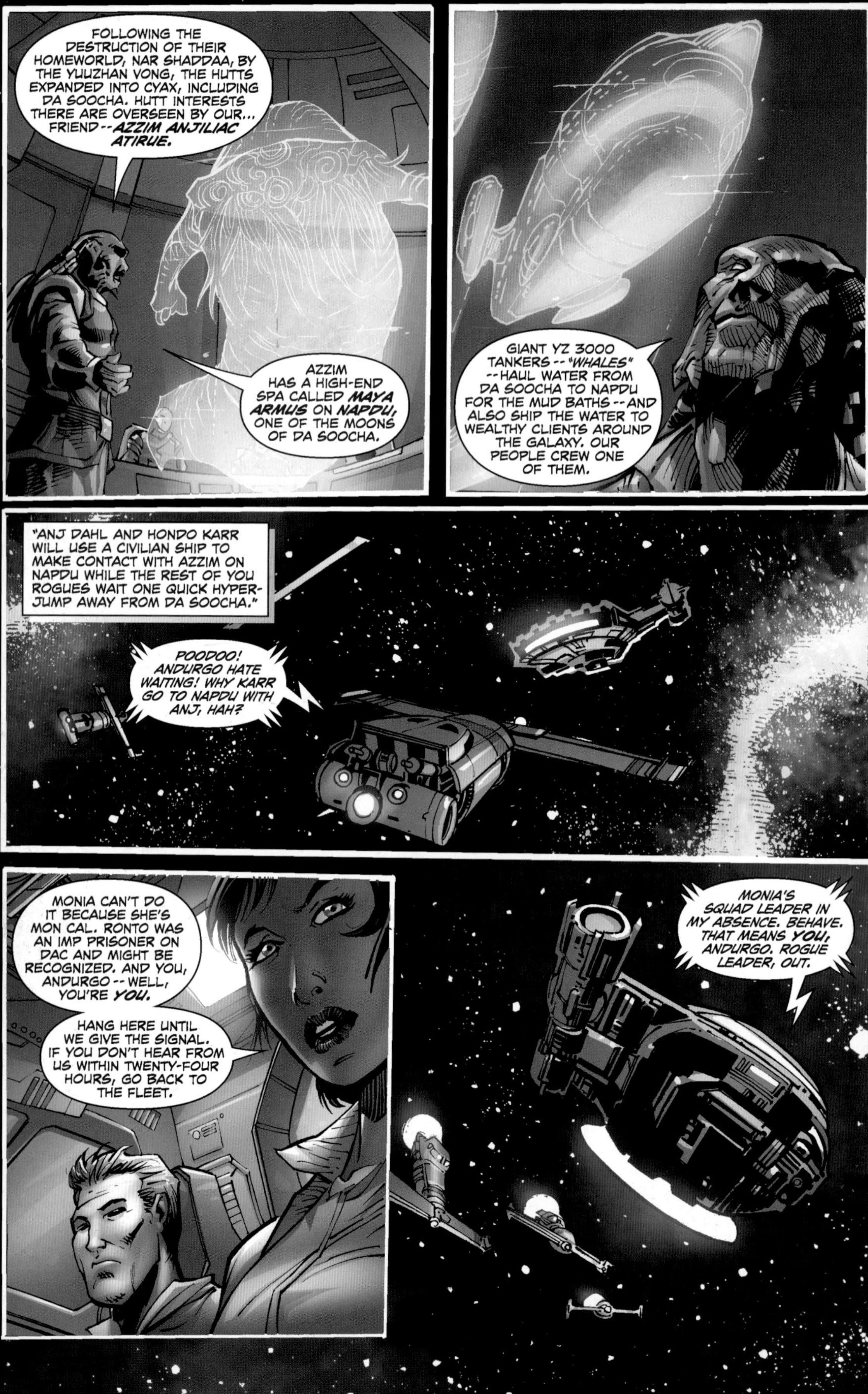
FOLLOWING THE DESTRUCTION OF THEIR HOMEWORLD, NAR SHADDAA, BY THE YUUZHAN VONG, THE HUTTS EXPANDED INTO CYAX, INCLUDING DA SOOCHA. HUTT INTERESTS THERE ARE OVERSEEN BY OUR... FRIEND--AZZIM ANJILIAC ATIRUE.
AZZIM HAS A HIGH-END SPA CALLED MAYA ARMUS ON NAPDU, ONE OF THE MOONS OF DA SOOCHA.
GIANT YZ 3000 TANKERS--"WHALES"--HAUL WATER FROM DA SOOCHA TO NAPDU FOR THE MUD BATHS--AND ALSO SHIP THE WATER TO WEALTHY CLIENTS AROUND THE GALAXY. OUR PEOPLE CREW ONE OF THEM.
"ANJ DAHL AND HONDO KARR WILL USE A CIVILIAN SHIP TO MAKE CONTACT WITH AZZIM ON NAPDU WHILE THE REST OF YOU ROGUES WAIT ONE QUICK HYPER-JUMP AWAY FROM DA SOOCHA."
POODOO! ANDURGO HATE WAITING! WHY KARR GO TO NAPDU WITH ANJ, HAH?
MONIA CAN'T DO IT BECAUSE SHE'S MON CAL. RONTO WAS AN IMP PRISONER ON DAC AND MIGHT BE RECOGNIZED. AND YOU, ANDURGO--WELL, YOU'RE YOU.
HANG HERE UNTIL WE GIVE THE SIGNAL. IF YOU DON'T HEAR FROM US WITHIN TWENTY-FOUR HOURS, GO BACK TO THE FLEET.
MONIA'S SQUAD LEADER IN MY ABSENCE. BEHAVE. THAT MEANS YOU, ANDURGO. ROGUE LEADER, OUT.

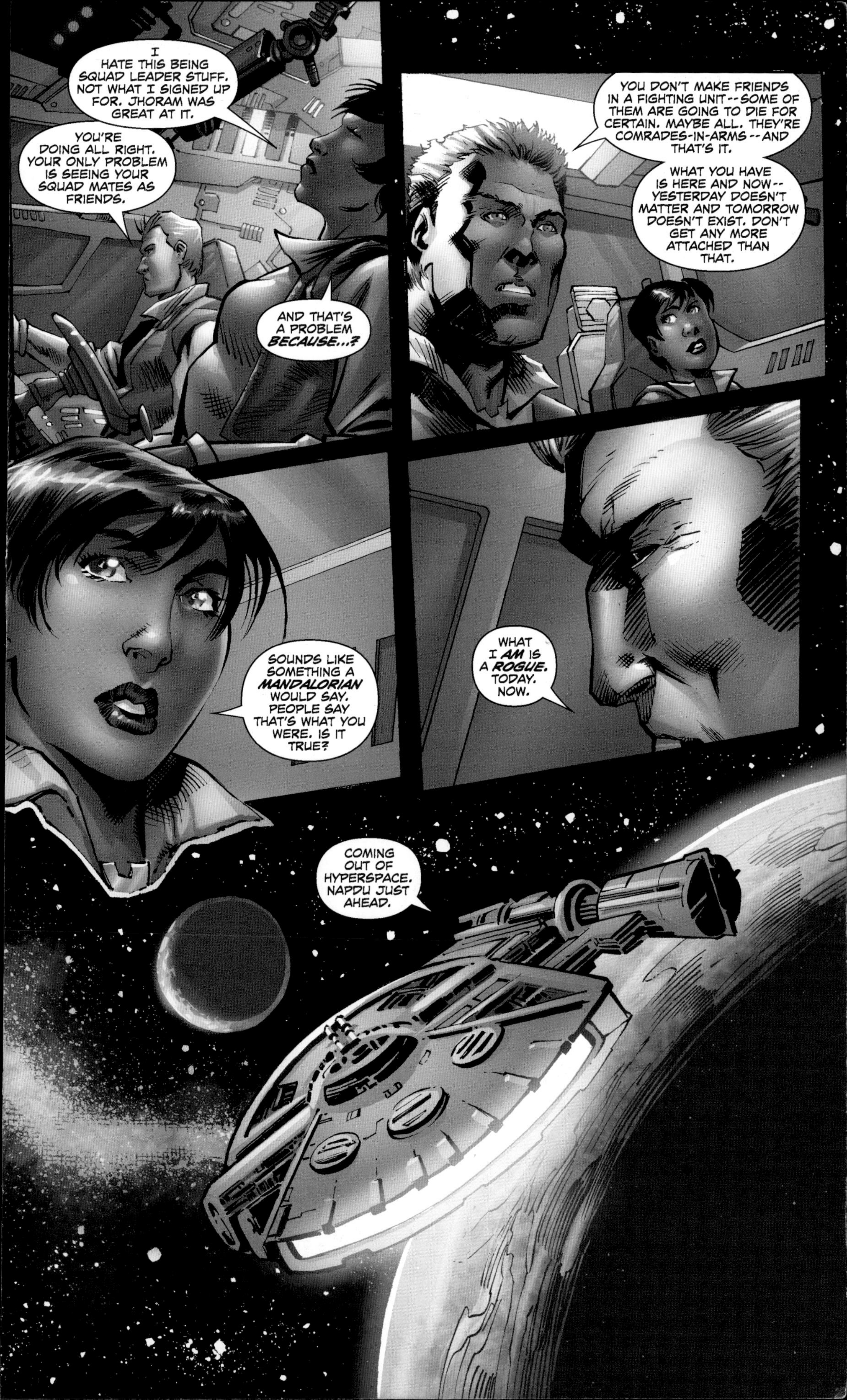

I HATE THIS BEING SQUAD LEADER STUFF. NOT WHAT I SIGNED UP FOR. JHORAM WAS GREAT AT IT.
YOU'RE DOING ALL RIGHT. YOUR ONLY PROBLEM IS SEEING YOUR SQUAD MATES AS FRIENDS.
AND THAT'S A PROBLEM BECAUSE...?
YOU DON'T MAKE FRIENDS IN A FIGHTING UNIT--SOME OF THEM ARE GOING TO DIE FOR CERTAIN. MAYBE ALL. THEY'RE COMRADES-IN-ARMS--AND THAT'S IT.
WHAT YOU HAVE IS HERE AND NOW--YESTERDAY DOESN'T MATTER AND TOMORROW DOESN'T EXIST. DON'T GET ANY MORE ATTACHED THAN THAT.
SOUNDS LIKE SOMETHING A MANDALORIAN WOULD SAY. PEOPLE SAY THAT'S WHAT YOU WERE. IS IT TRUE?
WHAT I AM IS A ROGUE. TODAY. NOW.
COMING OUT OF HYPERSPACE. NAPDU JUST AHEAD.

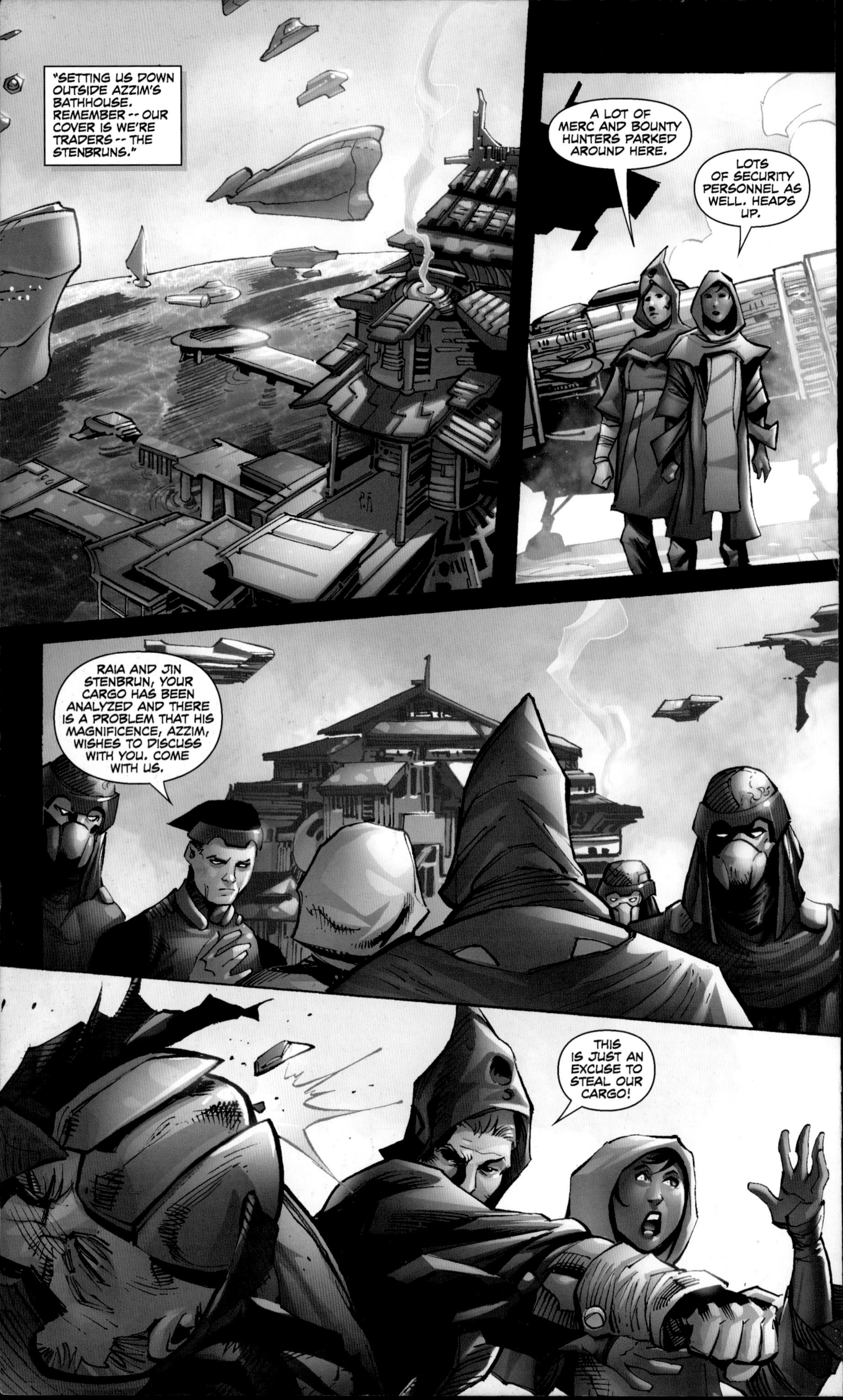
"SETTING US DOWN OUTSIDE AZZIM'S BATHHOUSE. REMEMBER -- OUR COVER IS WE'RE TRADERS -- THE STENBRUNS."
A LOT OF MERC AND BOUNTY HUNTERS PARKED AROUND HERE.
LOTS OF SECURITY PERSONNEL AS WELL. HEADS UP.
RAIA AND JIN STENBRUN, YOUR CARGO HAS BEEN ANALYZED AND THERE IS A PROBLEM THAT HIS MAGNIFICENCE, AZZIM, WISHES TO DISCUSS WITH YOU. COME WITH US.
THIS IS JUST AN EXCUSE TO STEAL OUR CARGO!

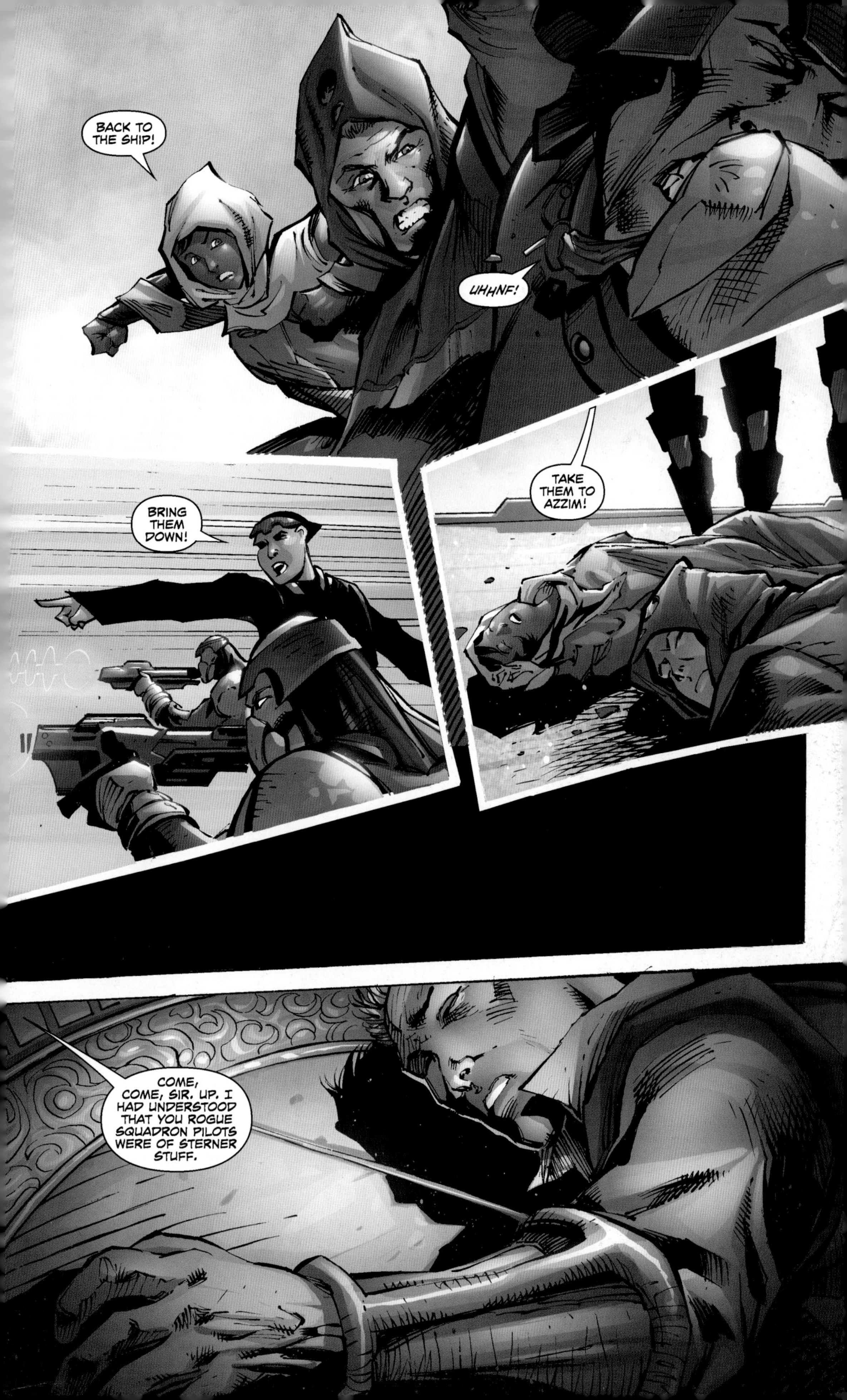
BACK TO THE SHIP!
UHHNF!
BRING THEM DOWN!
TAKE THEM TO AZZIM!
COME, COME, SIR. UP. I HAD UNDERSTOOD THAT YOU ROGUE SQUADRON PILOTS WERE OF STERNER STUFF.

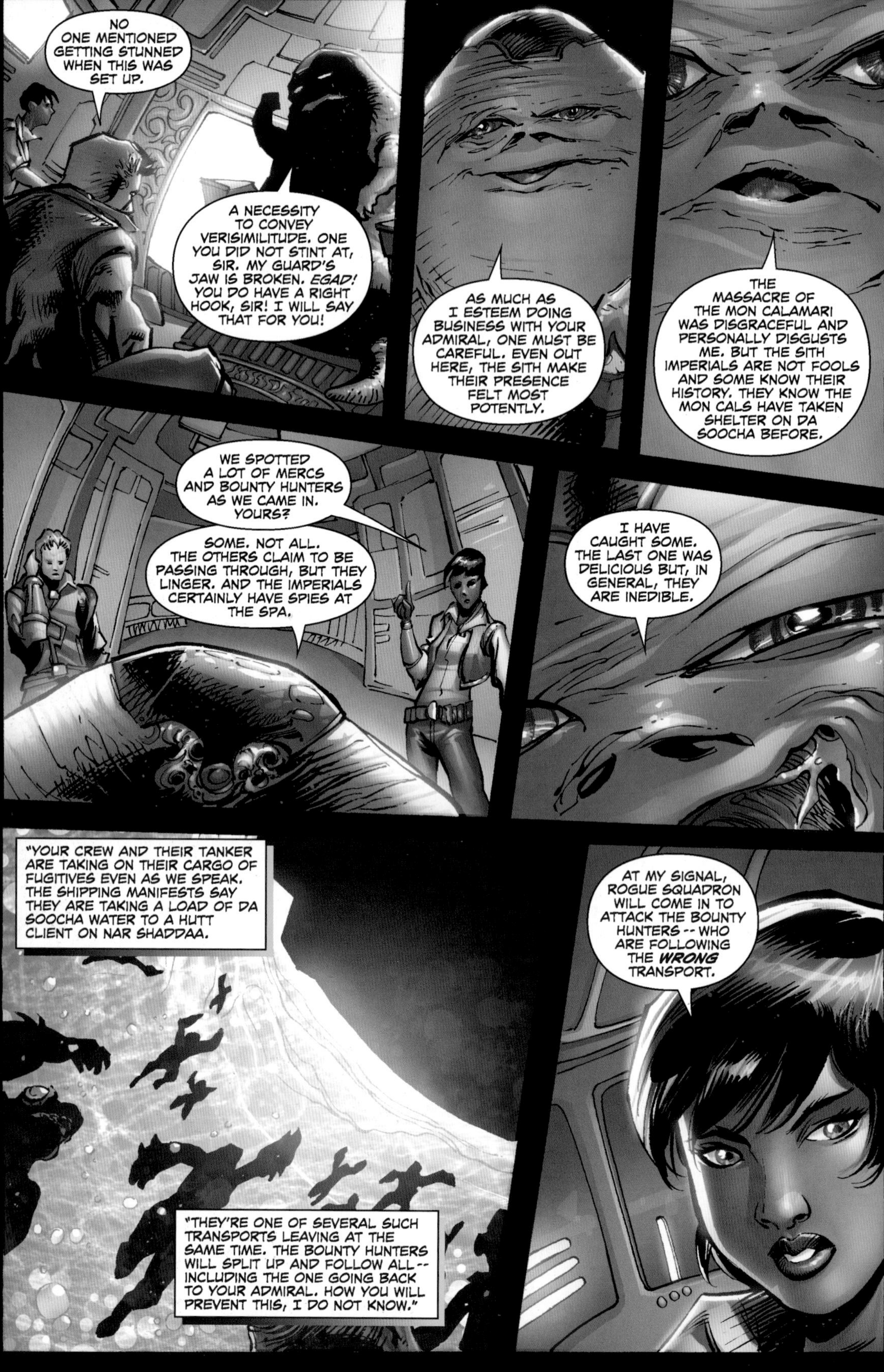
NO ONE MENTIONED GETTING STUNNED WHEN THIS WAS SET UP.
A NECESSITY TO CONVEY VERISIMILITUDE. ONE YOU DID NOT STINT AT, SIR. MY GUARD'S JAW IS BROKEN. *EGAD!* YOU DO HAVE A RIGHT HOOK, SIR! I WILL SAY THAT FOR YOU!
AS MUCH AS I ESTEEM DOING BUSINESS WITH YOUR ADMIRAL, ONE MUST BE CAREFUL. EVEN OUT HERE, THE SITH MAKE THEIR PRESENCE FELT MOST POTENTLY.
THE MASSACRE OF THE MON CALAMARI WAS DISGRACEFUL AND PERSONALLY DISGUSTS ME. BUT THE SITH IMPERIALS ARE NOT FOOLS AND SOME KNOW THEIR HISTORY. THEY KNOW THE MON CALS HAVE TAKEN SHELTER ON DA SOOCHA BEFORE.
WE SPOTTED A LOT OF MERCS AND BOUNTY HUNTERS AS WE CAME IN. YOURS?
SOME. NOT ALL. THE OTHERS CLAIM TO BE PASSING THROUGH, BUT THEY LINGER. AND THE IMPERIALS CERTAINLY HAVE SPIES AT THE SPA.
I HAVE CAUGHT SOME. THE LAST ONE WAS DELICIOUS BUT, IN GENERAL, THEY ARE INEDIBLE.
"YOUR CREW AND THEIR TANKER ARE TAKING ON THEIR CARGO OF FUGITIVES EVEN AS WE SPEAK. THE SHIPPING MANIFESTS SAY THEY ARE TAKING A LOAD OF DA SOOCHA WATER TO A HUTT CLIENT ON NAR SHADDAA.
"THEY'RE ONE OF SEVERAL SUCH TRANSPORTS LEAVING AT THE SAME TIME. THE BOUNTY HUNTERS WILL SPLIT UP AND FOLLOW ALL-- INCLUDING THE ONE GOING BACK TO YOUR ADMIRAL. HOW YOU WILL PREVENT THIS, I DO NOT KNOW."
AT MY SIGNAL, ROGUE SQUADRON WILL COME IN TO ATTACK THE BOUNTY HUNTERS -- WHO ARE FOLLOWING THE ***WRONG*** TRANSPORT.

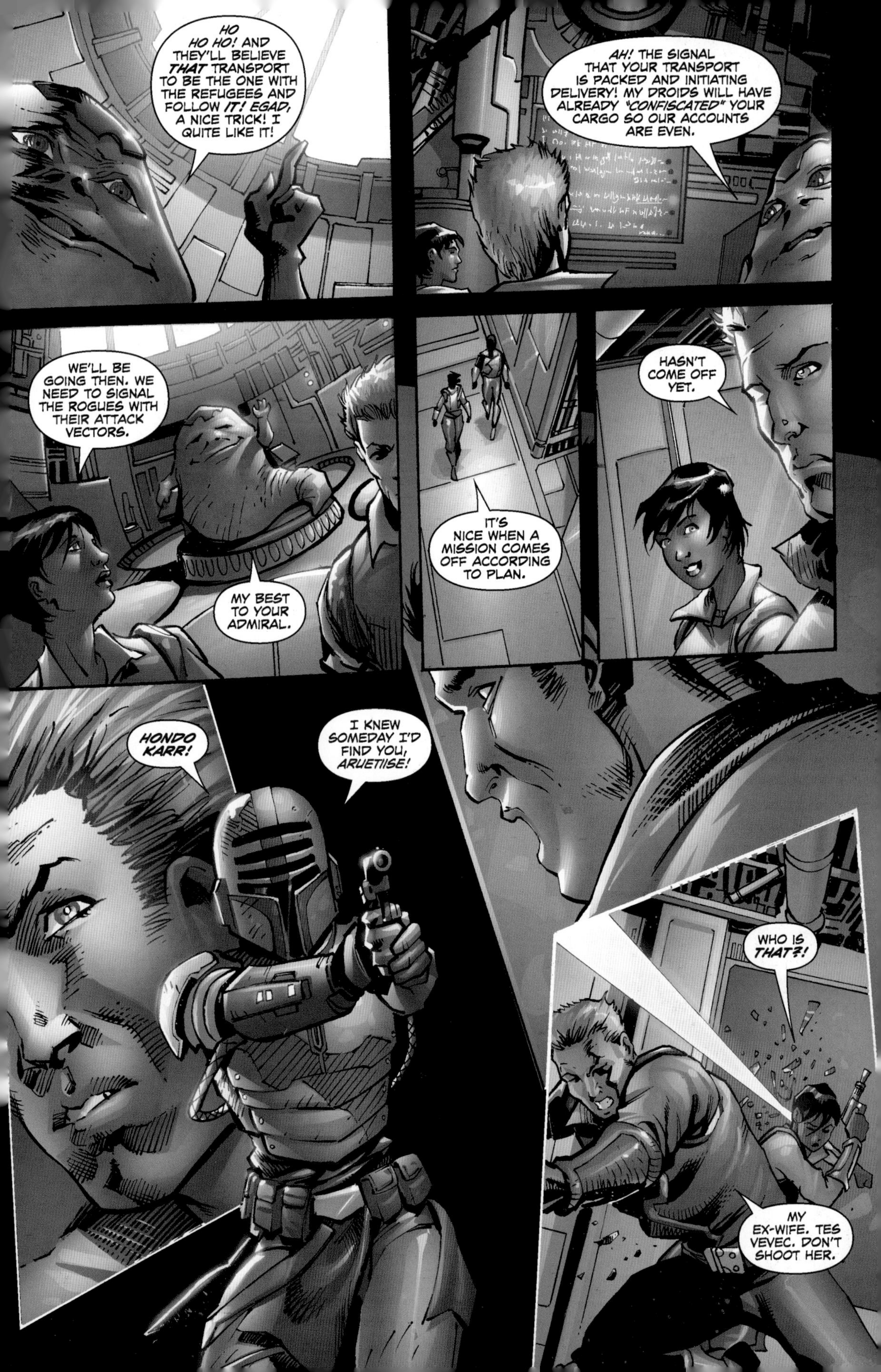
HO HO HO! AND THEY'LL BELIEVE THAT TRANSPORT TO BE THE ONE WITH THE REFUGEES AND FOLLOW IT! EGAD, A NICE TRICK! I QUITE LIKE IT!
AH! THE SIGNAL THAT YOUR TRANSPORT IS PACKED AND INITIATING DELIVERY! MY DROIDS WILL HAVE ALREADY "CONFISCATED" YOUR CARGO SO OUR ACCOUNTS ARE EVEN.
WE'LL BE GOING THEN. WE NEED TO SIGNAL THE ROGUES WITH THEIR ATTACK VECTORS.
MY BEST TO YOUR ADMIRAL.
IT'S NICE WHEN A MISSION COMES OFF ACCORDING TO PLAN.
HASN'T COME OFF YET.
HONDO KARR!
I KNEW SOMEDAY I'D FIND YOU, ARUETIISE!
WHO IS THAT?!
MY EX-WIFE. TES VEVEC. DON'T SHOOT HER.

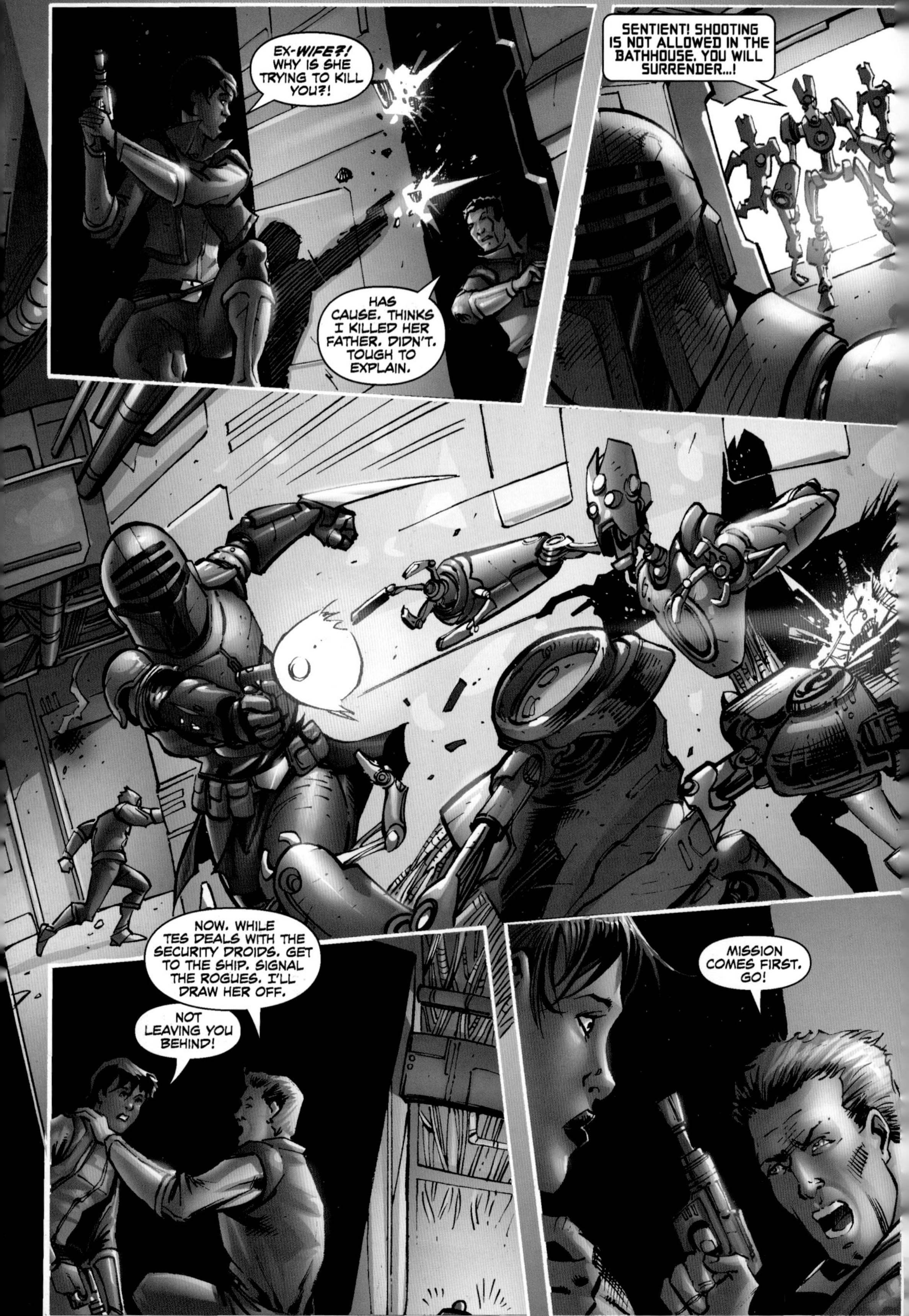
EX-WIFE?! WHY IS SHE TRYING TO KILL YOU?!
HAS CAUSE. THINKS I KILLED HER FATHER. DIDN'T. TOUGH TO EXPLAIN.
SENTIENT! SHOOTING IS NOT ALLOWED IN THE BATHHOUSE. YOU WILL SURRENDER...!
NOW. WHILE TES DEALS WITH THE SECURITY DROIDS. GET TO THE SHIP. SIGNAL THE ROGUES. I'LL DRAW HER OFF.
NOT LEAVING YOU BEHIND!
MISSION COMES FIRST. GO!

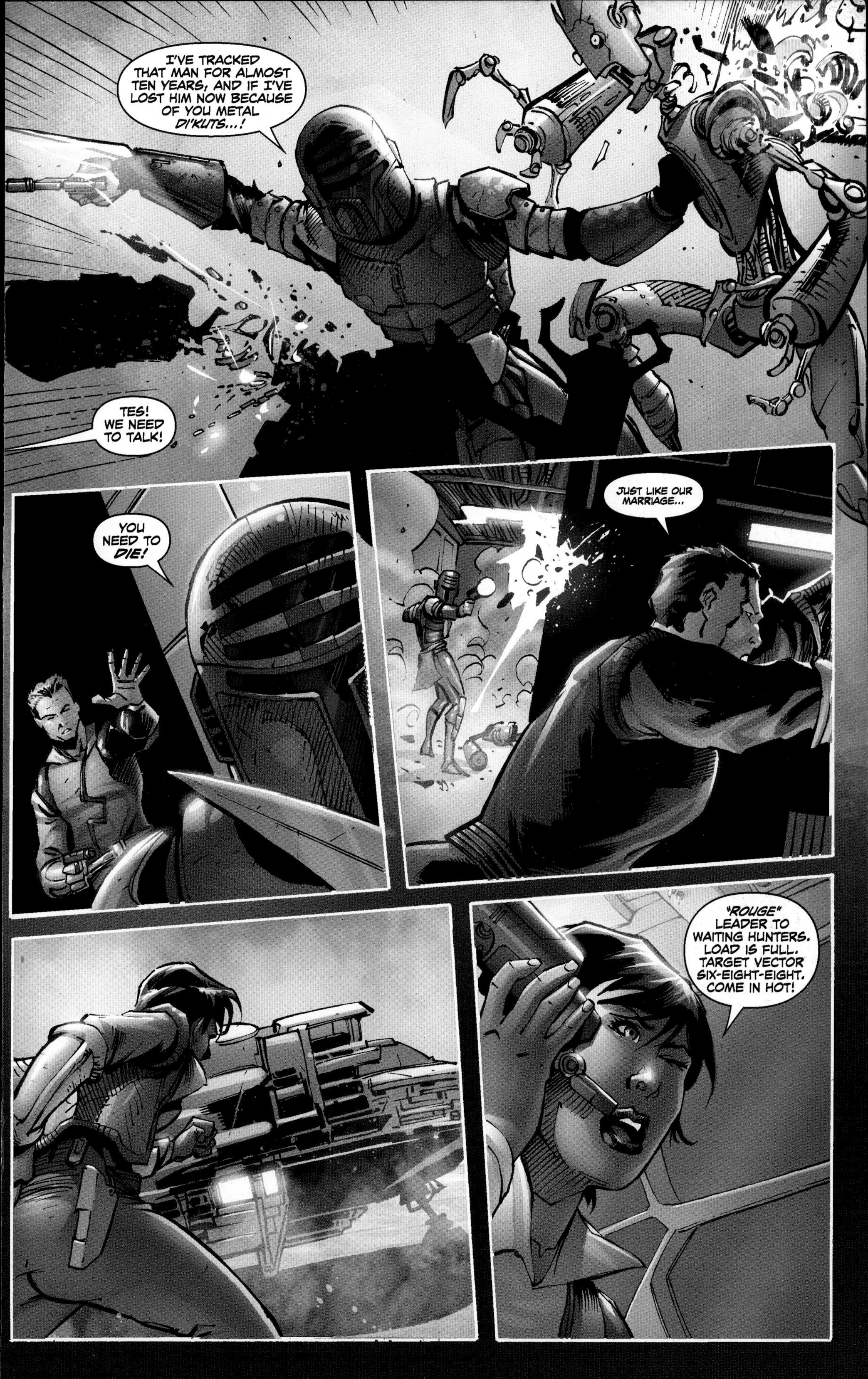
I'VE TRACKED THAT MAN FOR ALMOST TEN YEARS, AND IF I'VE LOST HIM NOW BECAUSE OF YOU METAL *DI'KUTS*...!
TES! WE NEED TO TALK!
YOU NEED TO *DIE!*
JUST LIKE OUR MARRIAGE...
"ROUGE" LEADER TO WAITING HUNTERS. LOAD IS FULL. TARGET VECTOR SIX-EIGHT-EIGHT. COME IN HOT!

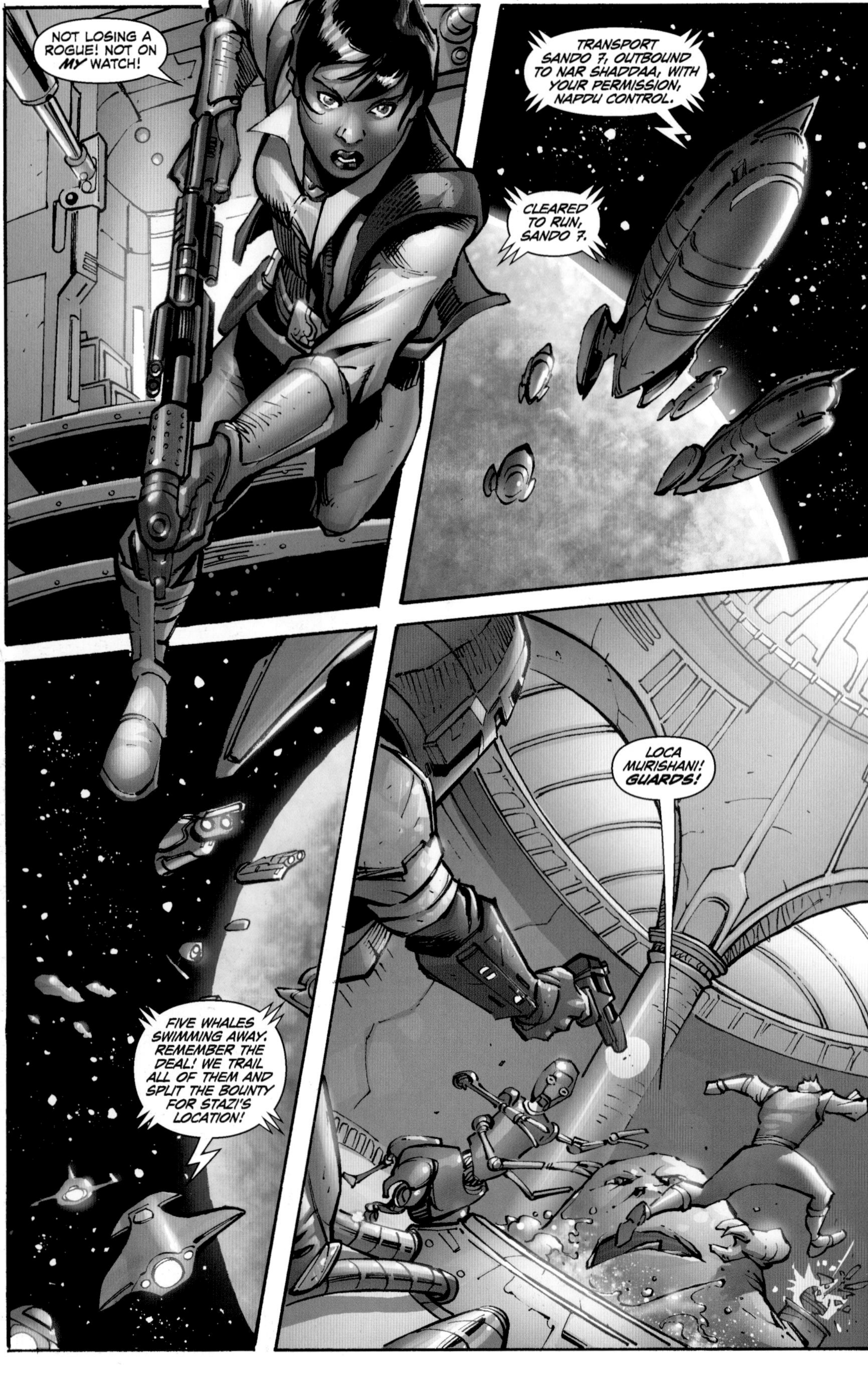
NOT LOSING A ROGUE! NOT ON MY WATCH!
TRANSPORT SANDO 7, OUTBOUND TO NAR SHADDAA, WITH YOUR PERMISSION, NAPDU CONTROL.
CLEARED TO RUN, SANDO 7.
LOCA MURISHANI! GUARDS!
FIVE WHALES SWIMMING AWAY. REMEMBER THE DEAL! WE TRAIL ALL OF THEM AND SPLIT THE BOUNTY FOR STAZI'S LOCATION!

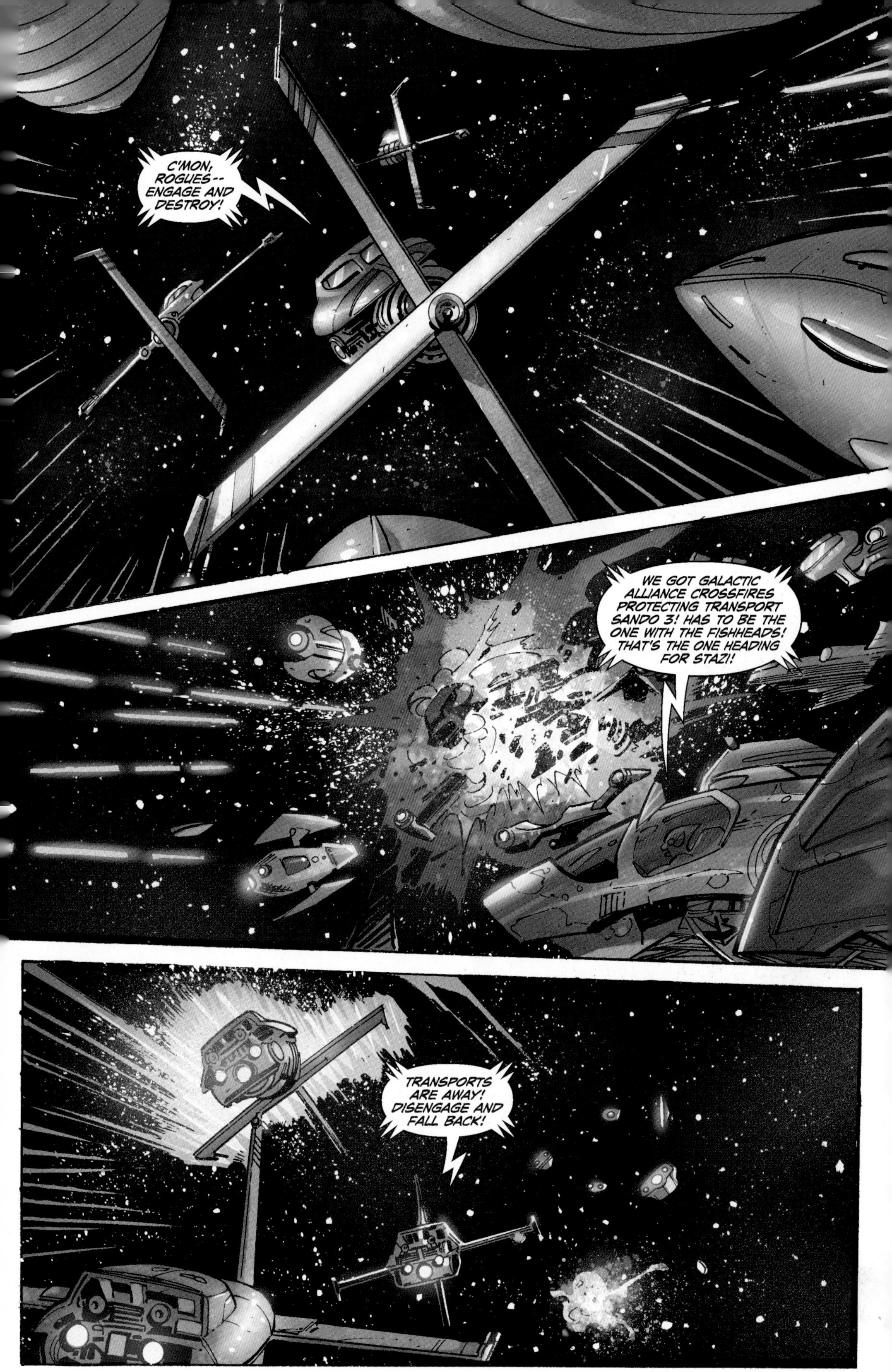
C'MON, ROGUES-- ENGAGE AND DESTROY!
WE GOT GALACTIC ALLIANCE CROSSFIRES PROTECTING TRANSPORT SANDO 3! HAS TO BE THE ONE WITH THE FISHHEADS! THAT'S THE ONE HEADING FOR STAZI!
TRANSPORTS ARE AWAY! DISENGAGE AND FALL BACK!

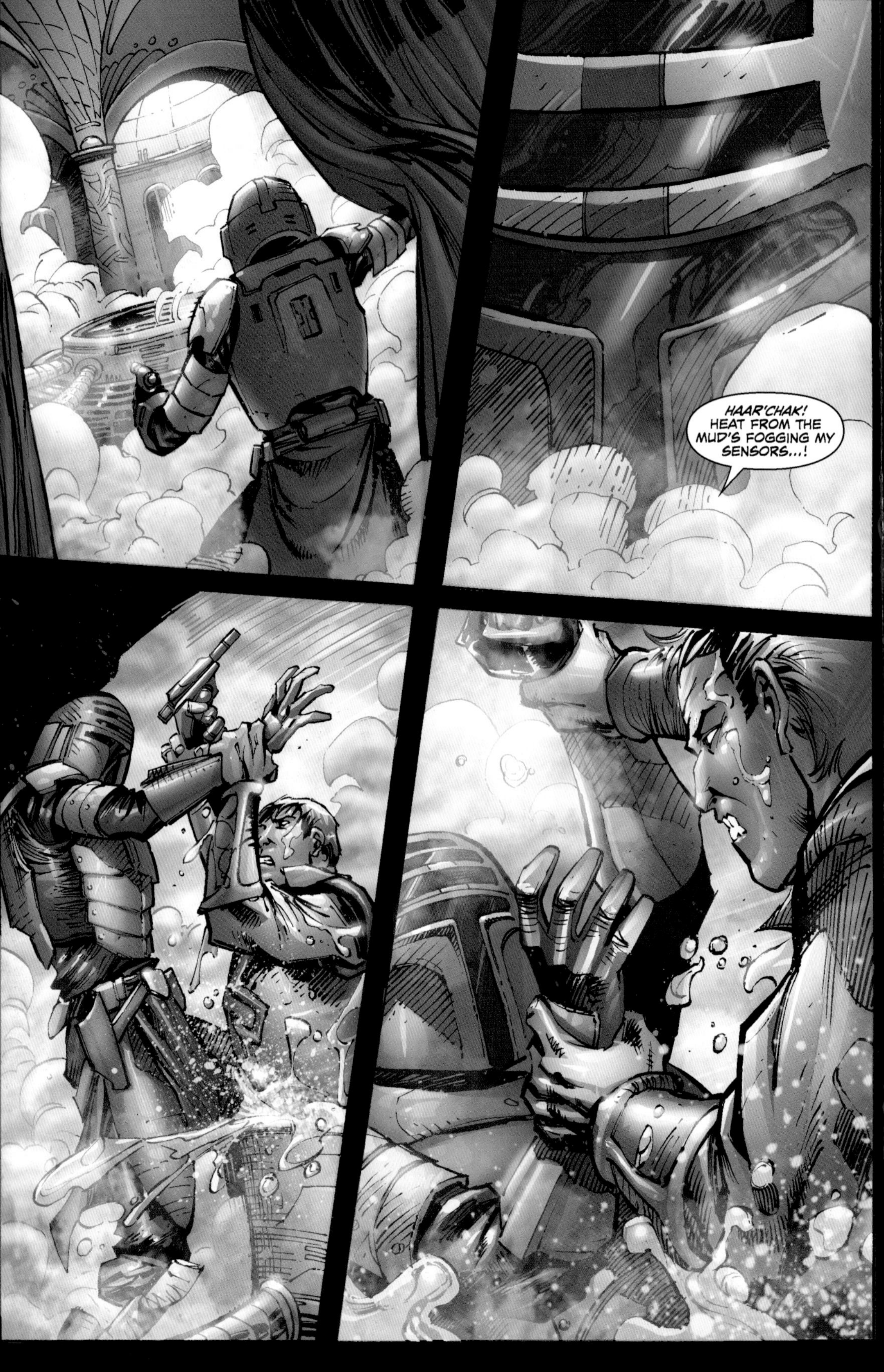
HAAR'CHAK! HEAT FROM THE MUD'S FOGGING MY SENSORS...!

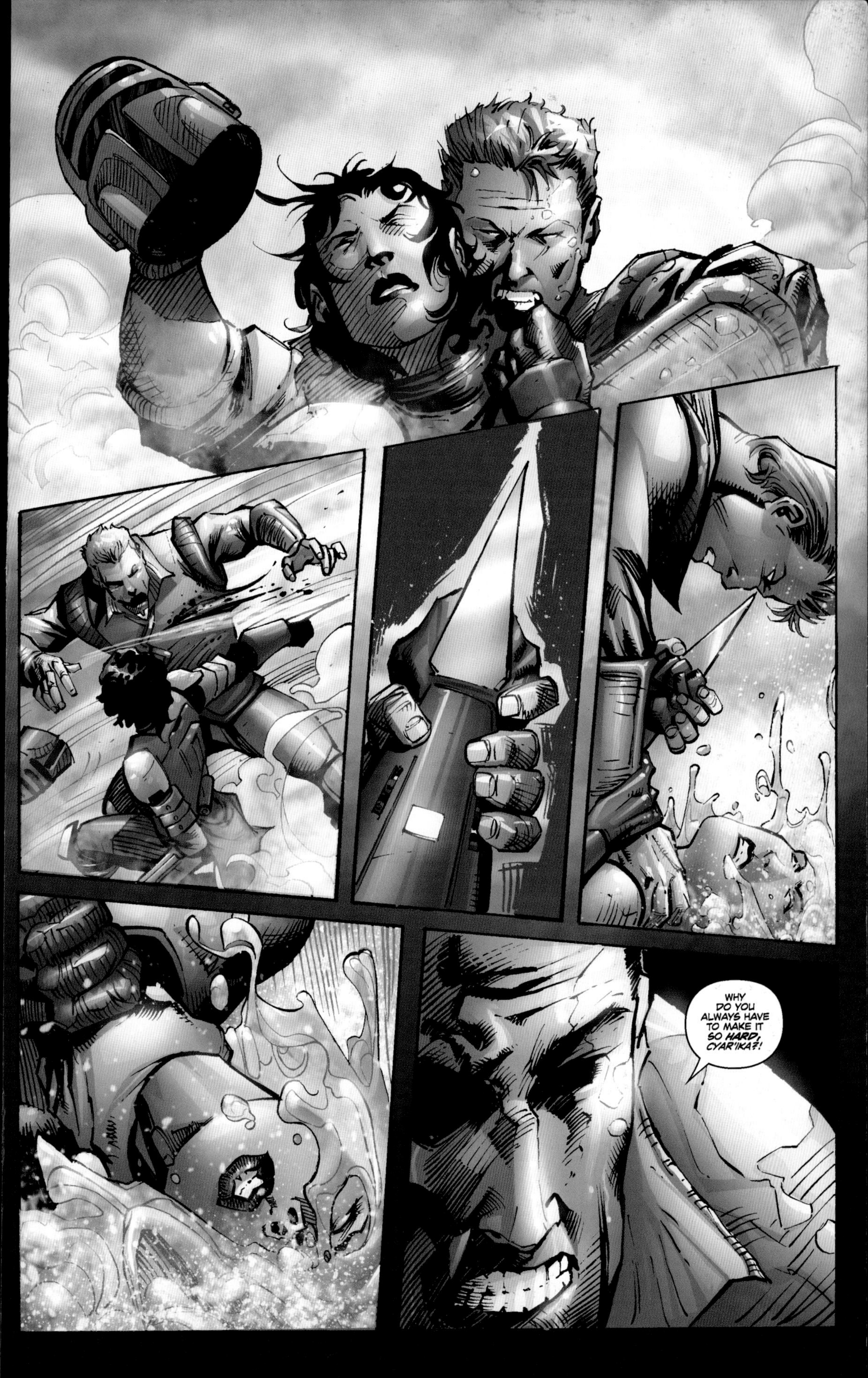
WHY DO YOU ALWAYS HAVE TO MAKE IT SO HARD, CYAR'IKA?!

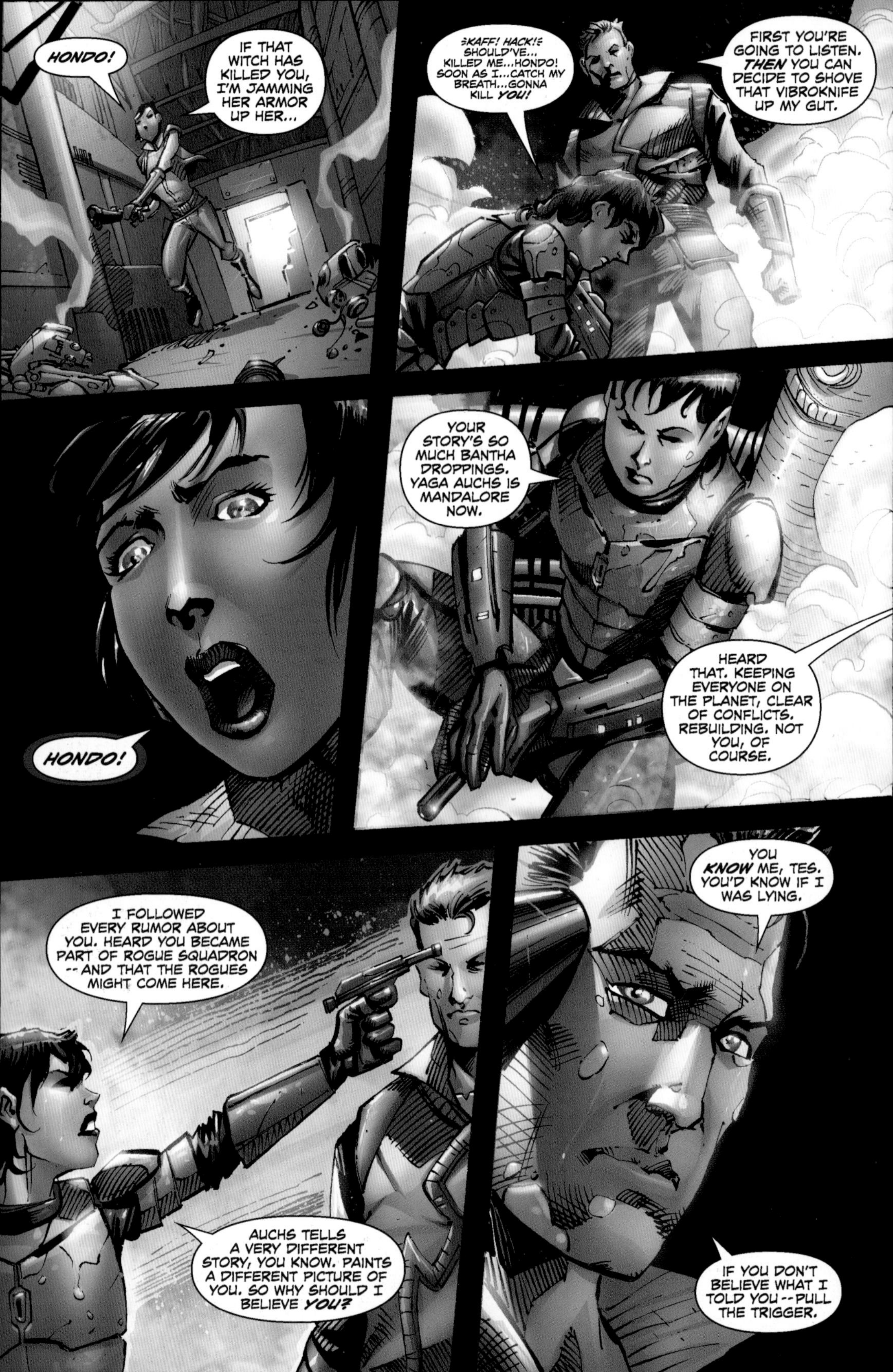
HONDO!
IF THAT WITCH HAS KILLED YOU, I'M JAMMING HER ARMOR UP HER...
KAFF! HACK! SHOULD'VE... KILLED ME...HONDO! SOON AS I...CATCH MY BREATH...GONNA KILL *YOU!*
FIRST YOU'RE GOING TO LISTEN. *THEN* YOU CAN DECIDE TO SHOVE THAT VIBROKNIFE UP MY GUT.
HONDO!
YOUR STORY'S SO MUCH BANTHA DROPPINGS. YAGA AUCHS IS MANDALORE NOW.
HEARD THAT. KEEPING EVERYONE ON THE PLANET, CLEAR OF CONFLICTS. REBUILDING. NOT YOU, OF COURSE.
I FOLLOWED EVERY RUMOR ABOUT YOU. HEARD YOU BECAME PART OF ROGUE SQUADRON -- AND THAT THE ROGUES MIGHT COME HERE.
AUCHS TELLS A VERY DIFFERENT STORY, YOU KNOW. PAINTS A DIFFERENT PICTURE OF YOU. SO WHY SHOULD I BELIEVE *YOU?*
YOU *KNOW* ME, TES. YOU'D KNOW IF I WAS LYING.
IF YOU DON'T BELIEVE WHAT I TOLD YOU -- PULL THE TRIGGER.

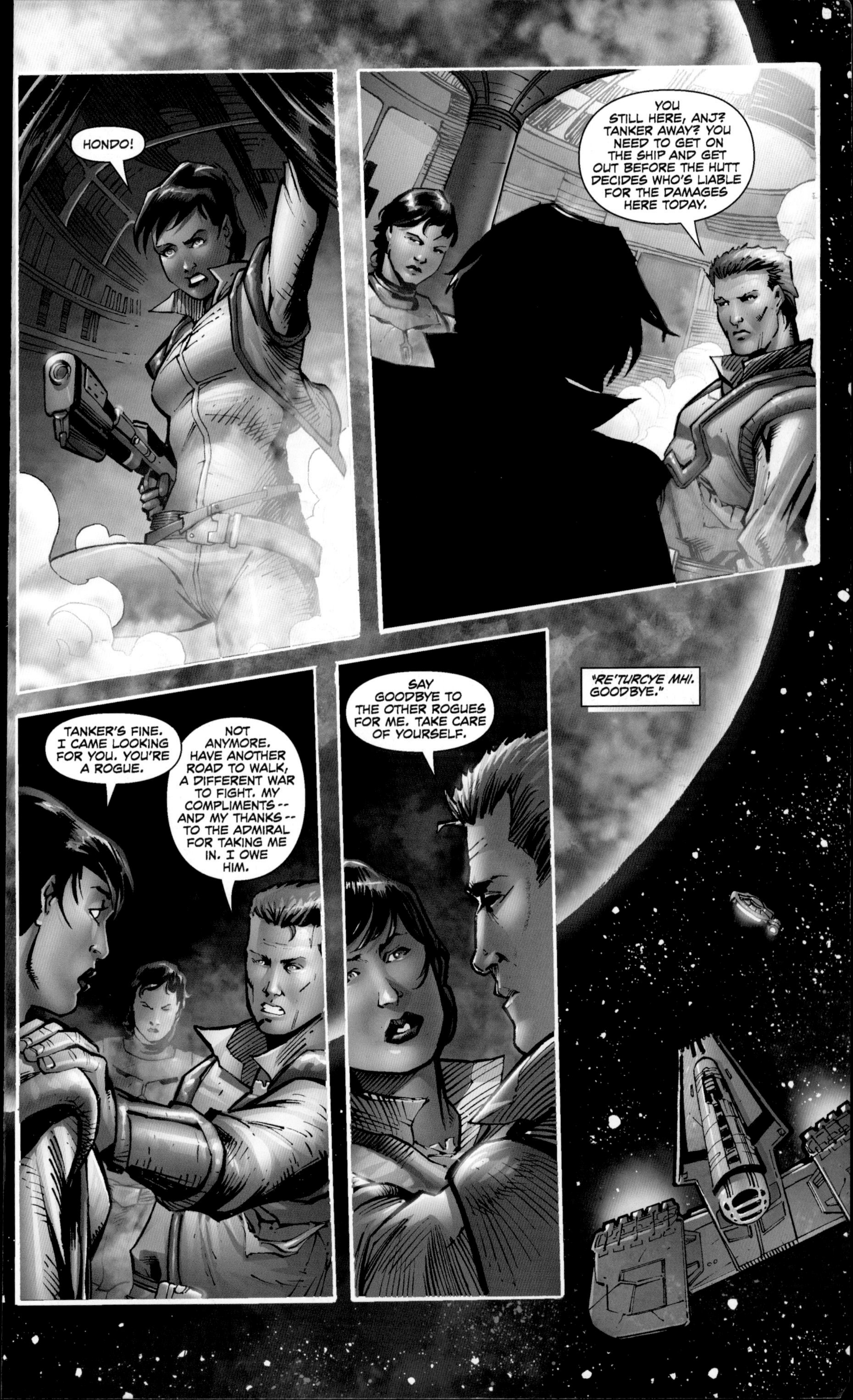
HONDO!
YOU STILL HERE, ANJ? TANKER AWAY? YOU NEED TO GET ON THE SHIP AND GET OUT BEFORE THE HUTT DECIDES WHO'S LIABLE FOR THE DAMAGES HERE TODAY.
TANKER'S FINE. I CAME LOOKING FOR YOU. YOU'RE A ROGUE.
NOT ANYMORE. HAVE ANOTHER ROAD TO WALK, A DIFFERENT WAR TO FIGHT. MY COMPLIMENTS -- AND MY THANKS -- TO THE ADMIRAL FOR TAKING ME IN. I OWE HIM.
SAY GOODBYE TO THE OTHER ROGUES FOR ME. TAKE CARE OF YOURSELF.
"RE'TURCYE MHI. GOODBYE."

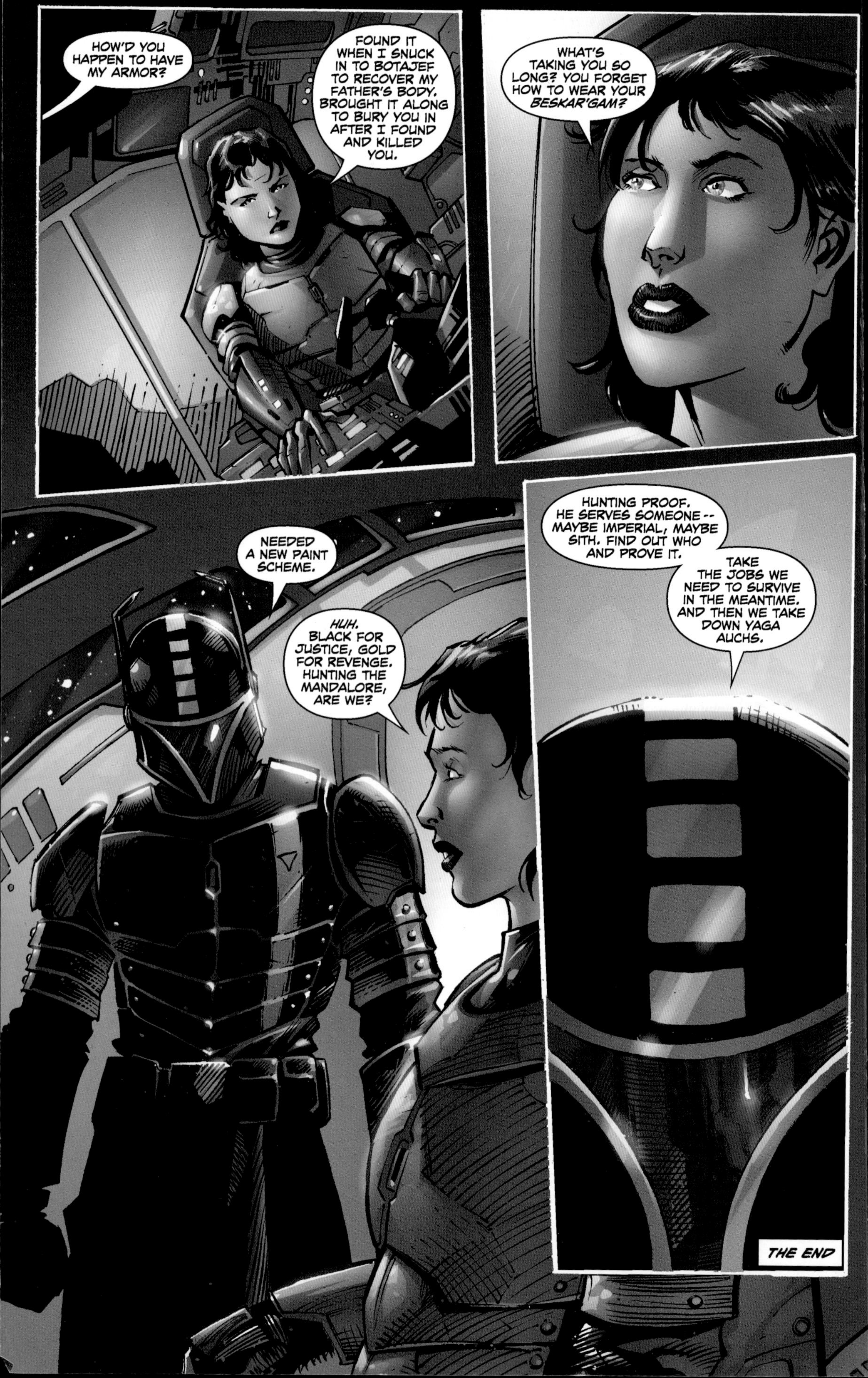
HOW'D YOU HAPPEN TO HAVE MY ARMOR?
FOUND IT WHEN I SNUCK IN TO BOTAJEF TO RECOVER MY FATHER'S BODY. BROUGHT IT ALONG TO BURY YOU IN AFTER I FOUND AND KILLED YOU.
WHAT'S TAKING YOU SO LONG? YOU FORGET HOW TO WEAR YOUR *BESKAR'GAM?*
NEEDED A NEW PAINT SCHEME.
HUH. BLACK FOR JUSTICE, GOLD FOR REVENGE. HUNTING THE MANDALORE, ARE WE?
HUNTING PROOF. HE SERVES SOMEONE -- MAYBE IMPERIAL, MAYBE SITH. FIND OUT WHO AND PROVE IT.
TAKE THE JOBS WE NEED TO SURVIVE IN THE MEANTIME. AND THEN WE TAKE DOWN YAGA AUCHS.
THE END

❖ GLOSSARY ❖

aruetiise: traitor

beskar'gam: armor

cheeka: woman

cheespa bo coopa: better watch it

chuba: a *gorg*; amphibian food source

chut chut: never mind

cyar'ika: darling; sweetheart

fofo: double

di'kut: foolish person; idiot

gorg: a *chuba*; edible amphibian

gornt: domesticated, omnivorous creature raised for meat

gusha: lucky

haar'chak: expletive: dammit

kreetle: sand-dwelling bugs native to Tatooine

kung: scum

loca: crazy

muna ja: pretty

murglak: derogatory spacer term

murishani: bounty hunter

nagoola: not bad

narglatch: dog-like predator

pateesa: sweetie; friend

patogga: pie

peetch goola: too bad

re'turcye mhi: goodbye; maybe we'll meet again

schutta: insult specific to Twi'lek females

skocha: burnout

stoopa: stupid

wakamancha: cowardly

wermo: stupid person, idiot; worm; slang: boy

STAR WARS GRAPHIC NOVEL TIMELINE (IN YEARS)

Omnibus: Tales of the Jedi—5,000–3,986 BSW4

Knights of the Old Republic—3,964–3,963 BSW4

Jedi vs. Sith—1,000 BSW4

Omnibus: Rise of the Sith—33 BSW4

Episode I: The Phantom Menace—32 BSW4

Omnibus: Emissaries and Assassins—32 BSW4

Twilight—31 BSW4

Bounty Hunters—31 BSW4

The Hunt for Aurra Sing—30 BSW4

Darkness—30 BSW4

The Stark Hyperspace War—30 BSW4

Rite of Passage—28 BSW4

Jango Fett—27 BSW4

Zam Wesell—27 BSW4

Honor and Duty—24 BSW4

Episode II: Attack of the Clones—22 BSW4

Clone Wars—22–19 BSW4

Clone Wars Adventures—22–19 BSW4

General Grievous—22–19 BSW4

Episode III: Revenge of the Sith—19 BSW4

Dark Times—19 BSW4

Omnibus: Droids—5.5 BSW4

Boba Fett: Enemy of the Empire—3 BSW4

Underworld—1 BSW4

Episode IV: A New Hope—SW4

Classic Star Wars—0–3 ASW4

A Long Time Ago . . . —0–4 ASW4

Empire—0 ASW4

Rebellion—0 ASW4

Boba Fett: Man with a Mission—0 ASW4

Omnibus: Early Victories—0–3 ASW4

Jabba the Hutt: The Art of the Deal—1 ASW4

Episode V: The Empire Strikes Back—3 ASW4

Shadows of the Empire—3.5 ASW4

Episode VI: Return of the Jedi—4 ASW4

Mara Jade: By the Emperor's Hand—4 ASW4

Omnibus: X-Wing Rogue Squadron—4–5 ASW4

Heir to the Empire—9 ASW4

Dark Force Rising—9 ASW4

The Last Command—9 ASW4

Dark Empire—10 ASW4

Boba Fett: Death, Lies, and Treachery—10 ASW4

Crimson Empire—11 ASW4

Jedi Academy: Leviathan—12 ASW4

Union—19 ASW4

Chewbacca—25 ASW4

Legacy—130–137 ASW4

Old Republic Era
25,000 – 1000 years before
Star Wars: A New Hope

Rise of the Empire Era
1000 – 0 years before
Star Wars: A New Hope

Rebellion Era
0 – 5 years after
Star Wars: A New Hope

New Republic Era
5 – 25 years after
Star Wars: A New Hope

New Jedi Order Era
25+ years after
Star Wars: A New Hope

Legacy Era
130+ years after
Star Wars: A New Hope

Infinities
Does not apply to timeline

Sergio Aragonés Stomps Star Wars
Star Wars Tales
Star Wars Infinities
Tag and Bink
Star Wars Visionaries

BSW4 = before *Episode IV: A New Hope*. ASW4 = after *Episode IV: A New Hope*.

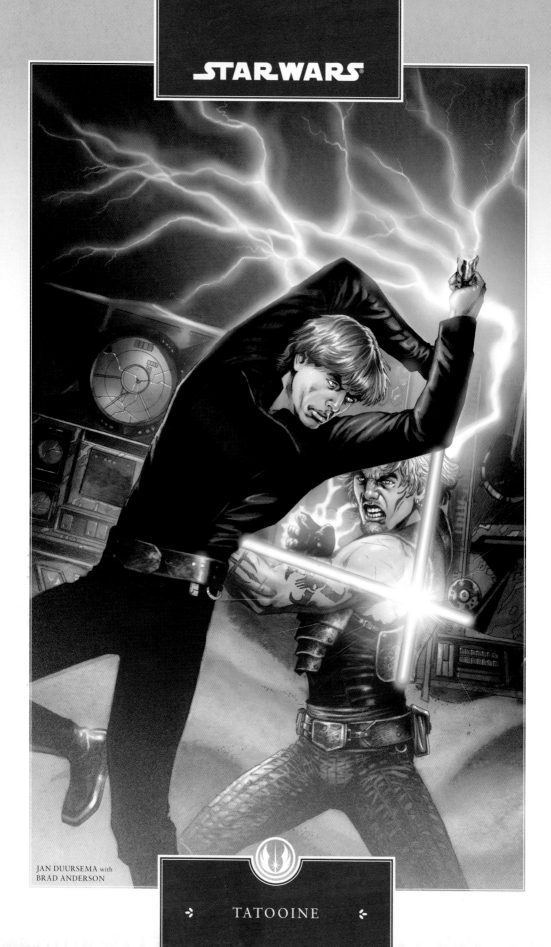

STAR WARS®

JAN DUURSEMA with
BRAD ANDERSON

❖ TATOOINE ❖

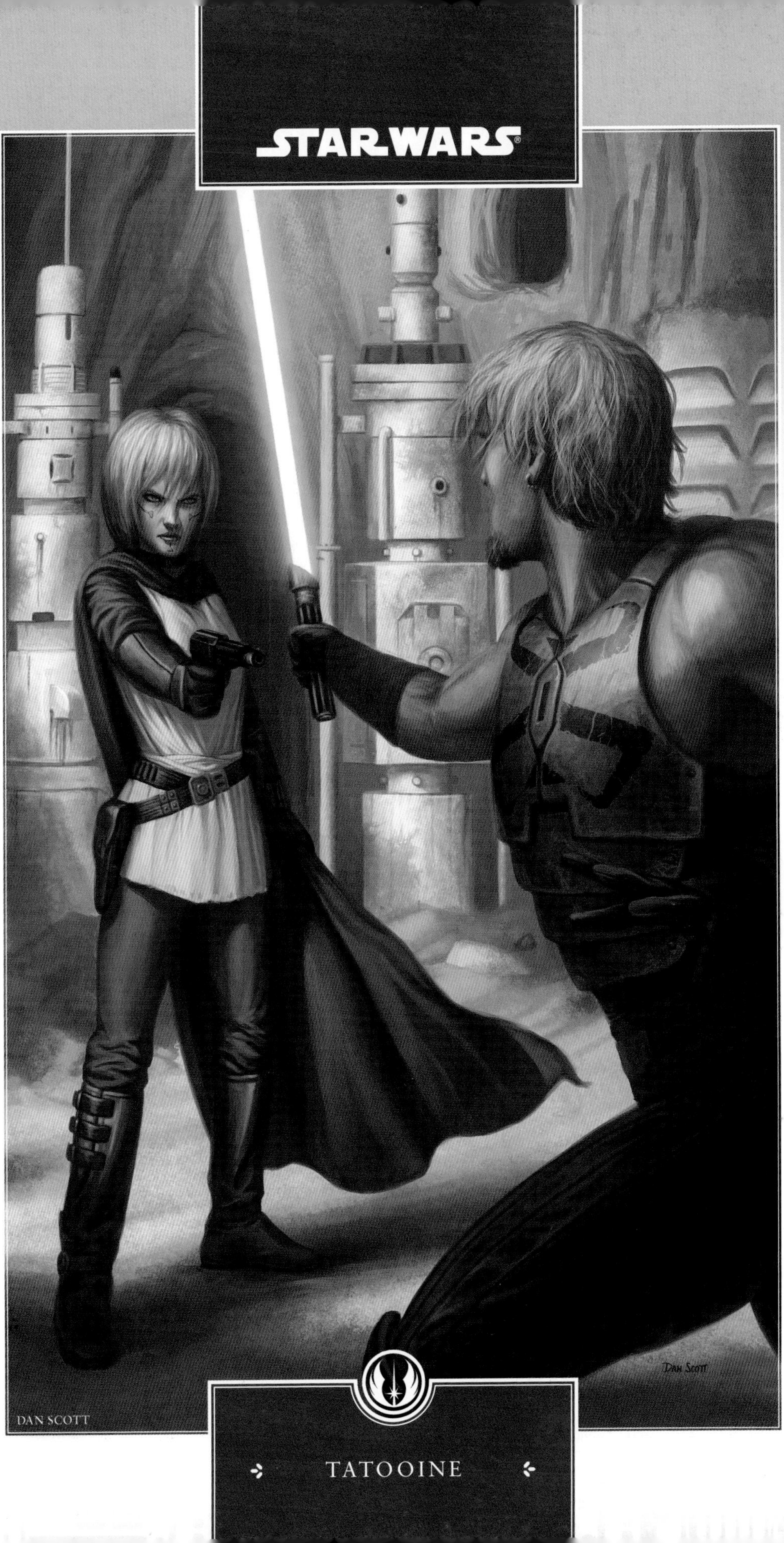
STAR WARS
DAN SCOTT
DAN SCOTT
TATOOINE

STAR WARS
VECTOR

An event with repercussions for every era and every hero in the *Star Wars* galaxy begins here! For anyone who never knew where to start with *Star Wars* comics, *Vector* is the perfect introduction to the entire *Star Wars* line! For any serious *Star Wars* fan, *Vector* is a must-see event with major happenings throughout the most important moments of the galaxy's history!

VOLUME ONE
(*Knights of the Old Republic* Vol. 5; *Dark Times* Vol. 3)
ISBN 978-1-59582-226-0 | $17.99

VOLUME TWO
(*Rebellion* Vol. 4; *Legacy* Vol. 6)
ISBN 978-1-59582-227-7 | $17.99

KNIGHTS OF THE OLD REPUBLIC

Volume One: Commencement
ISBN 978-1-59307-640-5 | $18.99

Volume Two: Flashpoint
ISBN 978-1-59307-761-7 | $18.99

Volume Three: Days of Fear, Nights of Anger
ISBN 978-1-59307-867-6 | $18.99

Volume Four: Daze of Hate, Knights of Suffering
ISBN 978-1-59582-208-6 | $18.99

Volume Six: Vindication
ISBN 978-1-59582-274-1 | $19.99

Volume Seven: Dueling Ambitions
ISBN 978-1-59582-348-9 | $18.99

Volume Eight: Destroyer
ISBN 978-1-59582-419-6 | $17.99

REBELLION

Volume One: My Brother, My Enemy
ISBN 978-1-59307-711-2 | $14.99

Volume Two: The Ahakista Gambit
ISBN 978-1-59307-890-4 | $17.99

Volume Three: Small Victories
ISBN 978-1-59582-166-9 | $12.99

LEGACY

Volume One: Broken
ISBN 978-1-59307-716-7 | $17.99

Volume Two: Shards
ISBN 978-1-59307-879-9 | $19.99

Volume Three: Claws of the Dragon
ISBN 978-1-59307-946-8 | $17.99

Volume Four: Alliance
ISBN 978-1-59582-223-9 | $15.99

Volume Five: The Hidden Temple
ISBN 978-1-59582-224-6 | $15.99

Volume Seven: Storms
ISBN 978-1-59582-350-2 | $17.99

Volume Eight: Tatooine
ISBN 978-1-59582-414-1 | $17.99

DARK TIMES

Volume One: The Path to Nowhere
ISBN 978-1-59307-792-1 | $17.99

Volume Two: Parallels
ISBN 978-1-59307-945-1 | $17.99

Volume Four: Blue Harvest
ISBN 978-1-59582-264-2 | $17.99

DARK HORSE BOOKS

darkhorse.com
AVAILABLE AT YOUR LOCAL COMICS SHOP OR BOOKSTORE.
TO FIND A COMICS SHOP IN YOUR AREA, CALL 1-888-266-4226
For more information or to order direct: On the web: darkhorse.com
E-mail: mailorder@darkhorse.com • Phone: 1-800-862-0052 Mon.–Fri.
9 AM to 5 PM Pacific Time. STAR WARS © 2004–2010 Lucasfilm Ltd. & ™ (BL8005)

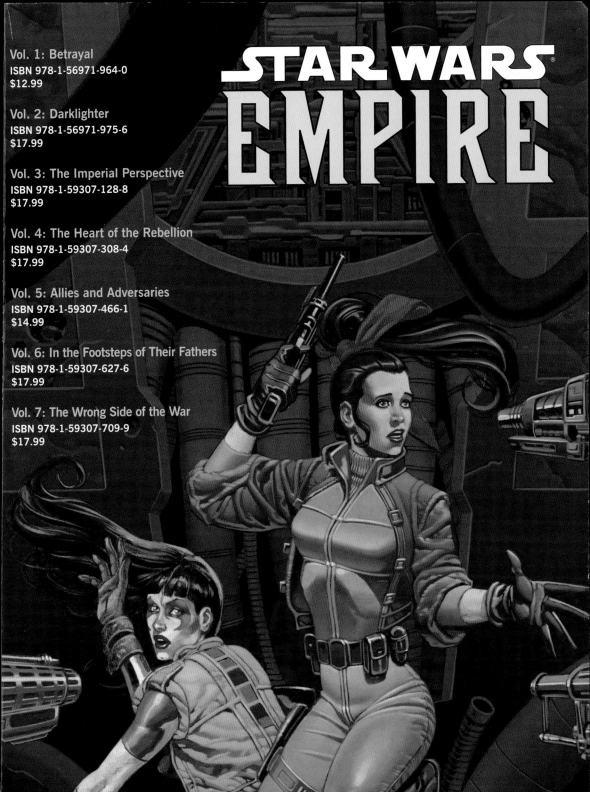

Vol. 1: Betrayal
ISBN 978-1-56971-964-0
$12.99

Vol. 2: Darklighter
ISBN 978-1-56971-975-6
$17.99

Vol. 3: The Imperial Perspective
ISBN 978-1-59307-128-8
$17.99

Vol. 4: The Heart of the Rebellion
ISBN 978-1-59307-308-4
$17.99

Vol. 5: Allies and Adversaries
ISBN 978-1-59307-466-1
$14.99

Vol. 6: In the Footsteps of Their Fathers
ISBN 978-1-59307-627-6
$17.99

Vol. 7: The Wrong Side of the War
ISBN 978-1-59307-709-9
$17.99

STAR WARS
EMPIRE

DARK HORSE COMICS

TO FIND A COMICS SHOP IN YOUR AREA, CALL 1-888-266-4226.

For more information or to order direct:
*On the web: darkhorse.com
*E-mail: mailorder@darkhorse.com
*Phone: 1-800-862-0052 Mon.-Fri. 9 A.M. to 5 P.M. Pacific Time.

STAR WARS
OMNIBUS
TALES OF THE JEDI

STAR WARS
OMNIBUS
X-WING ROGUE SQUADRON

STAR WARS
OMNIBUS
DROIDS

STAR WARS
OMNIBUS
EARLY VICTORIES

STAR WARS
OMNIBUS
RISE OF THE SITH

STAR WARS
OMNIBUS
EMISSARIES & ASSASSINS

STAR WARS
OMNIBUS
MENACE REVEALED

STAR WARS OMNIBUS COLLECTIONS

STAR WARS: TALES OF THE JEDI

Including the *Tales of the Jedi* stories "The Golden Age of the Sith," "The Freedon Nadd Uprising," and "Knights of the Old Republic," these huge omnibus editions are the ultimate introduction to the ancient history of the *Star Wars* universe!

Volume 1
ISBN 978-1-59307-830-0

Volume 2
ISBN 978-1-59307-911-6

STAR WARS: X-WING ROGUE SQUADRON

The greatest starfighters of the Rebel Alliance become the defenders of a new Republic in this massive collection of stories featuring Wedge Antilles, hero of the Battle of Endor, and his team of ace pilots known throughout the galaxy as Rogue Squadron.

Volume 1
ISBN 978-1-59307-572-9

Volume 2
ISBN 978-1-59307-619-1

Volume 3
ISBN 978-1-59307-776-1

STAR WARS: DROIDS

Before the fateful day Luke Skywalker met Artoo and Threepio for the first time, those two troublesome droids had some amazing adventures all their own!

ISBN 978-1-59307-955-0

STAR WARS: EARLY VICTORIES

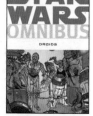

Following the destruction of the first Death Star, Luke Skywalker is the new, unexpected hero of the Rebellion. But the galaxy hasn't been saved yet–Luke and Princess Leia find there are many more battles to be fought against the Empire and Darth Vader!

ISBN 978-1-59582-172-0

STAR WARS: RISE OF THE SITH

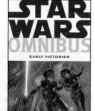

Before the name of Skywalker–or Vader–achieved fame across the galaxy, the Jedi Knights had long preserved peace and justice . . . as well as preventing the return of the Sith. These thrilling tales illustrate the events leading up to *The Phantom Menace*.

ISBN 978-1-59582-228-4

STAR WARS: EMISSARIES AND ASSASSINS

Discover more stories featuring Anakin Skywalker, Amidala, Obi-Wan, and Qui-Gon set during the time of Episode I: *The Phantom Menace* in this mega collection!

ISBN 978-1-59582-229-1

STAR WARS: MENACE REVEALED

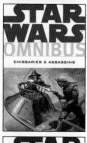

This is our largest omnibus of never-before-collected and out-of-print *Star Wars* stories. Included here are one-shot adventures, short story arcs, specialty issues, and early Dark Horse Extra comic strips! All of these tales take place after Episode I: *The Phantom Menace*, and lead up to Episode II: *Attack of the Clones*.

ISBN 978-1-59582-273-4

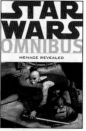

$24.95 each

DARK HORSE BOOKS

AVAILABLE AT YOUR LOCAL COMICS SHOP OR BOOKSTORE!
To find a comics shop in your area, call 1-888-266-4226
For more information or to order direct: • On the web: darkhorse.com • E-mail: mailorder@darkhorse.com • Phone: 1-800-862-0052 Mon.–Fri. 9 AM to 5 PM Pacific Time